THE PALACE
OF TOPKAPI
IN ISTANBUL

Entrance to the Tile Kiosk

THE PALACE
OF TOPKAPI
IN ISTANBUL

BY FANNY DAVIS

CHARLES SCRIBNER'S SONS

NEW YORK

For John Earl Davis

Acknowledgment is made to George Allen & Unwin Ltd.
for permission to quote from *The Meaning of the
Glorious Koran* by Marmaduke Pickthall.

Decorations used as chapter ends are adapted
from illustrations in *L'Art turc décoratif* by
Celâl Esat Arseven, drawn by Shehtap Güngör
Floor plans drawn by Yılmaz Güngör

A-10.70 [MJ]

*Printed in the United States of America
Library of Congress Catalog Card Number 75-113613*

PREFACE

THE IDEA of writing a book on the Palace of Topkapı came to me while I was sitting in the palace library engaged in certain research and from time to time watching the swarms of visitors pass by its windows. Topakı Palace has always fascinated me since the first time I was guided through it, now many years ago. Later I found there was very little to read about it in English—aside from the booklets that can be bought at the entrance to the museum, only two modern works, both written more than thirty years ago before much of the restoration had taken place or much modern research on the palace was available. It was high time, I thought, for a new book on the palace in English, and so I set about becoming more fully acquainted with its many buildings, rooms and exhibits.

For the privilege of researching the entire palace and for much of the information I gathered there my thanks go first to Hayrullah Örs, director of the Topakı Palace Museum, to Kemal Çiğ, assistant director, and to Firuze Preyger, second assistant director. They not only passed on to me considerable of their knowledge of the palace, but they patiently answered my numerous questions. I also owe thanks to the curators and assistant curators who helped me in many ways, especially to Ünsal Yüsel, Curator of Arms and Armor, who set me straight on many matters, and Jale Özbay, assistant curator of Chinese and Japanese porcelains, who advised on the selection of porcelains photographed. There was in fact no member of the museum staff, including the guards, who did not fully cooperate in my research. The little verse recited by the princes at the start of their day's schooling I owe, for example, to İhsan Bey, chief guard of the harem.

I am happy to extend thanks to Seniha Sami Moralı who saved me untold hours by translating Abdurrahman Şeref's articles on Topakı Palace written in the Ottoman alphabet in *Türk Osmanlı Encümeni Mecmuası*

(Magazine of the Ottoman-Turkish Historical Society); to Neşrin Moralı who aided me in many ways; to Nuri H. Arlasez who gave me the benefit of his insight into the palace. I also want to express thanks for help to Professor Hilary Boyd, Nezih Filatlı, Professor Thomas Goodrich, Ahmet Gürün, Priscilla Soucek, Professor Sıdıka Tezer, and many others I have not room to list. Permission to translate the passage on the visit to the Pavilion of the Blessed Mantle from Ayşe Osmanoğlu's book, *Babam Abdülhamit*, I owe to her eldest son, Ömer Nami Bey.

It is my pleasure to acknowledge the debt I owe to Professor Tibor Halasi-Kun, Turkologist of Columbia University, who generously shared with me his extensive knowledge of the Ottoman Empire, and to Professor Kathleen Burrill who taught me to read Turkish. Without the first I should have been unable to bring a background of understanding to the palace, and without the second I should have been unable to read the Turkish literature on the subject. To Professor Ernst Grube, former teacher of Islamic art at Columbia University, I owe much of what I know about Ottoman art, especially tiles and miniatures.

The color photographs in the book are by Halûk Doğanbey of Istanbul. The greater part of the black and white photographs are by Necati Urbay of the museum's staff. Exceptions are the pictures which are by courtesy of the Turkish Republic's Press Department and the pictures of the *tuğra* of Mahmut II, the shot of Osman III's Kiosk taken from Gülhane Parkı, and the scene of the present Golden Horn shoreline by Nuri H. Arlasez of Istanbul and reproduced through his courtesy. The reproductions of the engravings in the old albums of Grelot and Choiseul-Gouffier and Melling were taken from books in the possession of the Library of the School of Architecture of Columbia University.

Both floor plans of the palace are by Yılmaz Güngör, that of the harem based on the newly made floor plan of İlban Öz, present harem architect, and that of the Second, Third and Fourth Courts adapted from the floor plan in the museum's guide and one provided by the museum. The decorative Ottoman designs that spot the book are by Şehtap Güngör. My thanks go to all three of these creative people.

On my latest trip to Istanbul in the fall of 1969 the Sultan's Hall and the Kiosk of Ahmet I were filled with scaffolding, and hence it was impossible to get photographs of them at that time. The pictures of these rooms are therefore before the most recent restoration.

I am grateful to Elinor Parker of Charles Scribner's Sons whose advice and patience throughout the writing of the book have been invaluable. Finally I want to thank my husband, John Earl Davis, whose understanding of my interest in the Palace of Topkapı and whose forebearance at the absences necessitated by my stays in Istanbul to study the palace have made the book possible.

A word about pronunciation in modern Turkish: c has the value of English j, ç of ch, ş of sh; ğ is almost entirely elided; the undotted i has the sound of our short a, as the initial a in away. Otherwise the letters are pronounced like ours. Syllabic stress is, however, quite different and too complicated to go into here.

Since there is so much controversy about Turkish spelling, I should like to add that all Turkish words, including those transliterated from Ottoman, have been spelled according to the *Spelling Guide (İmlâ Kılavuzu)* of the Turkish Linguistic Society. Because this book has been written for the general public it has not been burdened with footnotes. For those who would like to look further into the history and restoration of Topkapı Palace, an annotated bibliography, in both Western languages and Turkish, is appended.

For some time the Imperial Harem of Topkapı Palace has been closed for restoration. By the time this book reaches the public, it may or may not be open. In any event, certain sections of it are due to be opened soon. The watch display in the Second Court, and the embroidery display, the Throne Room and the Library of Ahmet III in the Third Court, which were undergoing restoration when the author last saw them in the fall of 1969, are now, she has been informed, also soon to be opened.

FANNY DAVIS

Warwick, N.Y.
January, 1970

CONTENTS

[ix]

CONTENTS

ILLUSTRATIONS

ILLUSTRATIONS

ILLUSTRATIONS

THE PALACE
OF TOPKAPI
IN ISTANBUL

INTRODUCTION

TOPKAPI means Cannon Gate. The palace that looms on the point of Istanbul where the Bosphorus, the Marmara, and the Golden Horn meet and mix came to that name late in life, unsurprisingly if indirectly from the two cannon that guarded the most important of its water-gates. Until then people knew it first as the New Saray and then the Old Saray. Europeans called it the Grand Seraglio, an Italian corruption of *saray*, a Persian word for palace taken over by the Turks. By now all have united on Topkapı Sarayı, the Palace of the Cannon Gate. Within its walls dwelt, disciplined almost to silence, anywhere from five hundred to several thousand persons, all in the service of their lord, the Ottoman sultan, who was answerable only to God, to himself, and sometimes to the mobs of Istanbul.

There are certain buildings that have drunk in so much of the life about them that they are no longer mere structures of stone or wood but rather stilled organisms that have captured the past, solidified it and held it for the present. Such is Topkapı. For almost five hundred years east Mediterranean history was forged behind its massive gray-buff stone walls. Its floor plan, which runs from the series of courts and buildings laid out by Mehmet the Conqueror in the fifteenth century to the mélange of kiosks, courts and rooms added by later sultans, mirrors the development of the Ottoman Empire from a simple state of tightly organized frontier warriors to an intricate governmental establishment with far-reaching interests that ex-

[3]

tended at times from the outskirts of Vienna to the Red Sea, from the Caspian to the north coast of Africa.

Topkapı Palace was originally a well defended castle, as one can see from the battlements of its outer wall. However, in addition the Conqueror built within the fortress seven defense towers. As time passed and the Ottoman Empire's command of the waterways of Istanbul became unchallengeable, the character of the complex of buildings changed from fortress to palace. The towers were either incorporated into later buildings or allowed to fall to pieces. Only the tower of the head physician in the Fourth Court and that of the Divanhane or Council Hall in the Second Court still stand free. Both have undergone many changes.

When Topkapı is viewed from any of the many hills of Istanbul two dominant features stand out—the quadrangular appearing, spire-topped Divan tower we have just mentioned that reminds the viewer this was a military state, and the many chimneys of the kitchens which hint at the thousands of servitors fed there, the enormous retinue that made up the pomp of this Eastern empire.

Topkapı lies in historically the richest part of Istanbul—near Santa Sophia, the Byzantine church once turned mosque and now a museum, a fine old *hamam* or Turkish bath, and the famous Blue Mosque of Sultan Ahmet I. Along one of its borders, up a hill, runs Divan Yolu, the Council Road, which was once the scene of state processions. This and a number of lesser streets, plus the open area before the Imperial Gate, are its neighbors along the land wall. The palace is a triangle with a blunt point, and its other sides flank the busy harbor.

In the fifteenth century when England was being rent by the Wars of the Roses and Columbus had yet to find America, Mehmet II, the Conqueror, was setting up a system for governing an empire. In the sixteenth century, when François I was struggling to unite France and the American colonies were still largely a dream, Süleyman was governing a centralized, vigorous empire with a feared fighting arm. In the empire's citadel, Topkapı, a succession of sultans lived and ruled from the time the palace was built in the 1470's to the time it was abandoned as the ruler's residence in the 1850's. Even then, until the end of the Empire, it was still sometimes the seat of ceremony.

Its first stones were set under the direction of Mehmet II who, by his conquest of Byzantine Constantinople, earned the title of Fatih or Conqueror. He laid the palace out in a series of connecting rectangular courts, like the

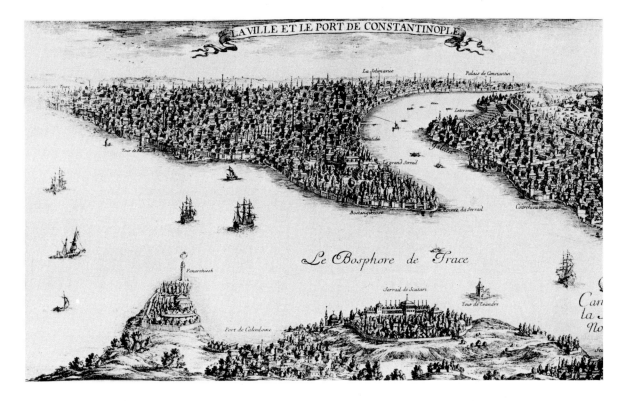

A view of seventeenth-century Istanbul by Grelot. Topkapı Palace is shown on the point, with the Sea of Marmara to the left, the Golden Horn to the right, and the Bosphorus where they join. The Cannon Gate (Top Kapı) with its twin towers appears on the point. The building along the Marmara shore marked Bostangikiosc is in reality the Pearl Kiosk (İncili Köşk).

military camps of his ancestors. His successors elaborated on this. Thus Topkapı is not one building but a group of buildings.

Mehmet had found the city in a state of advanced dilapidation. Constantinople had never really recovered from the sacking it suffered during the Fourth Crusade, and Byzantium as a whole had long been beset by the Balkan countries to the north and the Ottoman Turks to the south. There was little left of its former greatness. Mehmet, who combined a warrior's toughness with a connoisseur's enjoyment of beauty, determined to rebuild it. He looked over the city he had captured, the city that had resisted Islamic armies since the days of the Abbasid Caliphate, and chose three sites for his

[5]

outstanding edifices. First he built himself a palace, the Old Palace (Eski Saray), long gone, on the broad-topped hill where the University of Istanbul now stands. At a later time he built his mosque, the Mosque of Fatih, atop the city's highest hill, and then his New Palace (Yeni Saray), which became Topkapı. For that he chose the site that had been the acropolis of Constantinople, then in ruins.

It is tempting to speculate why he picked this spot, but one need go no further than its situation, the point of land projecting into historic waters of which he was now master. In addition to its beauty, it offered a site from which a fortress could guard the entire city. It is apt that Turks call a prom-

A seventeenth-century view of the Golden Horn side of Topkapı Palace by Grelot. On the point at the left may be seen the twin towers of the Cannon Gate (Top Kapı). The building on the shore marked Caikana is the Kayıkhane or Boathouse. Sinan Kiosc is actually the Basketmakers' Kiosk, and the Alai-kiosc is the Yalı or Shore Kiosk. The Appartements des femmes du Grand Seigneur, or the harem, is not where he has located it but to the front and left of the Divan Tower marked Chambre du Diwan. The Appartements des Officiers, with the conical towers, is obviously the Middle Gate. What Grelot has marked Entrée du Serrail, with the dome, is the old Armory or the Church of St. Irene, just inside the Imperial Gate.

ontory *burnu* or nose, and therefore the location of Topkapı Sarayburnu or Palace Point. Besides warrior and connoisseur Mehmet was also a scholar. He knew Greek and considerable of Byzantium's past. Where grandeur had been he would have grandeur again. He made the palace not only the center of government but a center of art and learning, a tradition that would persist with his successors.

Mehmet the Conqueror was the seventh in the line of Ottoman sultans. Even before him his forebears had greatly increased their holdings in Asia Minor and added territory in Europe. What the Conqueror accomplished was to bind this all together with the city of Istanbul its center, set up an administration, and make the Palace of Topkapı the seat of power. As his successors added the Balkans, Hungary, a good slice of Austria, all of Asia Minor, parts of the Caucasus, the Arab lands, Egypt, the Aegean islands and the north coast of Africa, the lines of power would all run to Topkapı.

The New Palace was Mehmet's office, where he received ambassadors, held council with his ministers, issued commands, and ruled his empire. How much leisure living he did here we do not know, but it is probable that he slept here from time to time since he built a Has Oda or Privy Chamber for the sultan's personal attendants. So far as we know there was no permanent harem for the palace's first century, although it is likely favorites visited their sultan here on occasion. We know that Süleyman the Magnificent, whom Turks call, perhaps erroneously, the Law-Giver, sometimes brought to Topkapı his clever, conniving and fascinating favorite, Hürrem, the Joyous One. The West calls her Roxelana, a name we have twisted out of her probable Russian origin. The rest of the harem, except likely her retinue of slaves, stayed behind in the Old Palace, an arrangement that doubtless made it easier for her to keep her hold on this least polygamous of Ottoman sultans. The statement one sometimes sees that Roxelana was transferred permanently to Topkapı is false. Women did not continuously live here until the reign of Süleyman's grandson, Murat III. From then on there grew up, piece by piece over the years, the whole harem complex of corridors, courts and rooms that open from one another haphazardly, built here and there, now and then, with no basic plan.

Murat's was a fateful move because it marked the beginning of what history knows as the Kadınlar Saltanatı, the Women's Sultanate, a period in which the paramount influence on the sultan and the grand vizier consisted of women—the sultan's mother and his favorite consorts. It was in Murat's time that the Old Palace became the Palace of Tears. To it were sent the harem of a deceased or deposed sultan to live out their manless lives, and upper palace servants too old to perform their duties.

Topkapı harem apartments were the site of much intrigue and dramatic history. Here Selim III, an enlightened and progressive monarch of the turn of the nineteenth century, was murdered while a callous—or perhaps frightened—palace woman looked on. He was killed in a prayer room he had built for himself near the suite that had been his mother's.

Down along the water were a series of handsome kiosks and the outer gardens of the palace that rose a short way up the hill. On the next rise were smaller gardens and the pavilions of the Fourth Court which, like the harem, were built from time to time by various sultans. In their heyday when the grounds were scrupulously tended, these gardens were made for love. Yet for most of the women masculine love did not exist. The only lover was the sultan, and he, however susceptible—and most of them were susceptible—could get around to only a selected number. Besides, although the sultan might take to bed any woman of the palace he chose, the whole matter was so elaborately guarded by court etiquette, and the sultans, by and large, so proud of their prowess as romantic lovers, there was no atmosphere of orgy about their relations with women. Thus some few women knew what it was to be romanced in a handsome kiosk in a beautiful garden, but most had to be content with the garden's visual beauty.

Up the incline from this Fourth Court lies the Third Court which, with the fourth, comprises the House of Felicity, the private domain of the sultan. Many of the small buildings that once filled it are gone, but others and its graceful portico still stand. Around it range the Pavilion of the Blessed Mantle, where the relics of the Prophet Muhammed are kept, and opposite this the Treasury where wealth was stockpiled. Just inside the Gate of Felicity stands the Throne Room where foreign ambassadors were received.

Outside the Gate of Felicity, going up the hill toward the At Meydanı (Horse Arena) or Byzantine Hippodrome, lies the Second Court or Court of the Divan. At one side of it stands the Kubbe Altı, the Place under the Dome, where the sultan's viziers held their councils of state, and on the other side the several kitchens that cooked for the thousands of people the *saray* fed.

Farthest inland is the First Court, a long area that was open to the public and sprinkled with detached edifices. Its main gate is the Bab-ı Hümayun, the Imperial Gate, just a few steps from Santa Sophia and overlooking the At Meydanı.

[8]

The Hippodrome, today's Sultanahmet Square, is physically without but culturally a part of the palace. It was along its length that enormous spectacles were staged by the sultan to celebrate important events. One of the first such, and one of the greatest, was the fête for the circumcision of three of Süleyman's sons, Mustafa, Mehmet and Selim. In later years Mustafa would, in his young manhood, be executed because of his father's ill-founded suspicions of disloyalty. Mehmet would die a natural death. Selim, the least able of the three, would succeed to the throne.

Among Muslims circumcision is performed not at birth but anywhere between the ages of five and eleven, in odd years, and it is a gala occasion. In the old days it was the custom for the rich to pay for the circumcision of a number of poor boys of their neighborhood, and the accompanying party was for all. Naturally the greatest circumcision parties were those held for the imperial princes.

For his sons' circumcision festivities Süleyman, on June 27, 1530, rode out of the Bab-ı Hümayun to the accompaniment of fanfares. The great of the Empire and the representatives of foreign states were at the At Meydanı awaiting him, and of all the assembly only Süleyman was on horseback. He received the salutations of his chief officials who walked forward to

The original Shore Palace of Topkapı in the mid-nineteenth century, after the towers of the Cannon Gate had been removed, photographed from a watercolor in the possession of the Topkapı Sarayı Museum. Directly above the shore palace is perhaps the Hasan Pasha Kiosk and to the left perhaps the Şevkiye.

NECATI ORBAY

[9]

greet him, and mounted his throne with its gold canopy held up by lapis columns. Around it were set the vari-colored tents of conquered rulers, his tributaries.

The first two days of the spectacle were spent in the sultan's accepting the congratulations of the eminent men of his domain. The third day he received the gifts sent for the occasion: cotton from Egypt, damask (a word derived from Damascus) from Syria, fine fabrics from India, porcelain from China, cups set with precious stones, goblets of crystal, furs, horses, slaves.

The fourth day was a military review that included displays of fencing and equestration. On the fifth came war games. Two towers had been built to be assaulted and captured in mock battle, and finally consumed in pre-arranged holocaust, only to be rebuilt overnight so that the performance could be repeated the next day.

The seventh day provided a procession in which palm branches, the sign of a circumcision or a wedding, were carried, decorated with gold filigree and reproductions of flowers, fruits, birds, and animals. Dances and concerts took place on the eighth and ninth days, together with a juggling performance and a contest in which sailors and Janissaries tried to climb a greased pole to gain the prize fastened to the top. On the tenth day there was a feast for retired officials; on the next three entertainment consisting of tricks of clowns and jugglers and the Karagöz, a performance of two-dimensional puppet figures on a lighted screen.

Finally, on the fourteenth day, the three little princes were brought from the Old Saray and presented to their father. On the fifteenth day a banquet was given to the assembled grandees. On the sixteenth the sultan presided over a learned discussion on the first chapter of the Koran. It is reported that one of the savants, in a fit of frustration when the right words would not come, toppled over with apoplexy. Nothing is reported for the seventeenth day, so perhaps the learned held forth for two days or perhaps the assembly rested. At any rate on the eighteenth the actual circumcision took place, not at the At Meydanı but in the nearby palace of the grand vizier, İbrahim, a subtle, clever, quick Greek who was the sultan's great friend until ambition led him to his death.

The final event was a few days of races out at the Sweet Waters of Europe at the head of the Golden Horn. All in all the *sünnet düğünü* or circumcision festivities had lasted three weeks. When they were over Süleyman asked İbrahim, who was married to his sister, "What in your opinion was the more beautiful, your marriage with my sister or this fête of my sons?"

[1 0]

İbrahim answered, "There never was and never will be a fête like mine, for mine was honored by the presence of the padishah of Mecca and Medina, the Solomon of our epoch." No wonder such a fast-thinking man was grand vizier. So trusted was his position that he entered and left the *saray* by a small side gate which ever after has been known as İbrahim's Gate.

İbrahim was but one of the figures who risked and won and lost to have a hand in the wielding of the great power that rested in Topkapı. Its greatness lasted through the eighteenth century. Then in the early nineteenth Mahmut II took a dislike to the palace. Its bloody history, climaxed by the recent killing of his cousin, Selim III, depressed him. Mahmut, whose aim in any event was to set the Empire on a new course, built new palaces. There he spent his time and honored Topkapı only on state occasions. From then on Topkapı became the new Palace of Tears where the consorts and slaves of the sultan's predecessors lived cut off from the stimulus of the court.

The sultan who followed Mahmut, Abdülmecit, built the Europeanized Palace of Dolmabahçe across the Golden Horn in the newer part of the city. In 1853 he made it the official imperial residence. History had turned away from Topkapı. From then on until the Republic of Turkey rescued it, its story was a sad one of neglect and even destruction. In 1924 Topkapı became a museum, and so it is today, alive again—with Turks and Europeans and Americans come to see the site and experience the feel of history.

THE OTTOMAN DYNASTY

THE FAMILY that lived in Topkapı reigned for seven centuries, beginning in the thirteenth and lasting into the twentieth. The West calls them Ottoman, but their Turkish name is Osmanlı from their eponymous ancestor, Osman, the first ruler of the Ottoman state. Born for the most part of non-Turkish mothers, they were nevertheless Turkish in training, language and custom. Unlike most dynasties they ruled in an unbroken line, thirty-six of them, for although there were abdications and depositions, there was never a hiatus, never a time when a usurper gained the throne or a foreign power overthrew them.

Legends have grown up about their beginnings, legends that came into being after the Ottoman state had gained some importance and its ruler therefore deserved a genealogy. They were written down by early Ottoman historians and from them passed into the histories of the West. The most widely prevalent, at least in the West until recent times, is the tale that the Kayı tribe of nomad Turks was chased west out of Asia by the Mongols and filtered into the Euphrates River country of eastern Asia Minor. There their supposed leader, Süleyman, was drowned in the river, and his son, Ertoğrul, led four hundred families of the tribe up across Asia Minor. Somewhere on their way they came across a battle in progress which their warrior horsemen joined, valiantly on the weaker side. The fresh nomad horsemen brought the embattled forces victory. Happily for Ertoğrul the forces' leader

[12]

turned out to be the Seljuk sultan, Alaeddin, ruler of the Seljuk Turkic state that encompassed central Anatolia. Alaeddin rewarded the nomads by enfiefing Ertroğrul with land on the Byzantine border in northwestern Asia Minor in the country watered by the Sakarya River south of the Sea of Marmara. Osman was Ertoğrul's son. The only actual facts in this story are that the Ottomans did actually start in this region and that there was a thirteenth-century Seljuk sultan named Alaeddin.

Another legend—which used to be the official Ottoman tradition—traces Osman back through fifty-two ancestors through Oghuz Khan, the legendary progenitor of the widespread Oghuz Turkic group, to the Biblical Noah. There were still other genealogies, some contradicting each other. Only in modern times has the early history of the Ottomans come to light, and, so far as historical fact goes, it starts with Osman. Far from being the son of the leader of a tribal band, he has been identified as a fighter for the faith of Islam, a ghazi.

Ghazis were a feature of medieval Islam. In the thirteenth century the Byzantine Empire, weakened but still a recognized power, was holding on to all it had left in Asia Minor, which was the region along the northwestern coast. The rest was cut up into small states, most of them Turkic. In the march or frontier lands between the Byzantines and the Turks a constant warfare of border raids took place, carried on on the Turkic side by the ghazis, warriors for Islam, and on the Byzantine side by the *akritai*, warriors for Christianity. Both were motivated by a passionate desire to extend the boundaries of their faiths; both were avid for booty. Certain of these ghazis won fame for their exploits, and young men, fired by faith or hungry for adventure, clustered around them. They seem to have been loosely organized into an order with a bond of common ideals and customs. Otherwise the ghazi leaders acted independently. Osman was such a man. Like the others he was undoubtedly invested with the title of ghazi by a religious figure, in his case Sheikh Edebali who was to become his father-in-law. From Edebali he must have received the ghazi symbol, a war-club, which he would have held over his head while he repeated the ghazi oath: "With this club will I first subdue all my passions and then kill all enemies of the faith." His son Orhan, in an inscription which is the earliest Ottoman document to come down to us, called himself a ghazi and the son of a ghazi.

Where Osman's family actually was from has not come to light. It may have been anywhere in Asia Minor, for the Turks had been pouring in from western Asia ever since the Seljuk Turks of Iran had defeated the Byzantines in the Battle of Manzikert in 1071. Originally a Central Asiatic people, the Turks had steadily moved westward until some of them reached the Aegean. Osman's ancestors could have been any of these.

The little Ottoman state he founded, then one of the lesser principalities of Asia Minor, grew first by conquering territory from the Byzantines. In 1326 Orhan captured the city of Bursa at the foot of one of the several Mount Olympuses of the eastern Mediterranean—this one is now called Ulu Dağ, the Great Mountain—and made it his capital. The success of the small principality drew to it the elements needed for a viable state. Other frontier warriors, merchants, artisans, the dervishes who were the proselytizing religious figures, and fragments of tribes all gravitated to the Ottoman district because its location, on the border of the decaying Byzantines, and the leadership of its sultans provided the best hope of victories and all of the opportunities for soldiering and looting, proselytizing or commerce or pasturing, whatever one's profession. Among these early comers were members of the *ulema*, the orthodox religious establishment of Islam. They interpreted Islamic law, which became the law of the new state, and laid the foundations for the organization of the territory it would acquire.

The first ten sultans down through Süleyman followed the ghazi tradition. They were warrior sultans who led the army in person, and the victories they won built up an empire. On their way they moved their capital to Edirne (Adrianople) in Europe, but their proudest conquest was the city of Istanbul, the Byzantine Constantinople, which fell to Mehmet II in 1453. This then became their capital, which it continued to be as long as the Empire lasted. Until Mehmet the Conqueror the Ottoman rulers had been leaders of a frontier state, albeit a swiftly expanding one. With him they took on the panoply of empire. Heretofore they had been accessible to the people. From now on they would hide themselves behind the walls of Tokapı, appearing only in procession and on special occasions. Heretofore they had lived largely in tents, despite the palace built in Edirne. Now they would build more palaces, of which Topkapı would be the most important.

Down through Süleyman in the mid-sixteenth century the sultans were extraordinary men, intrepid, stern, but wise in their choice of advisers and skilful in their deployment of the army on the field of battle. They were trained to fight and to govern. In his youth each was taught horsemanship and the use of firearms. In his young manhood each was governor of a province so that he might acquire experience in ruling.

After Süleyman change shook the Ottoman sultans. They lost their

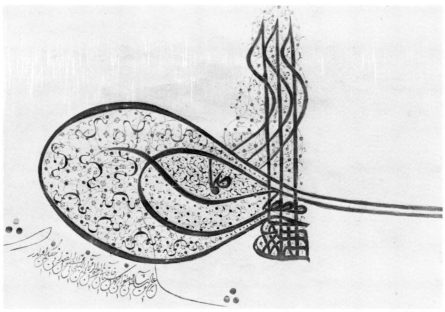

NECATI ORBAY

The tuğra *or signature of Süleyman the Magnificent.*

frontier characteristics. From martial they turned effete and gradually ceased to lead their armies. In the seventeenth century, when they no longer spent their youth afield but in the Kafes or Cage of Topkapi, some became the prey of harem women. Their cruelty was no longer the toughness of a ruler exercised in the interest of the state but a fault of character exercised by whim. They became self-indulgent and their own pleasure, rather than the good of the state, their aim. Concomitant with this came the time when European military power began to equal or even to exceed the Ottomans'. The conquests grew fewer, harder to come by, turned to defeat. Many reasons have been offered for the decline of the Ottoman Empire, and this is not the place to go into them, but surely the weakening of the character of the sultans was one of them. Yet able men appeared among them, and every now and again the dynasty threw up a truly far-sighted sultan. Such were Selim III of the turn of the nineteenth century and Mahmut II of the century's first half. When they came to power they struggled to put the Empire on its feet again, but reactionary forces at home and strong enemies abroad defeated them.

The last strong ruler was Abdülhamit II who ruled from 1876 to 1909.

[1 5]

By his time the sultans had deserted Topkapı. Abdülhamit lived in Yıldız Palace on a hill overlooking the Bosphorus. After him came two more sultans, but figureheads, for the Young Turks had taken power. The last sultan of the Osmanlı dynasty, Mehmet VI, left Istanbul on a British warship on November 12, 1922 to spend his remaining years in exile. The old Anatolian nucleus of the Ottoman Empire, plus Istanbul and a small strip of Thrace, had become the Republic of Turkey. There would be no more imperial ceremonies in Topkapı. It was fitting that it should become a museum.

THE IMPERIAL GATE

AT THE CREST of the hill that rises from Palace Point Mehmet the Conqueror pierced the outer wall of his New Palace with its most important gate, the Imperial Gate (Bab-ı Hümayun). Yet the first time I stood before it in the spacious area cleared of the debris of time and softened only by a few trees, I wondered what was imperial about it, or, for that matter, what was Ottoman. What I saw was a marble portal which, though set in high and massive and obviously very old walls, gave no suggestion of power or of a civilization different from my own. Later I learned that the portal is in fact a late addition to Topkapı, having been built in 1867 after a fire partially destroyed the old gate-house and when Western architectural ideas had become the fashion.

The portal itself is a pleasant enough work, ornamented with slender attached columns and shallow, carved niches. It rises to the height of the wall, around thirty-five feet, grafted onto what is left of the old gate-house. The actual entry, a little left of center, has not changed. A line of marble, underlined with small, chaste decorative pieces, tops the entire length of the gate-house, making a not very successful attempt to tie old and new together.

If the Imperial Gate gives no hint of the majesty within, this was not always so. Old engravings show the original gate-house as a two-storied pavilion of the same rough stone as the wall, tall and wide and dominating the square before it as the present gate could never do. Rivaling it for atten-

tion on the left is the Byzantine bulk of Santa Sophia and on the right the
Fountain of Sultan Ahmet, an exquisite example of the last period of true
Ottoman before the days of European influence, square with swelling circu-
lar corners where water was offered to passersby and a sloping, pinnacled
roof with a deep overhang. It has a truly Eastern quality that presages much
of what we shall see within the palace.

The old gate-house was simple and even austere, with two rows of
windows and the gate itself subsidiary to the building. Its second story and
its windows were never reconstructed so that it no longer towers above the
wall, and its interior is so dark few people tarry there. Cars of sightseers
usually drive right through without stopping.

Yet the gate is worth a closer look since it introduces certain features
that will be encountered again and again in the palace—the *tuğra* (tuh-ra) or
signature of the sultan and the calligraphic inscription. The gateway entrance
is so deep and its arch so high that one looks through it to a lower, flatter

*The old Imperial Gate (Bab-ı Hümayun) before it was destroyed by fire,
from Choiseul-Gouffier. To the right is the Fountain of Ahmet III, to the left
a corner of Santa Sophia.*

arch, obviously left from the old building, whose lintel carries the *tuğra* of Mahmut II of the early nineteenth century, the last sultan to live in the palace, and above this two inscriptions, the upper one that of the Conqueror, the first. These *tuğra*s are interlaced designs of a standard pattern. To the uninitiated they all look alike, but the sultan's name is intricately intertwined in the pattern. Drawing them was a special art. Mahmut's signature here indicates that repairs were made on the gate at his bidding.

Inscriptions are more decorative than legible, and even among those who can read old Turkish in the Arabic alphabet which Atatürk had the nation abandon, it takes a specialist to decipher them. This one tells us when and by whom Topkapı was built: "This is a blessed castle that has been put up with the consent of God and is secure and strong. May God the Most High make eternal the sultanate of the sultan of the two seas, the shadow of God in the two worlds [this world and the next], God's servant between the two horizons, the hero of the water and the land, the conqueror of the stronghold of Constantinople, Sultan Mehmet, son of Sultan Murat son of Sultan Mehmet Khan, and may He place his position above the north star. Done in the month of Ramazan the Blessed in the year 883 (1478/9)."

This must have been the date on which the palace as planned by the Conqueror was completed. We cannot be sure in exactly what year it was begun, but people who have studied the matter think it was sometime after 1465/6, that the construction took several years, and that the old gate-house and walls were the last portion built, having been finished in the year given in this inscription.

At present the gate-house is an entryway, nothing more. Although there are a few side rooms left, they display nothing and in any event are too dark to be of interest to anyone but a student of Ottoman architecture. With the old gate-house things were very different. It had many uses. For the Conqueror it was a place of pleasure with, in his time, an unbroken view of the Hippodrome. Under his successors it was at various times a storehouse for the belongings of people who died without heirs and for soldiers who died in battle, and for state archives. At one period it became the receiving station for the revenue from the crown lands set aside to provide personal spending money for the sultan's mother. This was called shoe money (*başmalık*) since it was for trifles.

The Imperial Gate was guarded by gatekeepers (*kapıcıs*), and they too used these rooms. They also guarded the Middle Gate which connects the First and Second Courts. Like all groups in Ottoman society they had their special headgear, a tall, cylindrical cap that folded over on itself and hung down the back. It was their duty to open the Imperial Gate at the morning call to prayer and to close it after night prayer. On days when the Imperial Council or Divan met they queried at the gate all those who had come to do business with it and ascertained that their business was proper to the occasion. At night the gatekeepers were reinforced by a company of Janissaries, foot soldiers, whose headquarters was a small board structure on wheels which could be rolled up to within a few feet of the gate.

The old days knew old cruelties. At times the gate displayed in its niches the heads of those who had rebelled against the Empire. In the seventeenth century when a series of rebellions had agitated Anatolia, so many heads of defeated rebels were brought to Istanbul that they were heaped in putrifying piles in front of the gate. It was up to the gatekeepers to remove them.

During uprisings in the city it was the gatekeepers' duty to close the great iron doors of the Imperial Gate. This they did not always do. In 1648 when there was a plot afoot against İbrahim, the sultan of the time, the head gardener (bostancıbaşı), who was also chief of the sultan's guard, was won over by the anti-İbrahim forces. He gave the order to the gatekeepers to open the Imperial Gate, and the men aiming at the deposition of the sultan passed through. At other times, other groups forced the gate and brought on those life-and-death crises that faced certain Ottoman rulers.

Today's Imperial Gate has left all this behind. The change is symptomatic of the change that came over the Ottoman Empire. In 1478 it was young and vigorous and bent on conquest, and the Conqueror's gate was large and stern and severe. By 1867 the Empire had run its course. Instead of conquering territory it was losing it, and the gate's rough façade had been softened with carved marble.

Yet the name, Bab-ı Hümayun, still tells us something about the Ottoman Empire. The word *bab* is Arabic for gate and *hümayun* Persian for imperial, the *i* that joins them the Persian genitive. Their use is an example of the Ottoman tendency to fuse into their own language and culture what they willed of Arabic and Persian. The result was the culture of the ruling class, the elite of the Empire. The palace within this gate was the place where many of them were trained and to which the most important of them were attached.

I remind myself that I am entering what was Turkish Wasp territory each time I walk over the cobblestones of the gateway, dodging taxis and met only by small boys who seem to find a fascination in its gloom.

[20]

The Imperial Gate.

The tuğra of Mehmet II at
the entrance of Topkapı Sarayı.

THE FIRST COURT

IT ALWAYS SEEMS to me that nowhere is the passing of the Ottoman Empire so evident as in the First Court of the *saray*. The only building one sees is the Byzantine Church of St. Irene, which is after all pre-Ottoman. The court is open to the public as it has always been, but the public today consists of taxi drivers loitering beside their cabs waiting for a tourist fare, sellers of postcards, and men who sidle up to foreigners and ask, "Change money?" On Sundays and holidays, when Turks visit the palace, there may be men selling *simit*, the bread ring the Turks have been eating for centuries, but on other days these are replaced by sellers of the modern *sandviç* (sandwich). A few tourists stroll through here but most come by bus or taxi along the curving, tree-shaded road that winds in from the Imperial Gate or a similar one that climbs the hill from a side entrance. They meet at the Middle Gate which is the entrance to the Topkapı Palace Museum. Inside, the museum has restored the palace. In the First Court, which does not belong to the museum, one has to do one's own restoration.

The First Court is the largest of the courts, too long to take in at a glance, about 1,000 feet and of varying widths, though roughly 500 feet. It follows the straight lines of Turkic military encampments except on the east or Sea of Marmara side where the contour of the land molds it. Most of it is given over to dusty ground where fig trees have sprung up since the feet of horses ceased to tread it. The rows of long disused cannon that lie on the ground, the old walls and the fountain or two that line it seem to claim little attention. Yet this was the Procession Court (Alay Meydanı) where gaily caparisoned horses carrying men in vari-hued costumes used to line up waiting to fall in to the cortèges that were so important a part of court life. Each day members of the Outer Service went about their duties here, men passed down it to press their claims for justice, and dignitaries traversed it on horseback.

For me an effective way to bring the First Court back to life is to look closely at the miniature of it from the *Hünername, The Book of Skills* of the sultans made in the late sixteenth century, which we reproduce here. Though like all Islamic miniatures it has taken liberties with space, foreshortening the court and placing the Middle Gate on a line with the Imperial Gate whereas it is actually a bit to the left, it pictures what the court contained when the Empire was at its height. Later other structures were added, and some subtracted. The Imperial Gate, in the mid-front of the painting, has the old pavilion over it and Bab-ı Hümayun written in Ottoman letters in its doorway. Gatekeepers, their headdresses falling down their backs, guard both this and the Middle Gate.

The large building inside the gate to the left is St. Irene, about where it stands today. Under Ottoman tenure it was the Imperial Armory and is so labeled. To the right of it on the ground is a set of scales marked State Wood Scales, and it is indeed weighing a piece of wood. To the right of the road is placed the infirmary for the pages of the Palace School, called here the Room of the Sick, with two pages and a eunuch outside it. One of the closed litters that brought in the sick is pictured before it.

Halfway down and a bit to the left stands a fountain, from the position of its trough on the ground a horse fountain, fountain *(çeşme)* clearly written along its base. Down on the left near the Middle Gate men are handing out long sheets of paper from a kiosk labeled Tower of the Commissioner of Stationery. He distributed the special colored and watermarked paper that court calligraphers used. There was apparently a portico at the upper left of which there is now no trace. It is interesting to see it here because porticoes are a salient feature of the Second and Third Courts.

The Middle Gate, unmistakable because of its twin towers, is here curiously marked Gate of Felicity (Babüssaadet) which is now and has long been the name of the gate to the Third Court. It would seem from this and another miniature that at some early period the names changed. The figures on horseback and afoot show the court a lively place and give a better idea than words could of the costumes of the period.

The *Hünername* miniature having coaxed the Ottomans back to life, it

Hünername *Miniature No. 1: the First Court.*

is less of a task to re-create the First Court in some detail, although one must remember that not all the buildings were here at any one time.

The site of the infirmary for the Palace School to the right as one enters is now a dust patch that once held several wards for the several halls of pages and a small garden. The Palace School was an extraordinary institution that trained men for government posts. It was located in the Third Court and we shall get to it presently. Borne to the infirmary in litters drawn by the men who manned the wood yard, which stood across the way, the ailing pages were here solaced by music and wine. Although alcoholic beverages were forbidden them in the rest of the palace, for some reason they were permitted in the infirmary, which was regularly supplied by the palace gardeners who made their deliveries by hoisting canteens over the garden wall. It is said the pages were so fond of the place measures had to be taken to prevent malingering. Only when the sultan gave his permission could a page be moved to the infirmary. Even a tooth could not be pulled without his sanction, and if the extraction was somehow found unnecessary, the physician lost one of his own teeth in recompense. The Department of Finance was located near here, but it too has disappeared, destroyed by fire.

Past the historic dust patch one comes upon an open space that was the Boot Gate (Cizme Kapısı). I have never come upon an explanation of the name and can only suggest that there may once have been a bootmaker's workshop down in this direction, perhaps behind one of the doors that once opened from the wall that goes downhill. An alternate name for it is the Garden Gate (Bahçe Kapısı), which is more understandable since it led to palace vegetable gardens. The first time I tried to follow the road that dips down from here I was brought up short by a sentry guarding the army installation near the shore. Later, through the kind offices of Kemal Çiğ, the assistant director of the museum, I was able to investigate old sites down here.

Near the Boot Gate some sources say there was once a grove of lemon trees. Be that as it may, beginning a bit past the gate and reaching all the way to the inner wall of the palace is a long grey stone wall, a little higher than a man, behind which the Imperial Bakery stood and the palace waterworks still stand. About a third of the way down it lingers an old doorway with a quatrain telling us the bakery was built in 1616, which puts it in the reign of Ahmet I, the builder of the Blue Mosque. From the bakery came a very fine white bread made of corn flour. The grain was transported for this special purpose from the city of Bursa in northwest Anatolia and grown in the surrounding countryside, once the Roman province of Bithynia. Bread baked from this flour and goat's milk went daily to the sultan, to his and his predecessors' married daughters, and to certain pashas and other men of importance as an indication of imperial favor. A coarser flour was imported from Greece, and a bread that was perhaps a mixture of the two, being of a medium color, went to persons of middling importance. Black bread, probably baked entirely from the Greek flour, was given to the court pages. Each person on the list had his daily allotment. How many loaves went to the sultan is not recorded, but the married daughters living outside Topkapı in palaces of their own each received twenty, the pashas ten each, the head of the religious hierarchy (şeyhülislâm) eight, and so on down the line to one per head for lesser folk. The bakery included a mosque for the bakers who were on a salary fixed according to rank and given a woolen outer garment each year at the bayram or holiday at the end of the holy month of Ramazan. The bakery continued in operation until 1880, after the sultans had forsaken the palace. Its mosque wall is now incorporated into a modern building which is the workshop for the Archaeological Museum. All the rest has disappeared. Farther along an old fountain hugs the outside of the wall underneath what appears to be a stone tower but which perhaps could have been a chimney. It is in such bad shape that not even its date remains.

Behind the wall, near its end, are the palace waterworks. The entrance to them, however, lies in the Second Court near the Imperial Kitchens. Here are the storage wells for water brought from distant springs. The wells connect with the large cisterns and canals that have supplied the palace with water for centuries. Today they are equipped with electric pumps and force water to those of the palace fountains that are now flowing. They also protect the palace from fire by means of a modern system based on the principle of ionization. It gives an alarm and indicates the location of the smallest sign of fire, even cigarette smoke, and sends water under pressure through the canals to the place endangered. None of this area behind the bakery wall is open to the public.

On the court side of the wall that hides the waterworks, flush against it, is the Executioner's Fountain (Cellât Çeşmesi), a grim reminder of the summary justice—or injustice as the case might be—that could be handed out. It is unadorned as befits its grim function, except for a tuğra and inscription added in the late nineteenth century in the reign of Abdülhamit II. Its date is unknown but its simplicity suggests antiquity. Among the many duties of the palace gardeners was the performance of executions. Men condemned to death by the Imperial Council were sometimes beheaded by them here and their heads exhibited on short columns in front of it, the Warning Stones (İbret-i Senkler). The executioner then matter-of-factly washed off his axe and knife under the faucet of the fountain. The executed were often political personages, the victims of the intrigue endemic in the Empire. Up to the nineteenth century the risk of losing one's head was great in high position. Yet it did not prevent men from maneuvering for important posts, so alluring were the rewards. Many a grand vizier fell victim to the executioner's sword, although he had the doubtful honor of being beheaded elsewhere. During the time of Selim I, the Grim (1512–1520), so many grand viziers were executed a favorite curse came to be, "May you be *sadrazam* to Sultan Selim." (*Sadrazam* was a title of the grand vizier.)

To return to the Executioner's Fountain, when the German Emperor Wilhelm II visited Istanbul in the late nineteenth century it was thought the sight of this might make a bad impression on him, and so the fountain was removed from the wall and stored in one of the rooms of the Imperial Gate. After the palace became a museum it was restored to its original setting.

Going back to the Imperial Gate and concentrating on the left-hand side of the road, one passes first the place where stood the dormitory of the Carriers of Silver Water Vessels and of the Straw-Weavers who wove the matting that covered the palace floors. The first carried the water with which the walls of the Room of the Blessed Mantle in the Third Court were washed down. Among the duties of the latter was, each year, to weave new matting for the Room of the Blessed Mantle in the Third Court for which they used special reeds from Lake Manyas in Anatolia. The old floor covering was brought out to the First Court and burned. To the rooms of these two services was added a wood yard that could hold five hundred shiploads of firewood cut from the imperial lands along the Black Sea and Mediterranean coasts. It was unloaded at the Wood Gate on the Marmara and then piled in the wood yard to be carried to the many fireplaces of the palace by the halberdiers. On one occasion, which we shall go into later, it was used as weapons.

In the year 1634/5 one of the great Ottoman tragedies took place in the wood yard, the execution of the Ottoman poet, Nefi. He has been called the greatest satirist in Ottoman literature, and this talent was his undoing. It was his custom to write lampoons which he called Arrows of Fate (Sıhan-ı Kaza) about persons of importance. Among his victims was the sultan's brother-in-law who was angry enough and influential enough to obtain Murat IV's consent to Nefi's doom. His execution was performed with the acquiescence of the religious hierarchy (*ulema*) who too had felt the poet's shafts.

In 1622 the wood yard's merchandise found tragic use when the Janissaries, who were not issued arms in times of peace because they could not be trusted with them, picked up the logs to use as weapons in storming the palace to unseat the young and promising Osman II and reinstate on the throne the demented Mustafa I. The Janissaries were an unruly corps and habitually signaled their unrest by overturning their soup kettles, huge metal cauldrons that can still be seen in a kitchen of the museum. A favorite spot for this was under a wide-spreading plane tree that used to stand in the First Court. Earlier in this century a stump and limb of it were left, propped up by concrete, but by now all of it has succumbed.

A little farther in the court the impressive Church of St. Irene still keeps its place, reddish on the outside but wonderfully light and spacious within. From the time of the Conqueror till the end of the Empire it was an armory. The Republic at first transformed it into a military museum but recently it has been so beautifully restored it is difficult to think of its ever having housed weapons. Yet in the seventeenth century the sultan's standard, flying the horsetails denoting his rank, was set up in front of it when he was about to go to war. The cannon that lie outside of it date from the time of Süleyman through World War I. They belong not to Topkapı but to the Military Museum, and one day will be moved to that museum's new quarters now being planned for the Conqueror's old arsenal in Tophane across the Horn.

Beyond St. Irene, still on the left, one passes the tall buff wall and arched gate of the Imperial Mint (Darbhane, literally Striking House). In early times it stood near the Old Palace but has been at Topkapı at least since the last years of the seventeenth century. In it not only were the Empire coins struck, but here craftsmen made some of the gold and silver vessels, the jewelry and jewel-set objects of the palace, and the doors inlaid with mother-of-pearl and tortoiseshell that one sees farther in. Here too was the Pavilion of the Weavers of Silver Thread who wove the silver and perhaps gold cloth used in the palace. It had once been in another part of the city but was moved to the Mint premises by Ummetullah, a concubine of Ahmet III, after the old building burned. The plague of fire followed it here, and it burned in Topkapı a few years later. It was rebuilt in 1723. Though the Darbhane no longer coins money, it sets the standards of purity of metal.

Nestling against the wall of the Mint a little farther on is a modest little fountain from the time of Selim III. It carries his *tuğra* and a verse stating that one İbrahim, Selim's equerry, had it built "so that he might be remembered kindly until the day of eternity."

At the end of this wall comes the second road to the court, passing, a short way down a hill, through the Gate of the Guardians of the Walnut Tree (Koz Bekçileri Kapısı). The road leads to the level now occupied by museums and the Tile Kiosk, thence to the Gate of the Fountain of Fresh Water (Soğuk Çeşme Kapısı), which opens onto the street siding the land wall. There is a story here, true or not. It goes that a slave girl escaped from the imperial harem, it does not say how, and one is at a loss to figure out in what way she could have slipped through those well guarded gates. The chances are good that, having lived the secluded life of the harem, she did not know her way around the palace grounds. It was inevitable that she should have been caught. Her captor was a palace attendant who hid her in a plane tree while he bargained for a reward for her return. What he wanted was the post of watchman at this gate. He won his point, the girl was returned, to what fate the story does not say, and the gate thereafter became known as the Gate of the Guardians of the Girl (Kız Bekçileri Kapısı). Time and the tendency to tease words changed kız (girl) to koz (walnut), and so it became the Gate of the Guardians of the Walnut Tree.

Besides guard duty these men carried beverages for the sultan, keeping them cool in metal pitchers in the summer and warming them over braziers in the winter. When the sultan mounted his horse for the Friday procession to an imperial mosque to pray, one of them handed him a drink in a cup of gilded bronze. These men also carried the clothing of the sultan, the chief black eunuch and the treasurer on excursions from the palace, and had the privilege of making coffee for the sultan in their quarters. After Mahmut II gave up Topkapı the Koz Bekçileri had little to do and were abolished in 1867/8. Their guardhouse has long since disappeared, but their gateway remains. To the right of this road, below where the wall of the First Court until recently stood, excavation is going on for an addition to the Archaeological Museum on the lower level. In the process they are coming upon remains from both Byzantine and the Conqueror's times.

The area between the road and the inner wall of the palace seems to have been a favorite site for small kiosk construction. At various times there were placed here the Palace Storehouse and the office of the commissioner who watched over palace maintenance (şehremini); two pavilions for members of the Outer Service; and the headquarters of the Pious Foundations (Evkaf), the government department that regulated property in religious trusts. Just in front of this, near the Middle Gate, stood the Hall of Lawsuits (Dâva Kasrı) where every day one of the viziers of the Imperial Council heard petitions from morning till evening and made summaries of them to be presented to the Council.

That is the extent of the information we have on the physical make-up of the First Court, but that is really only a part of its story. The rest consists of the events that went on here, the gathering of the imperial processions and the turbulence that from time to time engulfed it, usually led by the Janissaries. To understand how they could be so independent as sometimes to defy the sultan and why they figured in so many important happenings both within and without the palace, it is necessary to know something of their history.

The Janissaries were a venerable institution organized as early as the third quarter of the fourteenth century, about a hundred years before the taking of Istanbul, to provide a corps of standing infantry on which the sultan could rely. Their Turkish name, Yeni Çeri, of which Janissary is a Western corruption, means New Troops. Conscripted from the Christian population when boys, they were Islamized and trained in hardiness, archery, and small arms. From the earliest times they had a reputation for being hard to handle. At the accession of each sultan they demanded and were given presents of money as the price of their loyalty.

However intractable in peace, the Janissaries were a formidable fighting force in the stress of battle and important contributors to Ottoman victories. Their martial reputation lasted as long as the corps consisted of slaves. With no relatives at hand and forbidden to marry until retirement, they had no home but their hearth or *ocak* (ojak), no loyalty save to the sultan. Since when not on campaign one of their duties was to keep order, they came to be stationed around the Empire, but a large contingent was always in Istanbul, quartered in their barracks at the Et Meydanı (Meat Square), which lay up the hill from the palace a little to the west of what is now Hürriyet Meydanı (Freedom Square) where the University stands.

Their *ağa* or chief officer, so important he took part in the councils of state, was also head of the police of Istanbul, responsible for law and order in the entire city except for the palace and its environs. Rank and file Janissaries were a police force under him and as such could not be punished except by their own officers. Spoiled and headstrong, they were a law unto themselves.

They, too, had their distinctive headdress, a white felt cap mitered in the front, its division marked by an upright embellished shaft of silver, into which it is said they thrust a spoon, and a long tubular piece of cloth flowing in back. Legend has it that this headgear represents the sleeve of the Turkish saint, Hacı Bektaş, who was supposed to have blessed their initial organization by passing his sleeve over their heads. In point of fact Hacı Bektaş had died a long time before the Janissaries came into being. Their headgear was adapted from that of an Islamic guild of young men, and was not actually so very different from that of other early Ottoman services, except that it was white.

In 1622 Osman II, called Young Osman because he had yet to grow a beard, determined to replace them. They got wind of this and decided to stop him before he could stop them. That was when they charged the palace, picked up the logs in the wood yard, and raced their way into the Third Court, the House of Felicity, which was forbidden ground to all but members of the Inner Service. Here a palace page told them in which room of the harem Mustafa was being held. They climbed to the roof of this room, made a hole in the ceiling, and let down a man who found Mustafa sitting on a cushion with two slave girls at his feet. Out through the hole they pulled the madman. It was their purpose to put him on a horse and show him to the crowd, but he was too weak to sit a saddle. In all the tumult the palace people had forgotten to feed him. He was led instead to the Throne Room. Osman was transported to the Fortress of the Seven Towers, Yedi Kule, in the city walls. There he was eventually strangled. Strangulation was the accepted method of disposing of royalty, it being unthinkable to shed imperial blood.

Despite their unruliness the Janissaries had ceremonial duties. Every Friday when the sultan was in Istanbul he went to an imperial mosque to pray, and Janissaries in violet uniforms and startlingly white headgear lined his route. He chose different mosques at different times, sometimes Santa Sophia close by, sometimes a mosque farther off. In Süleyman's time the choice must often have fallen on the Mosque of Süleymaniye built at his direction by the famous Ottoman architect, Sinan. It lies at some distance from the palace and thus gave more people an opportunity to watch the procession.

A half-hour before the sultan emerged, two pages from the Privy Chamber of the Palace School appeared in the First Court, mounted their horses and rode out of the palace and along the route. They carried two imperial turbans, one with an aigrette and one without, which they bent slightly from time to time in the direction of the populace as if substituting

[31]

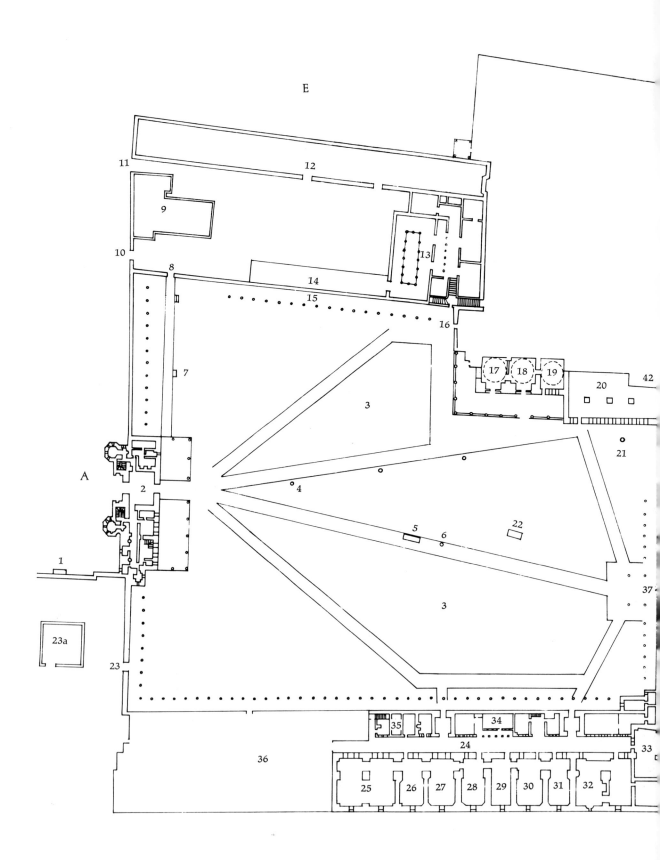

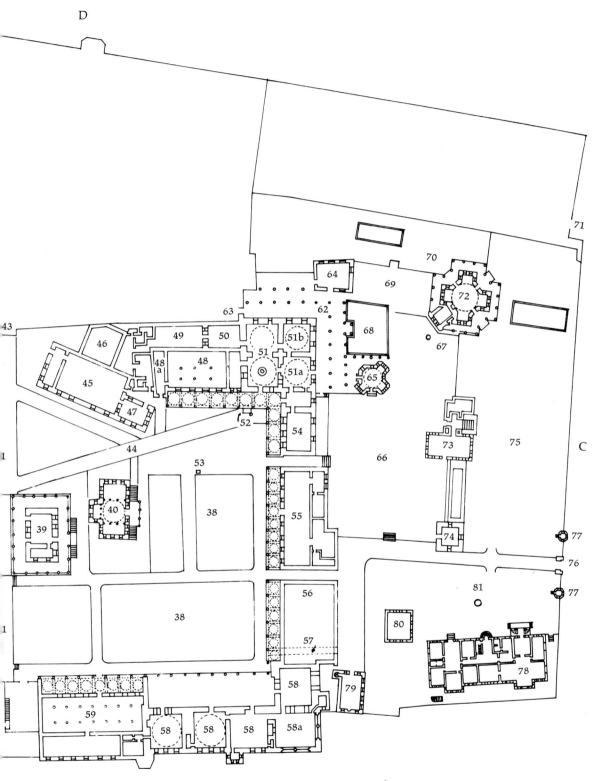

Key to Floor Plan of THE PALACE OF TOPKAPI

1. Executioner's Fountain
2. Middle Gate, entrance to the Topkapı Palace Museum
3. The Second Court
4. *Selâm* or Greeting Stone
5. Top of Byzantine cistern
6. Very old well, closed
7. Fountain
8. Death Gate
9. Mosque of Hacı Beşir Ağa
10. Mosque Gate
11. Outer Death Gate
12. Display of coaches, sedan chairs and horse trappings, formerly the Privy Stable
13. Quarters of the Halberdiers with Tresses
14. Their terrace
15. Arcade with old stone inscriptions
16. Carriage Gate to the harem
17. Divanhane or Council Hall
18. Scribes' Room
19. Display of watches, formerly room of the grand vizier
20. Arms and Armor, formerly Finance or Inner Treasury
21. Target stone marking where a sultan's arrow landed
22. Monument of Sukhum
23. Gate to the palace waterworks
23a. Waterworks
24. Kitchen Court
25. Display of Chinese porcelains, formerly the kitchens that cooked for the sultan, the princes, and the *valide sultan*
26, 27. Display of Chinese porcelains, formerly the kitchens for the harem women and the gatekeepers, respectively
28. Display of Chinese and Japanese porcelains and other objects, formerly the kitchen for the Divan
29. European porcelains, formerly the kitchen for the pages
30. Display of European objects, formerly the kitchen for the lowest palace servants
31. Display of gifts to Abdülhamit II on the 25th anniversary of his accession and other objects, formerly the kitchen for the harem serving women
32. Reproduction of an old kitchen, formerly the kitchen for the lower civil servants of the Divan, the room of the coffee-makers, and the confectionery
33. Display of Istanbul glassware and porcelain, formerly the confectioners' mosque
34. Dormitory of the apprentice cooks and dishwashers
35. Tinsmithing shop
36. This section is off limits to visitors; formerly used by members of the kitchen service
37. Gate of Felicity
38. The Third Court
39. Throne Room
40. Library of Ahmet III
41. Embroideries, formerly quarters of chief white eunuch
42. Kuşhane Gate to the harem
43. Kuşhane, the sultan's private kitchen
44. Marble Way from the Pavilion of the Blessed Mantle to the Throne Room
45. New Library, formerly the Ağas' Mosque
46. Former harem mosque
47. Reading room of the library, formerly a chapel
48. Display of calligraphy, formerly the dormitory of the pages of the Privy Chamber

48a. Special collection of calligraphy, formerly part of the Privy Chamber
49. Room of the Privy Chamber
50. Kerchief Room, now displaying religious relics and formerly a part of the Privy Chamber
51. Pavilion of the Blessed Mantle, formerly the Conqueror's Privy Chamber and now displaying religious relics
51a. Formerly the Reception Room of the Privy Chamber, now displaying religious relics
51b. Room of the Blessed Mantle itself
52. Mounting stone for the sultan and closed well beside it
53. Fountain, the gift of a harem woman
54. Display of a sultan's canopy, throne, and silver mounting block, formerly the Treasury of the Sacred Trusts and previous to that the Armor Treasury
55. Painting and miniature section, formerly the dormitory of the pages of the Treasury
56. Office of the museum director and his staff, on the site of the dormitory of the pages of the Commissariat
57. Underground passage from the Third to the Fourth Court
58. Privy or Imperial Treasury
58a. Treasury porch overlooking the Sea of Marmara
59. Display of sultans' clothing, formerly the dormitory of the campaign pages
60. Home of the assistant director, formerly a conservatory
61. Museum facilities, former quarters of the white eunuchs
62. Corridor with Pillars
63. Door to the Mabeyn and the Golden Way
64. Circumcision Room
65. Revan Kiosk
66. The Fourth Court; this section was the Tulip Garden
67. Tiered fountain
68. Pool with jets on the terrace
69. Marble Terrace; the small jutting portion is the İftariye
70. Garden
71. Elephant or Garden Gate
72. Baghdad Kiosk
73. Kiosk on the Terrace or Kiosk of Mustafa Pasha
74. Tower of the chief physician
75. Garden of the Fourth Court
76. Third Gate, connecting the Fourth Court with the Fifth Place in the Outer Palace, now part of Gülhane Parkı
77. Guard houses
78. Mecidiye Kiosk in Fourth Court; restaurant on lower level
79. Small Mosque on the Terrace
80. Wardrobe Room, where visitors prepared to be received by the sultan in the Mecidiye Kiosk
81. Pool carved with sea life

A. The First Court
B. Former gardens, extending to wall along Sea of Marmara
C. Fifth Court, now part of Gülhane Parkı, extending to the Golden Horn at Saray Point; the sea wall has been demolished around Saray Point
D. Former gardens, now Gülhane Parkı, extending in part to the railroad yards, in part to the land wall
E. Level on which the Tile Kiosk and other museums stand

Rendered by Yılmaz Güngör from material supplied by the Topkapı Palace Museum

Imperial Harem: for detailed plan see pp. 210–211

for the sultan's greeting. The original purpose of this had been to provide the sultan with a change of turbans in the mosque, but it came to be simply a matter of display.

Finally the sultan himself rode through the Middle Gate on a spirited horse equipped with a saddle set with gems. With him came the principal officers of the Privy Chamber who, at least in Süleyman's time, consisted of the chief officer of the hall, the sword-bearer, the master of the wardrobe, the master of the stirrup, and the master of the keys. The master of the turbans, who ranked with them, was one of those who had gone on before. In the First Court they mounted horses that had been brought up from the Great Stable down near the Marmara and took their place in line. The chief officer of the hall had robed the sultan for the ceremony and would disrobe him on their return. Meanwhile his place in the procession was near the padishah, whom he accompanied on all excursions outside the palace. Somewhat to the sultan's right rode the sword-bearer, the ruler's jeweled sword over one shoulder, a long piece of fabric heavily embroidered in gold over the other. Whereas the other gentlemen-in-waiting wore turbans for the occasion, his headdress was a high affair that folded over on itself, not unlike that of the gatekeepers but taller and a bright red. Close to the padishah rode the master of the wardrobe who carried the ruler's raincoat and scattered money to the people as the cortège progressed.

The procession was swelled by numerous others—messengers, foot attendants and guards of the imperial stirrup who walked or ran beside or in front of him, and a contingent of gatekeepers. Their costumes changed over the centuries, but they were always complicated and always colorful. Most amazing were those from whose headpieces large brooms of feathers rose into the air.

The pièce de résistance of all this was of course the sultan, the most gorgeous of them all. None of them had more innate dignity than Süleyman who scarcely needed the pomp of the procession to give him grandeur. Nevertheless his head was invested with a wide oval turban of a type that later went out of fashion, to which was attached a peacock feather aigrette in one of the jeweled holders to be seen in the museum Treasury. Over a gown of heavy silk he wore a sleeveless robe, likely ermine-trimmed, and it was his fancy to ride a white horse. As he proceeded down the First Court his suite fell in around him, led by the heralds who made way for the procession once it emerged into the street.

Today, looking at the First Court, I have sometimes wondered how it accommodated all those people. But the fig-trees weren't here then, nor the cannon usurping the ground. Under Süleyman the court must have been much as it is shown in the *Hünername* miniature; the wall of both bakery and mint came later. Much of it was clear. The most cogent reason, however, must have been the infinitely detailed organization of all things Ottoman. Everyone knew his exact place. Everyone was quiet, for the discipline of silence that became more severe the deeper one went into the *saray* was first invoked here. Nothing was heard but the clip-clop of the horses' hoofs and the footsteps muffled by the earth—only the paths of the court were paved —as the various services passed through it, in attendance on Süleyman. An august figure of stately manner and stern countenance, his long beard whitening as the years passed, he showed the acquiline profile he shared with the rest of the Ottoman dynasty to the crowds that stood to watch him.

No one was ever more waited upon than the ruler of the Ottoman Empire. Once he reached the mosque his boots were removed by the Ağa of the Janissaries and slippers, perhaps velvet, perhaps soft leather, which had been carried for the purpose put on his feet. No more than any other man could the sultan defile the mosque's rugs to which the Muslim touches his forehead in prayer. His prayer rug had already been set down in the imperial pew which was an enclosed place usually up a flight of stairs from the general congregation. Held by the arms in traditional Ottoman fashion, he was escorted to it by the Janissary Ağa and the mosque's administrator. The pew had already been perfumed with incense and supplied with trays of flowers and fruits which would later be dispersed to the women of his family. After the service he was escorted back to the palace as he had come.

It was the custom, during the Friday prayer procession, for subjects with grievances to present petitions to the sultan. These were handed not to the sultan himself but to members of his suite. Back in the palace, the sultan read them and then turned them over to the grand vizier. It would be interesting to know whether he ever followed any of them up.

The Friday processions were by no means the only parades that originated in the First Court but only the most frequent. Similar processions, longer and grander and participated in by the grand vizier, took place on various festive days called *bayrams* and on the sultan's departure for war. Their details might vary from reign to reign, but not their general tenor.

There was one cortège, however, that went into the palace and not out of it. Moreover, what was extraordinary for the time and place, it centered

[3 6]

around a woman. It was the procession of the sultan's mother (*valide alayı*), which was instituted after the harem moved to Topkapı. Fortunately a detailed account of one of these has come down to us.

On a day in April, 1789, the procession of the mother of Sultan Selim III passed through the already three centuries old Imperial Gate and along the winding road of the First Court to the Middle Gate. She had been living in the Old Palace since the death of her husband, Mustafa III, fifteen years before. On the accession of her son she had become *valide sultan* (val–ee–deh sool-tan, mother sultan), and now, a few days after his enthronement, she was passing in panoply from the Old Palace to the New.

Mihrişah—her name means ruler of the sun—rode in a closed carriage; in an earlier day her vehicle would have been a sedan chair. She is said to have been a Georgian from the Caucasus who entered the harem of Mustafa III, became one of his *kadıns* or official concubines, and in 1761 gave birth to Prince Selim. Before Mustafa's death banished her to the Old Palace she had had thirteen years to be near her son in Topkapı, and in those thirteen years a closeness had grown up between them that lasted until her death. This day was her time of triumph. From now on Mihrişah would have as her own the most important suite in the harem. She would be the undisputed mistress of all the women in the harem. She would have privileges other women of the Empire dared not dream of. Officials would court her favor, hoping for her intercession with the sultan, and members of both her own and foreign governments load her with gifts.

As her procession made its way down the hill of Divan Yolu, the Council Road that led from the Old Palace to the sea, her path was lined with Janissaries. In front of her carriage strode the Council heralds (*divan-ı çavuşlar*), in her day wearing a complicated turban boasting a feather in front. Following them were men whose duties had to do with the holy cities of Mecca and Medina, and then her steward (*kethüda*), the man who looked after her worldly affairs. These would be many, for the *valide* usually became a wealthy woman. His head was topped by the wadded turban of a pasha and his body clad in a long, wide-sleeved robe trimmed with sable. In his hand he carried a scepter. He in turn was followed by two ranks of halberdiers and finally, in long robe and tall, cylindrical turban, the Ağa of the House of Felicity or chief black eunuch. Next came the *valide sultan* herself in a closed carriage drawn by six horses, while around and behind her officials scattered bright coins to the populace. After her, in other carriages, rode daughters of former sultans and women slaves, filling eighty to a hundred vehicles in all and peeping out from the windows at a world they seldom saw.

At the Janissary guardhouses along Divan Yolu the procession halted for a ceremony in which the chief Janissary officer kissed the ground in front of the *valide* and was presented with a robe of honor *(hıl'at)*, a customary Ottoman manner of bestowing favor. At the same time presents were handed out to the individuals who manned the guardhouse and to the officer and his suite, all in accordance with a register which carefully specified who was to get what.

At the At Meydanı or old Hippodrome, the procession marched straight ahead between the Hippodrome and Santa Sophia. There it turned, with the great building on its left and the Fountain of Sultan Ahmet on its right, to enter the Imperial Gate. It halted a few minutes just inside the First Court while the head of the Armory saluted the *valide* and was rewarded with a present. The lady's escort withdrew at the infirmary and quietly arranged themselves in two rows according to rank, while her carriage passed between them to the Imperial Bakery.

Meanwhile Selim III, his long face and deep-set eyes solemn, walked slowly along this road in the opposite direction. He met his mother as her carriage reached the bakery's gateway. Striding to her right, he stretched out his hand for hers and carried it to his lips and then to his forehead in the traditional graceful Oriental salute, the *temenna*. The heralds cheered, calling out, "Long life to our padishah!" and Selim fell in front of his mother's carriage. On foot he led her through the Middle Gate and on to the imperial harem.

The processions one sees in the First Court today are the lines of cars, taxis and buses that drive up to the Middle Gate to debouch sightseers of all nations for the museum, on busy days creating a modest traffic jam. The tourists who climb the concrete ramp to the gate seldom look back. Often I have wanted to stop them and say, "Forget the taxis and the fig-trees and the street-sellers for a minute and in their stead people the court with long-skirted figures and prancing horses. This after all is part of the palace, what the Turks called Birinci (Birinji) Yer, the First Place."

THE MIDDLE GATE

THE MIDDLE GATE (Orta Kapı) has a military appearance and a Turkish name. The one is false, the other given to it at a late date. It was formerly called the Babüsselâm, which is Arabic and can mean either the Gate of Greeting or the Gate of Peace. Smooth with dressed stone, it consists of two octagonal towers topped by lead-roofed cones and connected by a deeply crenellated parapet. Below this is the face of the gate which contains a gateway through a larger outer and smaller inner arch much like that of the Imperial Gate, except that here the niches at right angles to the gate are much larger. It suggests defense, but that was a matter of style rather than function. What look like loopholes for weapons are actually only slits to admit light into the prisons the gate contains. The inner wall of the palace in which the gate is set is without battlements and built for privacy. Nevertheless there is a guard walk between the towers, and more gatekeepers manned this than the Imperial Gate. The grimmest part of it is unseen, the windowless dungeons under the turrets.

The original Middle Gate was built by the Conqueror and it does not seem to have been much changed. It used to be thought that Süleyman rebuilt it and added the towers, directly inspired by what he had seen during his campaigns in Central Europe. However, Barnette Miller, who made a study of the *saray* entitled *Beyond the Sublime Porte,* the first modern work about the palace in English, believes they were always there, basing her argument on a Nuremberg woodcut of 1493 which shows a gate with conical towers within the palace wall. Since this gate is so haphazardly situated in the woodcut, more convincing to me is the fact that many of the towers on and within the wall, not only in this woodcut but in a 1520 map of Palace Point by the Italian Vavassore, are conical. Both are before Süleyman's Central European campaigns and would seem to point to conical towers being indigenous to the palace. The argument for attributing them to Süleyman seems to rest on an inscription on the right leaf of the great, four-ton iron doors: "Made by İsa, son of Mehmet, in the year 936," which is 1524/5 of the Christian era, early in the reign of Süleyman I. What probably happened was that the doors were replaced then.

Above the doorway is the *tuğra* of Mahmut II who, although he eventually refused to live in Topkapı, nevertheless kept up certain portions of it. When a sultan had repairs made he affixed his signature to the place restored. Mahmut II's is found in many parts of the palace. At the Middle Gate above his *tuğra* is inscribed the *tevhit*, the Muslim doctrine of monotheism and the central Islamic belief: "There is no god but God, and Muhammed is the Apostle of God."

The outer façade of the gate marked the point at which all had to dismount except the sultan and certain elderly or ill persons to whom special permission was given to ride through. A few others, the sultan's mother and the princes, might be driven through in carriages. Even the grand vizier was reduced to walking here. Although he administered the Empire, his authority ended at the Middle Gate. An incident that took place in the reign of Selim III brings this home.

Şemseddin Bey, a chamberlain new to his job, submitted to Selim certain suggestions on foreign affairs which Koca (Koja) Yusuf Pasha, the grand vizier, thought should have been taken up with him. In the sultan's presence Koca Yusuf kept quiet, but once they left the imperial presence and reached the Middle Gate he turned to the chamberlain and told him sternly, "Şemseddin Bey, you cannot repeat to the sultan everything you hear. I can have your head chopped off right here."

With that Koca Yusuf Pasha mounted his horse and rode off to the grand vizier's palace, leaving poor Şemseddin Bey biting his lips until the blood ran.

By the mid-eighteenth century the Middle Gate was showing signs of decay and an extensive job, largely on the inside face, was done under Mustafa III. The only change on the side facing the First Court was the addition

[4 0]

of inscriptions beside the door. To the right, under Mustafa's *tuğra* and the line, "Keeper of the justice of the Holy Law, the shadow of God," is a poem commemorating this sultan. As summarized by Abdurrahman Şeref, the last imperial historiographer, who made a study of all the inscriptions in the palace, it says: "Sultan Mustafa's utmost desire was the prosperity of the world (the Ottoman Empire). He gazed upon the Imperial Divan. He looked at the ceiling, which his predecessors had not noticed. He saw that the painting and gilding were completely destroyed. The center of the universe (Istanbul), exposed to the eyes of all, should retain a most majestic appearance. He ordered the dilapidated roof to be demolished, and he renovated it completely." This refers to the Hall of the Divan in the Second Court, but more than telling us about a restoration there it shows how completely wrapped in its own image was the Ottoman Empire. It was the world, at least the civilized world, and Europe a barbarian country.

Another poem to the left of the door praises the sultan, which was never done in anything but the most extravagant terms, and ends with a prayer for his long life and prosperity. Over it is Mustafa's *tuğra* and the phrase, "Mustafa Khan, son of Ahmet, victorious forever."

This phrase, victorious forever, was a favorite with which to describe the sultan, even in the days when it was whistling in the dark. The inscriptions are dated 1758/9.

The Middle Gate has two sets of doors, one opening onto the First Court, one onto the Second. Between them is a fair-sized room, today the entrance to the museum, with a heavily decorated ceiling which most people don't take the time to notice. Here the tourist buys his admission ticket and pays a small fee to take along his camera. Printed guides to the museum and its collections are on sale, plus a variety of colored postcards and slides. It is not a place for absorbing palace decoration, though above the door are verses from the Koran and to one side what is left of a fountain from the time of Mustafa III. To the right of this central room were the vaulted quarters of the head gatekeepers, of which there were several. Here foreign ambassadors used to wait for their audience with the grand vizier, often, it is said, for hours. To the left were the small rooms of the ordinary gatekeepers and the cubicle of the executioner.

We have spoken of the slits in the walls of the gate's towers. They let small rays of light into the tower's upper dungeons where at times those whom the sultan had condemned to death awaited their execution. These dark and tragedy-laden cells were called the Gate Area (Kapı Arası), and

The Middle Gate.

anyone led there well knew the fate awaiting him. Perhaps the most famous man to be held in one of those horrid holes was Nevşehirli İbrahim Pasha, grand vizier to Ahmet III during the 1720's.

İbrahim, when a man of fifty, married the thirteen-year-old daughter of Ahmet III in a wedding that was one of Istanbul's great pageants. The difference in their ages was not unusual for the time. It took many years for a man to rise to the top of the Ottoman hierarchy of power, and it was only when he had reached one of the most important posts that he was given an imperial bride. This was a mark of favor for which they all strove, and many grand viziers and heads of the navy (kaptan paşa) married princesses. If a man already had a wife he simply put her aside. İbrahim had of course been married and had children older than his bride. Despite their disparate ages, Fatma was jealous of him, and on at least one occasion Ahmet III reassured his daughter that her husband was not carrying on with the dancers who entertained at the all-male banquets that were a feature of the times.

İbrahim was a man of cultivated tastes, and his and Fatma's palaces were the center of the social and intellectual life of the times. Under İbrahim's patronage literature flourished, translations were made from Arabic and French, printing was introduced, and pleasure palaces were built on French models. This was the Tulip Period (Lâle Devri) of which we shall speak later. The temper of the times is summed up by a verse by the court poet, Nedim, "Let us laugh, let us play, let us take joy from the world."

All this merrymaking and palace building did not set well with the plain people of Istanbul. To their way of thinking the court and the grand vizier had strayed from the simple Islamic way of life in which this world is but a pathway to the next. Feeling against the court's worldliness grew so strong that a mob demanded Nevşehirli's life. It was led by an Albanian bazaar broker, Patrona Halil, who was such a bully he had collected Patrona or vice-admiral as a nickname in his sea-going days. Ahmet III suggested exile, but when the mob refused to accept this he regretfully took back from Nevşehirli the imperial seal which was the requisite of the grand vizier and sent him to the Gate Area. There he was strangled and his body, after being exhibited to the rebels, left outside the Imperial Gate near the fountain where it was hacked to pieces. In the dark of the night a friend gathered up the grisly remains and gave him a proper burial in the garden of a library Nevşehirli had built.

The face of the Middle Gate toward the Second Court is quite different from the stern face it shows the First Court. The plain paneled wooden door is of old Ottoman inspiration and replaces a late painted one. On this side, which was once plastered, the now uncovered brickwork is embellished with medallions on either side of the door, scroll designs painted just under the roof, and in between them landscapes of Istanbul that probably date from Mustafa III. The portico, which is wide, is supported by pink and green columns that may have been first used elsewhere. The deep archways between them once had an all-over type of decoration which the museum has changed to the present more simple motifs that were found beneath. The result is a more clearly Ottoman portico, an imposing and pleasant starting point for exploration of the Second Court.

THE SECOND COURT

IF THE VISITOR to Topkapı needs his mind's eye in the First Court, in the Second Court his visual eye will do very well. Personally I always feel as if I had entered a park, its tall cypresses and plane trees for the moment screening the buildings, except for the lofty Tower of Justice that rises half-way down on the left. The court is a spacious, shady area, 459 feet long by approximately, since it varies, 361 feet wide and threaded by paved paths between which rose bushes make some compensation for the gazelles that used to graze on a lawn here. Straight ahead stretches a broad avenue be-tween two lines of centuries-old cypresses and plane trees, at one point intertwining like lovers, to the Gate of Felicity at the far end. Three other paths, like spokes, lead from the entrance to the grey stone buildings that surround the court, all but one of them fronted by a colonnade, mostly of marble pillars, that breaks the starkness of their façades and links them in a continuity. All have the tincture of age, and indeed all, even the colon-nade, go back at least to the sixteenth century.

They have known several restorations, the first after the fire that swept the palace in 1574 and the last accomplished by the museum. How extensive and how faithful to the old the museum's restoration has been I never ap-preciated until I ran across a series of before and after pictures in an article by Tahsin Öz, the former director. Out of what was at best dilapidation and at worst rubble has been re-created the court where much of the business of empire took place. Even today it is quiet, as if the old rule of silence still held. The guides who shepherd the tourists do not usually start their spiels until they have reached the buildings.

The Second Court had many names, the Court of the Divan because the Hall of the Divan or Council is here, the Second Place (İkinci Yer), the Old Place, and even the Court of the Processions, although in my opinion that appellation more properly belongs to the First Court. Here was enacted the great pageant when, every three months, the Janissaries received their pay, and here ended the processions of the foreign ambassadors who, when they came for an audience, arrived with the pomp due both the accrediting and the accredited powers. Here the sultan sacrificed sheep each year at the Sacrifice Festival (Kurban Bayramı), the feast day when Muslims reenact Abraham's sacrifice of a sheep in place of his son. In this court, on foot, gathered the processions for the circumcision of princes and the marriages of princesses.

Around it range in sequence on the left a gateway to a side court, the quarters of the halberdiers, of whom more anon, the Council Hall or Divan-hane with the tower behind it, and the Museum of Arms which used to be the Finance Treasury. On the right the massive imperial kitchens take up the entire length of the court.

The gateway on the left, down a slope past an old fountain, is called the Corpse Gate (Meyt Kapısı) because through it were carried the dead, except for the sultan. It also served as an auxiliary gate at night when the Middle Gate was closed, especially during the holy month of Ramazan when the fasting of the day was compensated for by the feasting of the night. It leads to a secondary court, the Court of the Halberdiers (Baltacıs), where the first thing one meets is a mosque built by a famous eighteenth-century chief black eunuch, Beşir Ağa. It is a square, reddish building with a low minaret, more like a tower, not particularly handsome on the outside, and closed. Two gates lead out from this side of the court, one a gate on the near side of the mosque and the other, or the far side, another corpse gate by which the dead passed onto a lower level and thence out of the palace grounds. Funerals were never held within the palace. The gates are useless now, since from them one would fall into the excavation for the Archaeological Museum.

The long expanse of stone construction that confronts one as one follows the path around the Beşir Ağa Mosque is the Privy Stable (Has Ahır). There are no extant documents about its origin, but Ekrem Hakkı

NECATI ORBAY

The cypress-lined main path in the Second Court looking toward the Gate of Felicity.

Ayverdi, the architect in charge of its renovation, thinks it dates from the Conqueror's day. Others would put it later. Certainly it is laid up with the rough stone much used by the Conqueror. Before its restoration it was one of the most decayed portions of the palace, its doorways crumbling, its interior a shambles. Only its outer wall seems to have had any strength left, and even it looked a little tired. All this one would never guess from today's sturdy structure. Even the bars on the windows have been replaced, suggesting the high value placed on the steeds and horse gear the stable once held. However, its white plaster interior scarcely brings to mind a stable.

That it was much made over after its original construction is attested both by the lack of early inscriptions and by one from the eighteenth century over a doorway. In summary it says: "The Imperial Stable was dilapidated. Each of the steeds there is of such imposing form that, on seeing it, the iron snake at the At Meydanı would melt in fright. One day Sultan Mahmut (I)

[47]

heard the noble steeds neighing in complaint. He immediately ordered the stable to be renovated."

The At Meydanı is the large open area fronting Santa Sophia known to Westerners as the Hippodrome, today's Sultanahmet Square, and the iron snake the Byzantine Serpentine Column of coiled bronze from which three snake heads used to strike out. It still stands on the Hippodrome, although perhaps not on its original site, but the snake heads have disappeared.

The Privy Stable consists of several rooms, the largest, very long, being where the horses were kept. Today it exhibits imperial coaches. Most of them are from the nineteenth century and indistinguishable from other handsome coaches of the period. Two, however, stand out, both used by imperial women. One is a glittering eighteenth-century coach of Selim III's time, its exterior set with diamond-shaped pieces of glass and inlaid with mother-of-pearl. It is called the Mirrored Carriage (Aynalı Araba). The other, of the same century, suggests femininity with its lattices and panels of green and gold and red. The room also has some old sedan chairs used by the women before carriages became the fashion. There is a pretty little eighteenth-century one of light green with gold filigree, its open sides screened by curtains. These were usually carried by poles on men's shoulders, but the museum has an even older one that was drawn by horses. On the walls is an interesting collection of horsecloths dating from the seventeenth to the nineteenth centuries, their patterns reminiscent of Turkish rugs. A nice touch, and evidence of the Turk's love of horses, is the tombstone Osman II erected for his favorite mount, Süslü Kara, the Fancy Black, that died at the age of four in 1622.

The rooms open onto one another, and one goes next into the much smaller private quarters of the Master of the Stables. It displays saddles, but is really more interesting for its decoration. Before restoration the old door and niches were still there but naked of decoration. They are now clothed with plaster work based on old models and give back to the room the grace it once had. The carved ceiling is not the original but an eighteenth-century work brought from a yalı or seaside house on the Bosphorus. The door is a perfect example of the woodwork of the Conqueror's time with its rectangular carved pattern. The carved surfaces remain untouched, although some of its planks have been repaired.

Next, after a small, in-between area, comes the Harness Treasury (Raht Hazinesi), ample but not huge, which once protected the sultan's jeweled horse trappings except for some so valuable they were stored in the Imperial Treasury. It still has a few jeweled harnesses, including one of silver set with turquoises, but these are late acquisitions. Mahmut II had the gems pried out of the old ones and sold to support the new Western-type army he organized in the nineteenth century.

In older times on festival days the *valide sultan*, the grand vizier, the chief black eunuch and other dignitaries presented jeweled gear to the sultan. Each piece was noted in a register and placed in the Harness Treasury, which was sealed with the Imperial Seal. These trappings have been described as reins of gilded silver, jewel-studded, and horses' headpieces that consisted of gold plaques set with precious stones and dangling with small chains merging into diamond sunbursts, and small, diamond-studded holders of aigrettes to sway over the horses' heads. There were also multitudinous saddles set with precious stones. Dr. Covel, an Englishman viewing a circumcision procession, wrote of it: "In the furniture and ornaments of men and horse . . . Diamonds, rubyes, emeralds, gold, silver, embroider'd work, etc., were common things." After each such ceremonial a count was made of the number of precious stones that had fallen off.

This stable held only twenty-five to thirty horses for the sultan's personal use when he was in Topkapı, fiery animals with long slim legs, sharply pointed ears, and large, lively eyes. The Great Stable (Büyük Ahır), where the pages' horses were kept, was down near the Marmara shore at the Stable Gate, and others lay outside the city. All were in charge of the Master of the Stables (İmrahor, a contraction of Emr-i Ahır, Commander of the Stable) who had under his jurisdiction an assistant and some three thousand grooms, stablemen, saddlers, apprentices and others.

In the latter years of the Empire the Privy Stable was given over to other uses—a hospital for the black eunuchs and a dormitory for the palace gardeners and halberdiers. Finally it was simply left to decay.

Going toward the Corpse Gate by which one entered, one passes a slope leading up to a terrace that once belonged to the halberdiers and from which their dormitory looks out. It is now simply overgrown with brush.

Back in the Second Court, up a few steps to one's left and under the arcade along the immediate wall is a collection of stone inscriptions taken largely from the old kiosks that once lined the shore. It is an excellent place to study *tuğras* if one knows how.

Behind this wall lies the terrace and quarters of the halberdiers with Tresses (Zülüflü Baltacıs), so named because of the long locks of hair (*zülüfs*) that hung down from their headdresses along their cheeks. In early times halberdiers, with or without tresses, were Christian conscripts who came up through the ranks of state service. Some rose to high place, one of them becoming grand vizier.

Their building or set of buildings is one of the oldest in the palace, but although it has been steadied on the outside it is not yet restored inside and is therefore closed. It is nevertheless an interesting old place, consisting of a wooden dormitory with a gallery around a central open space, its beams and posts still bearing their painted decoration; a flagged courtyard whose tiles are of mixed periods, some even Italian; a little coffee hearth; a bath; even an old wooden, two-story mosque. The most interesting is the square *çabuk odası* or pipe room for recreation. A wood bench runs around its sides, a large rectangular brazier stands in the center, and one wall is composed of tall, narrow cupboards in which the men kept their *nargiles* or water pipes. One can evoke them in their tall embroidered caps to which curls of hair were attached, sitting on the wooden benches, the bases of the water pipes at their feet and the long, snakelike tubes running up to their mouths, while charcoal embers glowed in the brazier.

Something of the history of the halberdiers' quarters is told by the twenty-three marble inscriptions Abdurrahman Şeref found in the courtyard when he examined the palace in 1910. They stretched over most of three centuries, from 1587 to 1847. We know from one that the quarters were repaired as early as the sixteenth century and from another that they were tiled in the seventeenth. This was done, so the inscription said, because "the walls and closets were old and full of bugs." The court's many fauceted ablution fountain which still stands in the courtyard was known as the Father Fountain (Baba Çeşmesi) from an old tradition. One day the sultan heard a veteran halberdier worrying because water for ablutions before prayer was in short supply. Straightway he ordered the fountain built. The story seems to be entirely legend, for the fountain has an inscription saying it was the gift of a chief officer of the hall. Most of the inscriptions told of endowments to provide for the reading of sacred texts, for supplies as varied as olive oil and rose jam, and for payments to men who served the hall such as water-carriers and coffee-makers. Inscriptions were often an attempt to achieve a kind of immortality, as may be seen by the one that reads "Fortune is fickle. I wrote this so that when I die my script will remain as a memorial. Written by the sultan's gentleman-in-waiting, Beşir Ağa, trustee of the Treasury." The better to be remembered, Beşir Ağa had this repeated in the cooks' prayer place on the kitchen side of the court.

The duties of the Halberdiers with Tresses were many. Once a month they carried wood into the harem, at which time the black eunuchs went before them to make sure no women were in sight. In addition to this precaution, their collars were turned up, and these, together with their pendant strands of hair, were supposed to keep them from looking to left or right. They were the caretakers of the Hall of the Divan which they swept, opened and closed on the days the Divan met. It was their duty to put out any fires that might occur in the harem, for which they were equipped with large hooks, buckets and axes. Two of them oversaw the cooks in the sultan's private kitchen. On days of Şeker (sugar, sweets) and Kurban (sacrifice) Bayramı they carried the imperial throne from its place in the Treasury to the Gate of Felicity. They offered sherbet on the day each year when the *Mevlût*, a poem in praise of the birth of the Prophet, was read across the square in the Mosque of Sultan Ahmet, and they looked after the Ağas' Mosque in the Third Court. When the grand vizier went on campaign thirty of them accompanied him to read the Koran.

Their most famous member was Deli (Mad) Hüseyin Pasha, who attained high rank not from brain but from brawn. The story is related by the Ottoman chronicler, Naima. Since his telling could scarcely be improved upon, we repeat it here:

In the reign of Murat IV [1623–1640] an ambassador came from Persia and brought a bent bow to prove his prowess. He unfastened the string and presented the bow, asking if there existed in the Ottoman Empire an athlete who could bend it again. They sought such a person. They could not find in Istanbul a man who could so much as move the string, let alone unfasten it and bend the bow. The bow was entrusted to the Ağa of the House of Felicity (the chief black eunuch). He did not wish to be humiliated by the Persian ambassador, and he gave secret orders to search for an athlete with strong arms.

Deli Hüseyin was serving then among the novice halberdiers whose duty was to carry wood into the room of the Ağa of the House of Felicity. One day when he brought wood into the room, he found it empty. He caught sight of the bow. He seized the bow and was bending it several times as in practice. When he was told that the Ağa of the House of Felicity was coming he was frightened; he left the bow and ran away.

When the Ağa came and saw that the bow had been handled, he asked, "Who played with this bow?"

[51]

Yahya Ağa, who was on duty, was frightened and answered, "The halberdier Deli Hüseyin brought wood to the fireplace. He was playing with the bow. When he heard you were coming he left it and ran away."

The Ağa rejoiced and ordered Deli Hüseyin to be called immediately.

The steward of the guild and the old members of the guild said to him, "You gallows bird, you go into the Ağa's room and you can't keep quiet. You meddle with this and that. You deserve to have your nails pulled off." Thus they scolded and rebuked him and sent him to the Ağa.

The Ağa handed the bow to him and said, "Now let me see you bend it."

Deli Hüseyin took it up again and bent it five or ten times as if in practice. The Ağa was full of astonishment and admiration, and he ordered, "Now quickly dress this fellow up in decent clothes. I shall introduce him into the Imperial Presence."

In the Imperial Presence he again bent the bow and showed his strength and was congratulated. Later, in the Imperial Presence, when he was bending the bow before the Persian ambassador, he got so excited that he broke it and laid the pieces before the ambassador. The sultan and the others were so astonished they remained with their fingers in their mouths. This incident was the beginning of Deli Hüseyin's fortune.

He was raised to the rank of pasha and became extraordinarily famous in Istanbul. Together with his strength and courage he was a very frank and jovial character. His merry manners and free speech amused everyone. One day when he was leaving Istanbul in a large procession to go to war, a huge crowd of men and women assembled to see him pass, riding proudly in full armor with helmet and cuirass. He loudly greeted the people who filed to see him, and he said goodbye and asked for their blessing. Then he addressed the women:

"Greetings to you, ladies, flowers of paradise, angels on earth! Scholars and wise men and heroes are born of you. God Almighty give you blessings and prosperity. Don't forget to pray for us."

Men and women lamented and cried, "God save you for the padishah. This is meet when a hero becomes a vizier." And they blessed him with all their hearts.

NECATI ORBAY

The wooden Persian bow that Deli Hüseyin broke.

Deli Hüseyin survived the campaign but not the envy and suspicion of the grand vizier. Thus could honor be won and life lost.

The doorway from the halberdiers' lodgings opens under a portico just before the wall turns at a right angle. Set into the immediate wall is an unassuming gate, the Carriage Gate (Araba Kapısı) which takes its name from the fact that the harem women stepped into their carriages here on their infrequent outings from the palace. Its iron door, framed in marble, is topped by an inscription telling us that it was rebuilt in 1587/8 by Murat III. This puts its present aspect after the fire of 1574 and also tells us that there was a former gate here, perhaps built by Süleyman who had considerable work done in this part of the courtyard. The gate gives entrance to the quarters of the black eunuchs and from there to the harem. It was through here that the Halberdiers with Tresses bore their wood.

Just past it begins the Hall of the Divan whose entrance is around still another corner. Its importance is such that it will be discussed separately. Abutting it is the Museum of Arms, once the Finance or Inner Treasury (Emanet or İç Hazinesi), an oblong stone building surmounted by eight domes and windowed drums. It is a strong structure, its walls thick, its windows barred, its stern front unadorned by a colonnade. Although as a whole it dates from the fifteenth or early sixteenth century, being built of the

[53]

same rough stone as the stable, its lower row of windows was added in the twentieth. This came to light through a study of the bricks used in them, which were made in a brick factory on the Golden Horn in the time of Mehmet V. This row was closed during the recent restoration. Even its domes were probably changed in a 1926 restoration when windows with small glass panes were inserted in the bases of their drums, replacing what were probably slits for defense. Until very recently it has been closed for investigation and the modernization of its display fixtures, but is now open, the most modern exhibit in the museum. During the restoration process an old tunnel was discovered that led underneath the back of the building from what was once probably the quarters of the sultans' cooks to the gate of the Kuşhane, the sultan's private kitchen. The cooks' area, which seems to have been in the basement of the building, burned under Abdülhamit I. It was rebuilt but not connected to the tunnel.

The building is made up of one long, high room and, at the back in one corner, a high domed room that was perhaps used by a treasury official. It could have been the place from which the treasury was guarded, since it overlooks the main room. Old wooden pillars once supported it and a balcony that has been taken down.

The interior of the Finance Treasury now displays, in its vaulted interior, 364 pieces of armor, most of which belonged to sultans, out of a collection of 11,000. Among them are decorated bows, some made by the sultans and one the Persian bow Deli Hüseyin broke to confound the Persian ambassador; quivers inlaid with mother-of-pearl and ivory or of gold-embroidered velvet; thimbles for pulling the bowstring; long, metal-tipped wooden lances and shorter ones for the game of *cirit*; and gold-headed standards plus a collection of rifles and swords, chain armor and helmets big enough to fit over a turban, and other objects. All are either Mameluke or Iranian or Ottoman. The Mameluke swords are unique pieces brought back from his conquest of Egypt by Selim the Grim. Most of the swords are engraved along the blade with verses from the Koran, usually the sura or verse of victory.

Among the most interesting exhibits are the metal frontal pieces that protected a horse's head in battle. There are three of these, one of bronze belonging to Selim I and two seemingly of gold. One of them is pictured here, probably sixteenth century and, to judge from its perfect condition, never used in battle. On the left of the nose section it bears the *damga* or brand of the Kayı, the Turkish tribe to which Osman, the first Ottoman sultan, belonged. Although it looks gold it is actually copper covered with a solution of gold dust and mercury. This was applied by first heating the copper and then rubbing the mixture on, the same technique used to tin copperware for cooking. The motifs on this particular frontal piece suggest that it was made in Süleyman's time.

In this display nothing is more revealing of the Turkic background of the Ottomans than the *tuğs* or horsetails to denote rank. To tie a *tuğ* to one's staff was an old custom the Turks brought with them from Central Asia. There the *tuğ* had been a yak's tail, but the Ottomans, perhaps because they were not in yak territory, used a horsetail instead. The number of tails attached to a staff varied with the rank. The grand vizier was entitled to three, other viziers to two, and the sultan to six or, some say, seven.

Come wartime, the ruler's *tuğs* were taken from the Imperial Treasury and set up in various places at various times. At one time the imperial standard with its *tuğs* was in front of the Imperial Gate, at another before the Armory in the First Court, or before the Gate of Felicity or even, in the nineteenth century, at the Middle Gate. On the occasion of bringing the standard forth sheikhs recited prayers, and sacrifices of lambs were prepared. Finally when all was ready the sultan appeared and, according to an old document, "prayed and eulogized and bestowed favors and picked up

The executioner's sword and case, from the Arms and Armor Section.

NECATI ORBAY

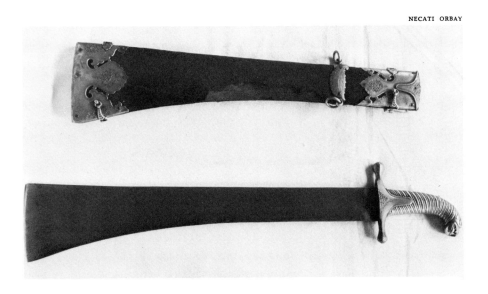

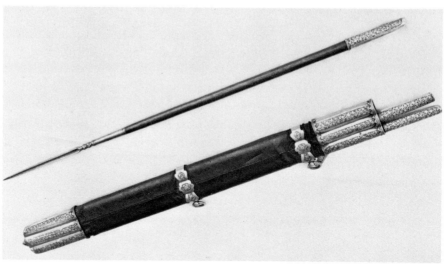

NECATI ORBAY

A cirit *and a case for three for the popular Ottoman horseback game, from the Arms and Armor Section.*

the *tuğ* full of glory and put it in its place and performed the sacrifices and gave the order to those whose duty it was to carry the *tuğ*." When the sultan was at the front his standard with its *tuğ*s was raised before his tent, having been transported by a corps of special *tuğ*-carriers.

When the Museum of Arms was a treasury it stored the various tax revenues of the Empire and a fifth of all war booty. Holding the bulk of the Empire's cash, it was the repository for funds to be paid out, as for war expenses and salaries for the military and officials. If it was short of funds it could borrow from the Privy or Imperial Treasury in the Third Court, but the money had to be paid back. The coins were kept in cistern-like vaults that are still under the floor. One can see their covers, to the right as one goes into the Arms Section.

At the corner of the Museum of Arms and the wall of the Third Court the first Hall of the Divan stood in the Conqueror's day. Its foundation and floor were discovered when an earlier restoration of the Finance Treasury was in progress. Later a wooden mosque, the Central Mosque much used by the *saray*, was put up on its site. It lasted until 1919. There are now no buildings at this end but a stone column, moved from another site, that once marked the spot where a sultan's arrow landed. The court is bordered here

[56]

only by the wall and the portico that extends on either side of the Gate of Felicity.

There is one other monument in this vicinity, however. Off the central path among the cypresses stands a bulky work of marble which, despite Ottoman inscriptions, does not seem quite to belong. Nothing the casual visitor can read identifies it, but it is in fact two eighteenth-century inscriptions from a fountain in the one-time Turkish fortress of Sukhum on the northeastern shore of the Black Sea. The fortress was lost to the Russians, but in a subsidiary action in the Ottoman-Russian War of 1877 the Turks managed to retrieve the inscriptions. They were their only gain in a disastrous war, and were set up here in this marble block.

Back at the Middle Gate and this time proceeding to the right, one finds today only the porticoed wall and the gate to the palace waterworks in the First Court. Once along here there was a building of considerable import-

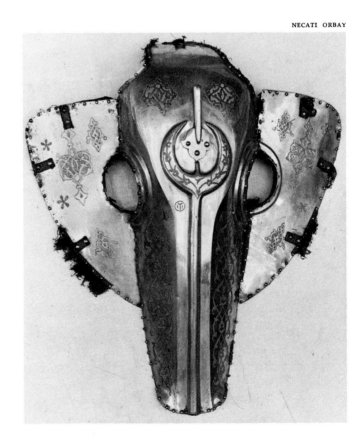

A horse frontal piece from the Arms and Armor Section. Note what looks like a letter T with a line on each side of it, all in a circle. This is the brand of the Kayı tribe to which Osman, the first Ottoman sultan, belonged.

A tuğ *or horsetail, an emblem of rank, from the Arms and Armor Section.*

NECATI ORBAY

ance, probably small but handsomely decorated. It was the guest room (*misafir odası*) where the sons of the Crimean khans were hosted on their yearly trip to Istanbul to bring tribute, part of which was young girls, to the sultan. And it was in this room that the bridegroom of an Ottoman princess awaited the formation of the great marriage procession which would escort his bride from the palace of her ancestors to the new palace he had provided for her. Some of these were enormous. Lady Mary Wortley Montagu, whose husband was British ambassador to the Porte in the early eighteenth century, describes one of eight hundred rooms.

Although the bridegroom was by now legally married to the girl, he had never seen her. At the marriage ceremony she had been represented by the chief black eunuch. It had perhaps taken place years earlier. Many a princess was married as an infant and given to her husband only when she

[5 8]

reached sexual maturity. These husbands were so much at the mercy of their wives, only the honor and political preferment the relationship conferred could have made the step worthwhile. An imperial son-in-law might have no other wives, although other men might have four, nor any slave girls. His inferior position was firmly established on the night of consummation when he had to await his wife's call before entering her room, then kneel at the foot of her bed, kiss the coverlet, and humbly creep in from the foot. However, unless he fell afoul of the sultan's displeasure, the imperial son-in-law or *damat* would be one of the circle of intimates whom the sultan invited to join him for evenings of discussion or entertainment in the kiosks of the Inner Palace or along the shore.

The guest room where the son-in-law waited probably fell to pieces after the sultan and his family left Topkapı. Only an occasional inquirer into things Ottoman, like me, stops to wonder where it stood.

Except for this ghost there is an uninterrupted path from the Middle Gate to the Imperial Kitchens. They are two long, ash-colored stone structures, one behind the other so that only the first is on view from the court, and separated by a narrow, elongated subsidiary court. The first is now made up of workrooms of the museum. In Ottoman times it contained the apartment of the superintendent of the kitchens, the tinning shop—the palace used copper utensils that had to be periodically retinned—and the dormitory of the palace cooks. Three passageways through it give access to the kitchen court.

The second building, which is wider and edges the cliff above the Marmara, is where the actual cooking was done. At the southern end were more dormitories and a cooks' mosque where now are stored the collection of rich robes of the sultans and the treasure trove of palace embroideries for which there is no room in the display areas of the Third Court. Down this way too are the Topkapı Palace archives.

The rest is kitchens, ten of them, to which was attached a mosque for the confectioners facing the kitchen court at the north end. The kitchens are all wide, very tall, and vaulted. Two chimneys rise from each, one from a dome and a higher one from a pyramidal cone. The latter are the ones that ascend into the sky to form one of the landmarks of Istanbul. Four of their domes go back to the Conqueror, and the other six were built by Süleyman.

After the fire of 1574 the kitchens were rebuilt by Sinan who added the cones and enlarged the rooms. In the last years of the Empire they had been allowed to decay to such an extent that some of the chimneys and domes were in ruins, their pointing fallen out. The confectionery was full of rubble. Nothing was left of the cooking facilities. Today, except for the lack of cooking hearths in all but one, the kitchens look much as they must have looked in Sinan's time.

Because Sinan was responsible for other parts of the palace, more, in my opinion, than can be proved, and also because he is an interesting character in himself, he is worth looking into a little. He was a Christian conscript from Asia Minor and for this reason was thought to have been Greek. Recent research has uncovered his true ancestry. He came from a Christian Turkish family, one of a group brought into Asia Minor in early medieval times by the Arabs to fight the Byzantines. Instead they were converted to the Greek Christian rite and came to be considered Greek.

Sinan arrived in Istanbul when he was twenty-two and was entered into a branch of the Palace School on the Hippodrome. It was the practice of the early Empire to encourage the salient characteristics of a conscript, and so Sinan studied with Turkey's best architects. He served for some years as a Janissary in the army. He went to Italy with the corsair-admiral, Barbarossa. Gradually promoted to master craftsman and then to architect, in 1539 when he was fifty he was appointed by Süleyman chief architect in charge of all the public buildings of the Empire. He left a short autobiography, *Memorandum of Buildings (Tezkere-ül-ebniye)*, in which he says he made repairs in the New Palace. This gives us wide scope to decide what is Sinan's work. Since he lived till 1588, it has always seemed to me that the entire rebuilding of the palace after the fire of 1574 must have been done under his supervision. Surely no less a person than the chief architect would have been trusted with construction in the palace.

The fire started when chimney soot caught while the daily lamb was being cooked in one of the kitchens. Flames engulfed the entire kitchen area, destroying "various curious and desirable things and porcelain holders and implements and other things." From there the fire seems to have swept through the palace, devouring whatever was made of wood and scorching much of the rest. It may well be that the Second Court as it looks today, pulled together by the marble colonnade, was Sinan's doing. The harmonious arrangement of space, which we see in the court and in the kitchens, was characteristic of him. That and his lavish but judicious use of decoration have become the mark of classic Ottoman.

The kitchens are at present display areas. Two of them show 4,584 pieces of Chinese porcelain alone, from a collection of 10,512 gathered by the sultans. Porcelains recorded in a Treasury register of 1495 in the reign of Bayezit II were the start of the collection. It was augmented by sixty-two pieces taken by Selim I from Shah Ismail's palace in Persia and further expanded by an unknown quantity of ware he brought back from his conquest of Egypt in 1517. Süleyman, who greatly fancied porcelain, purchased much of it from China, and some of the ware came as gifts. Even though much of the Chinese ware is in storage, in my opinion too much is on display. One cannot take in so great a quantity without many visits, for which most foreigners do not have the time. The museum's explanation is that their storage space is limited. They therefore show the most valuable ware in cases and the less valuable simply displayed on the walls. There are plans afoot to redo the porcelain section at some future date.

The collection is particularly rich in celadon. We find Dr. Covel, chaplain to the British ambassador in the late seventeenth century, eating from it at an audience of his ambassador with the grand vizier at Edirne (Adrianople) in 1675. Celadon was a great favorite with the court, perhaps because it was credited with the ability to change color if poisoned food was placed on it. The collection grew with the years, part of it kept in the Treasury and part in storage space known as the Porcelain House (Çinilihane) which was in the kitchen section. Some of it would go out as gifts, as four jeweled censors and two bowls with plates entered the trousseau of Ümmügülsün, a daughter of Mehmet IV, in 1693.

To give a taste of the collection, the oldest pieces are tenth-century celadon of that special celadon light green. This is T'ang, but the collection also shows green Sung and Yuan, some of it with a raised dragon design and some with fluted edges. There is cobalt blue and white Ming ware going back to the fifteenth century. The room also shows some fine jars and a large cobalt blue and white vase set on a metal tripod carved with turtles. Here too is what is called Emperor's Yellow, bowls and plates of a type on which Chinese emperors were served. There is also sixteenth-century white Ming, some of the bowls' interiors decorated with blue pines.

All this is in the southernmost room of the kitchens, a double room in which food was once cooked for the princes and the mother sultan and at some period for the sultan himself, although another kitchen was assigned to him in another part of the palace.

The next two rooms, the kitchens of the harem and the gatekeepers, display a good deal of cobalt blue and white Ming, some of it with a gold glaze, and a few Chinese bronzes and enamel on copper. At the entrance are large plates with Islamic inscriptions, special orders from China.

The kitchen that was used to cook for the Council or the Divan has later and rather less interesting ware, except for some ivories. The porcelains are Japanese pieces. There is one object, however, which cannot be overlooked, an exquisite miniature of a Chinese garden composed of gold inlaid with silver in which rise layer after layer of pavilions set with coral and interspersed with jade-tipped trees. It was a gift from the Emperor of China to Abdül-hamit II on the twenty-fifth anniversary of his enthronement, though sup-posedly much older, and quite outranks his other presents on display elsewhere.

Other kitchens, such as those of the pages and the various palace servitors, show European porcelain, much of it gifts from monarchs includ-ing a pair of large vessels with pictures of Napoleon in battle, and various bibelots. More interesting is the confectionary kitchen (helvahane) com-bined with a coffee kitchen, where one can see old kitchen equipment: large black kettles set on tripods, large cauldrons such as were used to cook for the Janissaries, great round trays on which food was delivered, and the tinned copper dishes in which it was served; old pestles, skimmers, ladles; copper saucepans and the like; the little vessels (cezve) in which coffee was made and still is; a fountain for the cooks to wash their hands; a drain in the floor, probably so that it could be washed; and an old fireplace set in a floral-tiled wall.

The final room, made out of the confectioners' mosque and a storeroom, has Istanbul porcelain and glassware. The porcelain comes from a factory Abdülhamit II established at Yıldız and is frankly imitative of Europe. To me the most interesting display is the group of glassware called Nightin-gale's Eye (Çeşm-i Bülbül) which consists of alternating spirals of color, often purplish, and white, very popular in Istanbul in the nineteenth century. Part of the Topkapı collection was put together by an American who was for years attached to the embassy in Turkey, G. Howland Shaw. Of all shapes and sizes—though none of the çeşm-i bülbül is huge—it is valued today at $2½ million.

When Topkapı was the heart of the Empire four to five thousand people were fed by the imperial kitchens on ordinary days, and on special days the number jumped. On the Janissaries' payday ten to fifteen thousand of the military were given soup, pilav, and zerde, a dish of sweetened rice colored with saffron. On the fifteenth of Ramazan the kitchens baked baklava, the flaky pastry filled with nuts and almonds, for ten thousand Janissaries. Cakes, jams, syrups came out of the confectioners' kitchen, and even perfumed soaps. The mosque for this kitchen once had a wealth of inscriptions, evidence of the generosity of many people. The one that hung to the left of the door will give the flavor:

"The stewardess Bedr-i Cihan (Full Moon of the Universe), second mistress of the linen of the court of His Majesty our Sovereign Lord, donated in her lifetime to the Guild of the Imperial Confectionery, by the agency of the medium-grade eunuch, Mahmut Ağa, the sum of 500 piasters to be paid to the reader of the complete Koran in this holy mosque. The interest of this sum is to be paid every month to the reader. The conditions are inscribed on this stone to inform all members. The chapter of the Îhlas (the 112th chapter of the Koran) is to be recited three times, and the chapter of the Fâtiha (the first chapter) once, as an offering of the founder. Dated the 17th of Cemaziülevvel in the year 1237 (1821/2)."

Accounts were kept for everything from food to jewels. From these we learn that the raw food sent daily to the imperial harem ranged from meat (presumably lamb), chicken and pigeon to almonds, celery and garlic. The harem also received a weekly supply that included sugar, olive oil, flour and spices. Every day the padishah was sent a wide variety of breads and ninety-five of the *simit* rings one still can buy. It is recorded that when Nevşehirli İbrahim Pasha and his wife, Fatma Sultan, were coming to dine with the padishah, his allotment of bread was increased.

The kitchens were serviced by various grades of cooks from plain to master cook whose salaries were fixed according to rank. At one time there were seventeen master cooks. The cooks were organized into companies, each with its special chore. One company cooked for the Privy Chamber, another for the Imperial Divan, and so on. We learn from a salary register of 1755 that there were ten companies of cooks, probably one for each kitchen, numbering more than three hundred in all, not including special cooks. Each had his specific job, one only baking bread, one cooking only pilaf, another only fish. Then there were the confectionery cooks who in the middle of the eighteenth century consisted of six master cooks and a hundred apprentices. Once a year they made peppermint, rose and poppy pastes for the sultan and certain palace officials. In their kitchen was made the best of the candy called Turkish delight, *lokum*.

The same register lists seventeen butchers and butchers' apprentices, twenty-three yogurt-makers and milk-handlers, thirty-one vegetable hand-

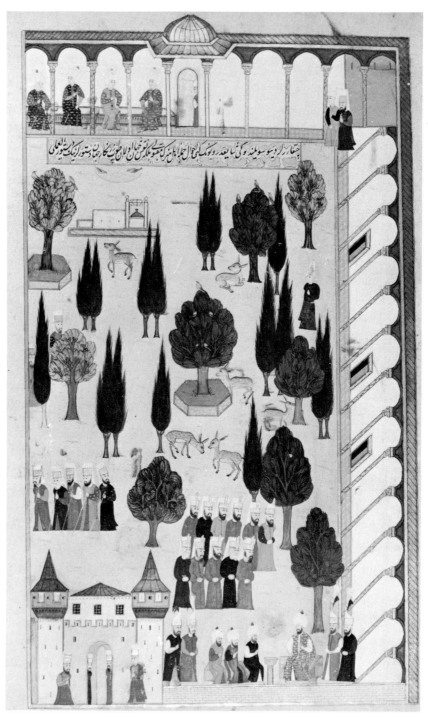

Hünername *Miniature No. 2: the east side of the Second Court.*

lers, seventeen chicken-handlers, twenty-three makers of *simit*, six providers of ice and snow to cool drinks in the summer, fifteen tinsmiths, twenty-seven candle-makers, and twenty-five water-carriers. Most of these people worked and were housed in the two buildings that stretch from end to end of the court.

The Second Court as it must have appeared in the late sixteenth century is transfixed for us in two *Hünername* miniatures. Miniature No. 2 pictures the gazelles, cypresses and plane trees, the gatekeepers at the Middle Gate, the chief heralds with their plumed headpieces, and the ranks of Janissaries with hands folded in respect. This is the attitude of respect the Turkish peasant will take even today. To the left are heralds with staffs, undoubtedly of silver, with which they struck the ground to announce arrivals. At the bottom right are seated a group of dignitaries, one, from his larger size, obviously more important than the rest. All wear an early type of turban. The Middle Gate is plain to see at the foot of the picture, the colonnade of the kitchens to the right with the same three entrances the building has today, and the Gate of Felicity at the court's far end. The miniature on page 72 shows the left side of the court with the Hall of the Divan, which we shall now take up.

THE COUNCIL HALL
OR UNDER THE DOME

IN THE MIDST of the solid, austere buildings of the Second Court stands the Council Hall (Divanhane), more important than any of them yet less solemn-looking. It is on the left-hand side about halfway down, and because it juts out into the court it has a corner position. This helps to give it lightness, for it appears to have more windows than walls. Its alternate name, Under the Dome (Kubbe Altı), aptly describes it; it was under its dome that the grand vizier and other councilors sat to hold a court of justice and to make the weighty decisions of the Empire. The men who participated were called Those Who Sit under the Dome (Kubbenişin).

It is a low building made to seem lower by the eaves that descend over its wide and pillared porch and by contrast to the Tower of Justice that rises behind it. Pillars of marble, porphyry and granite, that must have come from several sources, uphold its eaves. During one of its several renovations the porch was closed in by a grilled metal fence that gave it a caged look better suited to a zoo. This has been removed so that one walks onto the porch unimpeded. In fact the entire building has been returned by the museum to its sixteenth-century character.

The hall is actually a suite of domed rooms consisting of the council chamber, an adjoining room, the *divit odası* or pen room, where scribes kept minutes of the meetings, and a private lounge for the grand vizier, plus a coffee kitchen. The most important, the council chamber, has the corner. That gives it windows, wide ones, on two sides, and since it is divided from the scribes' room only by an archway and railing, it is left with only one solid wall. Thus it seems more spacious than it really is. Though by no means tiny, neither is it a great hall.

Along its back wall has always ranged a sofa for the chief members of the council. That and the general structure of the hall are the only things that have remained constant. Its decoration was unfortunately changed by Ahmet III in the early eighteenth century into a rococo that lasted until the museum, in 1942, undertook to restore it to its original state. Whatever else Westernization may have done for the Ottoman Empire, it certainly played havoc with its art, and the Divanhane was turned into a paneled and gilded imitation of somebody's idea of a European palace. Pictures of it from those days remain to give one an appreciation of the improvement brought about by the museum's work.

Now one sees along the back wall, above the sofa, a broad band of tiles in a small floral pattern that paneling had covered. On the arches that frame the windows and mark the division of the scribes' room the original decoration was discovered under plaster painted in oils which weather from a leaking roof had in any case ruined. The original decoration turned out to be oval floral medallions in white and gold and blue on a brown ground. These have been faithfully renewed and form a chain along the under sides of the arches. So, too, the pendentives have been restored to authentically Ottoman patterns of discs surrounded by twining flowers.

Above the tiling and over the center of the sofa, the place of the grand vizier, the wall is pierced by a lodge for the sultan set flush with the wall and protected by vertical and horizontal grating. The areas on either side of it are plain except for a chaste border. This is in happy contrast to the lodge the museum replaced, which projected into the room and was crisscrossed with fancy latticework, in all reminding one of the bay window of a boudoir. To further ornament it *tuğras* in curlicue gilt frames sided it.

Apparently in the early twentieth century the roof had been allowed to leak for years so that not much of the decoration of the dome was left, but it seems to have been carved and painted wood. Today its decoration is concentrated in a central medallion and a border along the edge. When the room was in use a gold sphere used to be suspended from the center of the dome that all might know the important matters of the world were decided here.

The council chamber now has the dignity that belongs to a room once

NECATI ORBAY

The Tower of Justice rises behind the Hall of the Divan in the Second Court.

the scene of grave ceremonies and weighty decisions. The sultan's lodge that overlooks it was named with typical Ottoman hyperbole the Bower of Justice, located in the Tower of Justice. Here, whenever he chose, the sultan sat unseen to listen to the discussions of the Divan and sometimes to look over foreign ambassadors being received by the grand vizier. If he disagreed at any point or wanted to make his ideas known, he rapped on the grating,

[68]

at which point the council members waited to hear his pleasure. The lodge is reached by a staircase in the tower via the quarters of the black eunuchs.

The sultan's sitting aside from the council seems to have originated from an incident in the Conqueror's day. Before they took Istanbul the Ottoman rulers had presided over the Divan in person. With the conquest of the imperial city they took on imperial ways. Thus when a Turk in simple clothes and sandals dodged the heralds and burst into the Divan chamber crying, "Which of you is His Majesty the Sultan? I have complaints to make," the Conqueror was annoyed and showed it. The grand vizier therefore suggested, "It is no longer suitable for our padishah to sit with us. It will be better for him to listen to his slaves from behind a lattice." This incident indicates that there must have been a lodge in the old Divan Hall down near the Gate of Felicity.

This Council Hall was built by Süleyman, destroyed in the great fire and rebuilt, I would guess, by Sinan. It underwent both eighteenth- and nineteenth-century restorations which are attested by high-flown inscrip-

The interior of the Hall of the Divan. Note the sultan's lodge.

NECATI ORBAY

tions. The one bearing witness to Mahmut II's work is particularly grandiose and says in part:

"The king of kings of the world, Mahmut Khan the Just, renovated the lofty place of the Divan. The grilled window is equal to the chain of justice, and without so much as moving indicates to the Emperor which cause is just. . . . The dome is a very heaven. . . . On the day of the Divan the Sultan's deputy, his vizier, and the treasurer and the chancellor are the brilliant stars in this heaven. In order to observe the influences of this majestic sphere the resplendent moon (the sultan) rises behind the golden lattice. . . . The Emperor, the ornament of the country, built this lofty tower as a sign that he is commanding the horizons." By Mahmut's time the Empire was shrinking, and to say that he commanded the horizons was a sad parody of fact. Ottoman inflated language continued long after Ottoman power had waned.

The scribes' room has not been restored, and its rococo paneling gives one an idea of how the Council Chamber used to look. The third room is used to exhibit the museum's watch and clock collection, but is now undergoing renovation.

The watch tower or Tower of Justice, contiguous to the back wall of the Divan, was a vantage point from which to watch for signs of disturbance in the city, particularly anything threatening the palace. Its lowest part, which is brick, goes back to the Conqueror and is unseen. Süleyman raised it with stone and put in the sultan's lodge when he built the Hall of the Divan. The lodge is small and dark, and the sultan must have had to stoop to enter it. Then in the nineteenth century Mahmut II added the upper section and its spire, or probably merely substituted his own for an older one. His addition resembles a European imitation of a Greek temple. It looks square, but is in reality an octagon enclosed in a square of pillars and pediments. Behind the pediments the lead-covered spire lifts into the sky. The pillared section is thus an architectural device for going from a square base to an octagonal spire, and scarcely Ottoman in feeling. The tower in all has a hundred and five steps that wind up past landings at twenty-step intervals and past windows that let in light. Though the number of steps scares one, actually the climb is easy, the steps are so low and broad and the landings offer so many resting places. So far as I know, the tower has never been open to the public, but since the museum is now working on it, I would guess that one day it will be possible for the visitor to climb it. It will be well worth the climb, for the view of Istanbul is stupendous. From the great windows on its four sides all the city lies before one.

For the Divan meetings, which took place at one period four times a week, Saturdays, Sundays, Mondays and Tuesdays, and at a later period on Tuesdays only, the viziers and certain other officials met in the corner room. The number of Viziers of the Dome varied with the epoch. Under Süleyman there were four, later the number increased, and at one period the rank for all but the grand vizier was abolished. Meanwhile they sat in the Divanhane on the sofa to the left of the grand vizier. To his right sat the two high judge advocates *(kazaskers)*, one for Anatolia (Asia Minor) and one for Rumelia (the European lands of the Empire). Also included at one time—membership changed over the centuries—were the state secretary, the chancellor, the admiral of the fleet, the chief treasurer plus the treasurers for Anatolia and Rumelia, and Janissary Ağa or chief officer, and the *kadı* or chief judge of Istanbul. Only those who had the rank of vizier had a right to the sofa; the others had appointed posts about the room. The state secretary's job was to record everything that went on. He passed what he had written over to the scribes in the next room who, hunched over their desks and inkwells, put it down in the state registers and made summaries for the sultan. To these he might add comments in the margin and, if he approved, would have the chancellor affix the imperial signature or *tuğra*. Sultans were in the habit of adding comments to whatever documents came their way. Selim III once wrote *eşek* or donkey on the margin of a report from an Ottoman ambassador to France whom Talleyrand had duped.

In the seventeenth century, the era called the Women's Sultanate, when women of the imperial harem wielded strong influence, the decisions of the Divan were often swayed by petticoat power. Kösem, who was the favorite of one sultan, the mother of two, and the grandmother of a fourth, came to have final power in her day, and historians have recorded that she sat in the lodge with her grandson when he was a small boy in the early years of his reign and handed down decisions.

A path leads to the Divanhane from the Middle Gate, along it at intervals three small rectangular pieces of stonework set on end. These are the *selâm* or greeting stones at which viziers were saluted, hand on breast, by members of the Divan staff. The stones are still in place. In former times there were two buildings in this area, the Kiosk of the Summaries (of the complaints heard in the First Court) which was pulled down in 1868, and a large room for the ubiquitous chief black eunuch.

Divan days were days of a pageantry that grew more complicated with time. The following description is a general one based on one by Abdurrahman Şeref who took his from a *Book of Ceremonies* by an eighteenth-century grand vizier and from papers in the archives of the Imperial

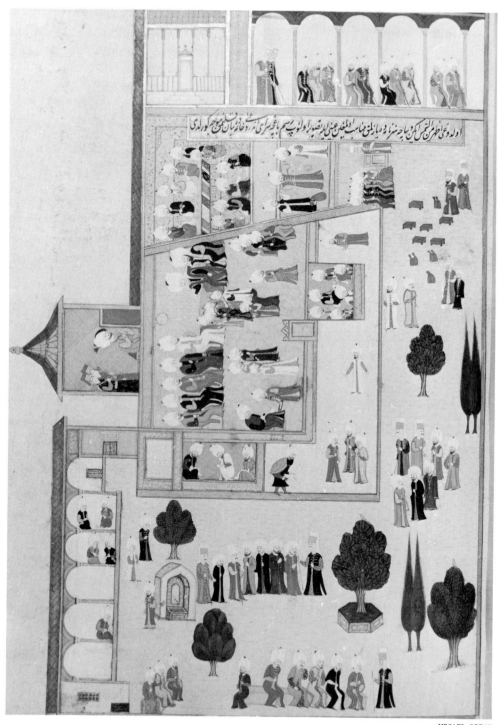

Hünername *Miniature No. 3: the west side of the Second Court showing the Hall of the Divan.*

Department of Ceremonies. Although certain details changed at times, it is on the whole the pattern throughout the life of Topkapı.

On such days all Divan members but the grand vizier met for prayer at Santa Sophia in their ceremonial clothes, the admiral of the fleet and the viziers in light green satin robes lined with fur, tall turbans on their heads, the two judge advocates in furred or plain robes depending on the season, on their heads the round, pleated turbans called örf peculiar to the religious hierarchy. Since the basis of law was the Holy Law of Islam, judges were members of the religious institution. After prayer they mounted their horses covered with homespun horsecloths special to the occasion and made their way to the Imperial Gate. The road between mosque and gate was lined with troops and functionaries, each group in its particular place and wearing its particular uniform. Color vied with color, the red robe of one with the gold of another, headdresses of sweeping plumes with high, conical caps.

The judge advocates reached the gate first and took their places at a corner. Then came the viziers, and as each approached, the Ağa of the Janissaries, who had been waiting at the gate, rode his horse forward a few steps in greeting; ceremony was that minutely regulated. The Janissary prayer leader recited a prayer, and the big iron doors of the Imperial Gate swung open. First the Janissaries and their clerks passed through, and then guardsmen on foot and the steward of the armorers, the chief armorer, the Janissary officers, the sergeants and officers of the cavalry, the weapons-bearers, the head gatekeepers, and a host of others. Finally the members of the Divan rode in and through the First Court to the Middle Gate where they dismounted and took the path with the selâm stones to the Divanhane. While they waited there for the arrival of the grand vizier they were served with iced fruit drinks in summer and cakes in winter, offered to each in order of rank.

Meanwhile after morning prayer the grand vizier left his residence, the Pasha's Gate (later the Sublime Porte) on Divan Yolu. At his horseblock he mounted a richly decorated horse to the cheers of the Divan heralds and rode up the hill along the tall outer wall of the palace and around Santa Sophia to the Imperial Gate. As the deputy of the sultan, he was resplendent in a white satin robe threaded with gold and on his head the kallâvi, a tall white turban with an oblique gold band, worn only by viziers and the chief treasurer.

He was followed the entire way by irregulars and volunteers on foot and their officers, in their special raiment, on horseback. These costumes are all but indescribable in their great variety, the head of the irregulars in a blanket-like robe of brown and cream stripes over grey *şalvar*, the baggy, ankle-length Turkish trousers, and a reddish sash into which pistols were thrust; the herald who led the way in a red robe over dark blue *şalvar* and a turban called *mücevveze*, a tall cylinder with ribs running up from the head. Numerous others swelled the procession—the steward of the gatekeepers, the salute officer, the running footmen, the chief saddler, to name a few. The head of the Hall of Gardeners was there wearing a robe of scarlet cloth and a sash glinting with gold thread. The Master of the Stables was there riding a horse with jeweled trappings, looking tall with the cylindrical *mücevveze* on his head.

When the grand vizier had passed the Imperial Gate and proceeded as far as the Imperial Bakery his steward dashed his horse up to the Middle Gate in order to be on hand to escort him to the gate's inner door. At this point palace personnel, the chief herald and the steward of the gatekeepers, took over, striking the ground with their staffs to announce the presence of the grand vizier. As he turned toward the Hall of the Divan the chief water-carrier welcomed him with typical Ottoman formality: "Deign to come in."

At this signal the viziers in the Hall of the Divan rose and walked out onto the porch to receive the state's chief officer, who greeted them with the words: "May your morning be auspicious." The members then sat, but still they were not ready for business, for the elaborate protocol of the palace demanded that they rise to be hailed by the grand vizier once again.

It was now time for the opening chapter of the Koran to be read, and outside the hall in the high chant that is the accepted manner of reading the Koran came the words, in Arabic:

In the name of Allah, the Beneficent, the Merciful,
Praise be to Allah, Lord of the Worlds,
The Beneficent, the Merciful.
Owner of the Day of Judgement,
Thee alone we worship; Thee alone we ask for help.
Show us the straight path,
The path of those whom Thou hast favored;
Not the path of those who earn Thine anger nor of those who go astray.

As the ancient words sang out attendants came up with a tureen of the Janissaries' soup and a loaf of their round, flat bread. Each member of the

Divan tasted them, and sometimes the grand vizier had the bread weighed in his presence to make sure the Janissaries were not being short changed. Next the viziers were offered a plate of candy. When this too had been tasted and it was therefore signified that the Janissaries' food was fit for their consumption, the Janissaries, who had been standing in ranks in the colonnade on the right side of the court, fell to. They rushed out into the court, a tide of men, hundreds and thousands of them. Foreign ambassadors who were sometimes present were hard put to it not to recoil in terror. Actually this rush toward the soup meant that all was well. If the Janissaries refused the soup, it behooved the statesmen to guard their heads.

Granted that they drank their soup, the business of the Divan could get under way. The state secretary slowly approached the grand vizier, kissed his skirt, placed beside him on the sofa the case with the summaries of the lawsuits, kissed his skirt again, and retreated to his place. The holder of the pen-and-ink case put at his side a handkerchief, a pen-box, and a fabric purse full of shining new coins to be distributed to converts and the poor. Finally the heralds led in the claimants. The grand vizier heard the pros and cons of the cases, sometimes asked the opinions of the other council members, and made his decision in accordance with the Holy Law and the civil law handed down by the sultans. He not only decided the cases, he pronounced the sentences, which might be flogging, imprisonment, or even execution. If it was flogging, where the punishment took place depended on who the culprit was. Janissaries, cavalrymen, armorers and artillerymen had the right to be flogged only in their own quarters and by their own officers. Others took their flogging right in the Divanhane.

Four times a year, on Divan days, the Janissaries received their pay (ulûfe), occasions of great display. Foreign ambassadors were often invited then so that they might see and be impressed by the grandeur of the Ottoman Empire. The pay was heaped up in leather purses in piles of ten, reaching from the grand vizier's seat to the door of the Divan. The handkerchief that the state secretary had previously placed beside the grand vizier was now put to use to tie up the authorization to pay, which had to be delivered to the sultan. When it was returned made official by the sultan's signature, the grand vizier arose and took a few steps toward the door, not to honor the bearer but rather the imperial rescript he brought. The grand vizier raised it to his lips, removed the handerkerchief and broke the seal. He now read it aloud, sat down and signaled that the Janissaries might come. After certain additional formalities the Janissaries designated for the task picked up the bags and distributed the coins they contained as the men came forward to receive them.

When the last man had been paid the noon meal was served to the Divan members. Kitchen attendants carried it in covered dishes on trays over which sumptuously embroidered cloths were thrown. Someone placed a tray to use as a table on a low stool before the grand vizier, another before the other viziers, and a third in front of the judge advocates. If a foreign ambassador was present, he had the honor of eating at the grand vizier's table. An almost endless variety of food was served. John Covel, who as the British ambassador's chaplain partook of such a feast in the seventeenth century, described it minutely in his journal. Though it took place in Edirne, the food was the same as at Topkapı for the cooks had the same training. He says the little tables or trays were covered with leather and set with wooden spoons, a salt cellar and pepper-box, four little saucers of pickled capers and olives, a carrot-like plant and parsley in a sweet sauce. Twenty dishes of meat were set before the group, one at a time, and whisked in and out so quickly Covel complained there was scarcely time to eat. He remembered roast chicken, roast pigeon, kebabs, dolmas or vine leaves stuffed with minced meat, puddings, pilaf, "a great *baked pye* in a platter, with puff paste above and minced beaten meat, wel season'd, underneath; a puf paste pudding in a platter, plain; *another*, seasoned with honey. About half way of this horse feast we water'd with a hearty draught of excellent Lemmon Sherbert, which was brought in a *fingeon (fincan,* a small cup) . . . gilt on the verge at the top." All this was eaten either with wooden spoons or with the fingers; knives and forks did not come into use in the Ottoman Empire until the nineteenth century.

All through the meal the chief chamberlain, the chief baker, and the intendant of the Imperial Kitchens were at hand to assure that everything went well. After it attendants brought around napkins, basin and ewer for washing the hands, and the master of ceremonies rose water and incense. The appearance of the Janissary Ağa dressed in a robe of honor was the signal that the sultan would receive them in the Throne Room. The Divan meeting was over. They might gather again in the afternoon to finish their business.

Again the *Hünername* brings the sixteenth century to life. Its miniature of the Divanhane shows the grand vizier in his white robe under the lodge where the sultan listens. To his right sit the four viziers in an early type of turban, the *horasanî*, to his left, at a little distance, the judges of the army

[7 6]

in their *örfs*. In one corner is the state secretary *(reis-ül-küttab)* writing busily, and in the next room sit the scribes, pieces of paper on their knees. Below them is a bag of Janissary pay, which one man holds by a cord. More bags are in the courtyard together with curious little stools. Officials and Janissaries stand about in separate groups, one of them by a fountain that no longer exists. The miniature scarcely suggests the crowds that filled the court on paydays, but however many the people it was never disorganized and never noisy. So pervasive was the silence in that great mass, Western visitors found it almost a palpable thing. Many mentioned it in the reports they wrote of their experiences in the *saray*.

In the sixteenth and seventeenth centuries, when the Divanhane was still Ottoman in appearance as well as in spirit, some of the Empire's greatest viziers presided over it. Two of them served Süleyman, İbrahim whom we met in the description of the circumcision fête in the Introduction, and Sokullu Mehmet of whom we shall hear more when we discuss the Palace School. A later outstanding grand vizier, Nevşehirli İbrahim, conducted affairs in the altered council chamber which, however debased in taste it may seem to us, was thought of as a place of grandeur in his time. The sofa had been extended along the rail of the scribes' room, and the grand vizier's seat seems to have moved to the corner.

In 1728, only a year before the end of his life, Nevşehirli İbrahim received the Persian ambassador in a Divanhane spruced up for the occasion. Its gildings were renewed. The entire portico of the Second Court, all the way around from the Middle Gate to the Gate of Felicity, was draped with scarlet cloth.

The Empire and Persia had just ended a long war, and the Ottomans were anxious to impress the Persian ambassador with their power and opulence. They therefore arranged his route through Istanbul so as to give him a view of the galleys of the navy and of the cannon that guarded the port. The day the grand vizier granted him an audience all was luxury. The floor of the room where the ambassadors waited was covered with rugs instead of the customary matting. The Divanhane itself shone with silk, gold and pearls.

"At the foot of the grand vizier," says the Austrian historian von Hammer, whose sources were Ottoman chronicles, "at the angle of the sofa which is reputed to be the place of honor, was extended a covering embroidered with pearls; on his right one saw a portfolio ornamented with precious stones, and an inkwell in which the emeralds and pearls projected that live and pure light which ought to gush from truly good writing; at his left was a reading desk sparkling with precious stones, on which was deposed a Koran whose black velvet binding was strewn with brilliants. . . .

"The footmen of the chamber wore precious girdles into which were fixed poignards and knives ornamented with precious stones; the ministers of State, the defterdar [treasurer], the reis-efendi [state secretary], the tschaouschbaschi [çavuşbaşi, chief herald] and the under secretaries of state, the chancellor, the masters of requests and the secretary of the cabinet rivaled the luxury; but all was obscured by the burst of diamonds that ornamented the rings, the girdle, the poignard, and the clasps designed to close the vestments of the grand vizier. 'He was,' says the historiographer, 'all resplendent and swimming from head to foot in a sea of pearls and precious stones.' "

Mohammed Khan, the Persian ambassador, was greeted by Nevşehirli İbrahim who rose to meet him, and he was seated on the sofa. If he had been representing a Christian country the grand vizier would have withdrawn until after his arrival to avoid getting to his feet for an unbeliever, and the ambassador's place would have been a backless stool.

It was the last time İbrahim was to show off the pomp of the Ottoman Empire. The next year he would lose his life in the Gate Area and his sultan, Ahmet III, be deposed.

After the middle of the seventeenth century the importance of the grand vizier increased at the expense of the Imperial Council. State business came to be transacted at his residence, and by the eighteenth century the Divanhane had become a place of ceremony rather than decision. Selim III and Mahmut II revived the Divan for their reforming purposes, but its new life was short. With the adoption of the Western cabinet system and the desertion of Topkapı, the Hall of the Divan was left to decay until the palace became a museum.

THE GATE OF FELICITY

IT WAS the prerogative of the sultan to have been born under a lucky star. He was the lord of the fortunate conjunction of the planets *(sahip kıran)* who brought felicity *(saadet)* to his empire. Thus his private quarters, which consisted of the Third and Fourth Courts and the harem, were the House of Felicity (Darüssaadet) and the entrance to them the Gate of Felicity (Babüssaadet.) Certain of the most imposing ceremonies of the Empire were centered here.

The Gate of Felicity dominates the north end of the Second Court by its wide and deep portico surmounted by a flaring roof with a gilded dome that culminates in the Turkish star and crescent. This is the most colorful of the palace gates. The wall it breaches is a sort of Pompeian red and the under side of its roof is painted in various colors perhaps softened by time. Under its curved wings lurk landscapes done by Italian artisans when the gate was restored in the 1770's by Abdülhamit I. His *tuğra* stands above a panel to one side of the door. Since Mahmut II's *tuğra* is on the other side it may reasonably be supposed that the gate saw restoration again in the early nineteenth century. It must have been then that there were added at each side dreadful *trompe-l'oeil* paintings of long colonnades which the museum has mercifully removed. They replaced a pair of graceful fountains of Selim III's time, and can be explained only by Mahmut's yen for Westernization in all things.

That this is not the original Gate of Felicity is attested by the *Hüner-*

name miniature of the Second Court which shows the portico more of a piece with the colonnade and topped by a lower dome that rises gradually from narrower eaves that are a simple extension of the colonnade roof. The pillars that support today's portico are different too, being set on higher pedestals and having round, un-Ottoman capitals. In the center of the portico floor is an indentation, now covered over, where the Sacred Standard of the Prophet's army used to be inserted on occasion. Over the door, which is wide, is the *besmele*, the Muslim prayer for beginnings: "In the name of God, the Merciful, the Compassionate." It opens every chapter of the Koran and is found frequently in the palace.

It is interesting that the Imperial Gate, the Middle Gate and the Gate of Felicity are not aligned with one another. One can only speculate on the reason for this broken axis. It may have been to prevent a view from the First Court of the sacrosanct precinct of the House of Felicity, should both the Middle and the Gate of Felicity be open.

Like the other gates, this one had other names: the Gate of the White Eunuchs (Ak Ağalar Kapısı) because they guarded it, and the Presentation Gate (Arz Kapısı) because its inner door opens directly across the portico from the Presentation Room (Arz Odası). In Western sources this is referred to as the Throne Room.

The interior of the gate between the outer and inner doors is unremarkable except for a restored ceiling of tree motifs. It seems to have had no particular use except as a guard room and a place to ornament the throne with its jeweled and embroidered coverings when it was on its way to be set up outside the Gate of Felicity.

It was under the portico of this gate that a new sultan received the allegiance of his dignitaries after the death or deposition of his predecessor. Until then he had been heir to the throne *(veliaht)*, in early times invested with the governorship of a province and after the sixteenth century confined to an Heir's Apartment in a section of the harem called the Cage (Kafes). To him there came the chief black eunuch to inform him of his accession, an event that brought with it a complete reversal of his way of life—from virtual prisoner to master of an empire. As soon as they could be summoned the two chief dignitaries of the Empire, the grand vizier and the chief religious figure *(şeyhülislâm)* accompanied the new ruler to the Room of the Blessed Mantle in the Third Court. There, before the holy relics, they prayed with him. One of these men was as important to the sultan as the other. The grand vizier administered the Empire for him, but he had to do it within the bounds of the Holy Law as interpreted by the *şeyhülislâm*.

The Gate of Felicity.

The chief astrologer (*müneccimbaşı*) set the day and hour for the enthronement, as he did for every important occasion, and the master of ceremonies (*teşrifatçı*) announced it. The participating officials adorned themselves in their furred robes of honor and gathered in the Hall of the Divan. A throne of beaten gold studded with green tourmalines was carried by the Halberdiers with Tresses from the Imperial Treasury in the Third Court to the Gate of Felicity. This throne had been presented to Süleyman's grandson, Murat III, by a governor of Egypt and is at least partly of Egyptian workmanship. Its ten gold plates cover a frame of walnut and are set with 954 tourmalines. The throne is on view in the Treasury section of the museum.

All were instructed by the master of ceremonies as to the order in which to move up to the throne and the exact place to stand. When the propitious hour had arrived the Ağa of the House of Felicity (the chief black eunuch)

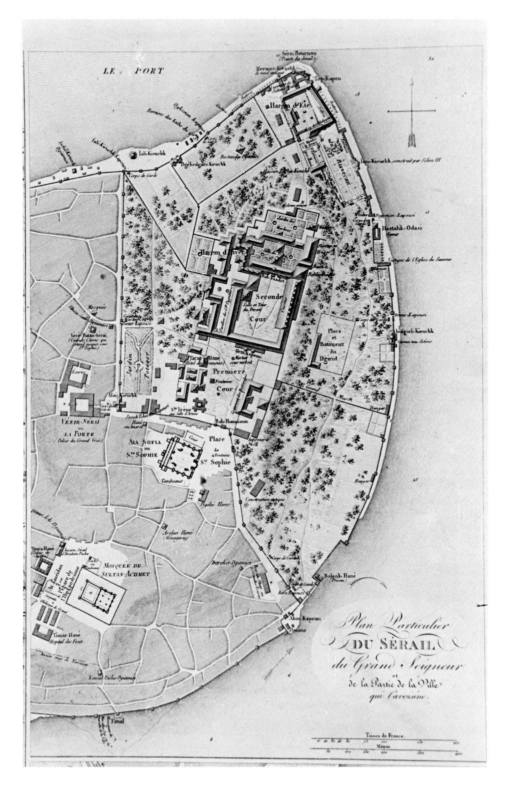

Map of Topkapı Palace and its environs from Melling's Voyage pittoresque. . . .
Though inaccurate in many details and revealing little knowledge of the build-
ings, it is useful for indicating how the gardens surrounded the Inner Palace and
the enceinte of the land and sea walls.

and the chief sword-bearer, each taking an arm, escorted the new sultan out to the portico. Over a garment of rich silk he wore a *kapaniçe*, a robe peculiar to the sultan, long and virtually sleeveless, its front pieces and its armholes edged with fur, its flat collar fur, and its breast adorned with rows of braid that resembled frogs, with jeweled buttons. On his head in the seventeenth and eighteenth centuries he wore a *Yusufî*, a complicated turban composed of a ribbed headgear that widened as it went up, around it wrapped a piece of fabric that gave it width. From its front center rose a high aigrette of peacock feathers in a jeweled holder. Tradition has it that this type of turban was worn by Joseph of Biblical days. Hence its name, pertaining to Joseph or Yusuf. Throughout the ceremony the Ağa of the House of Felicity stood at the sultan's right in a long furred robe and a tall turban, and the sword-bearer with his high, folded-over headgear at his left.

One by one the dignitaries came up the path from the Hall of the Divan to the portico of the gate and signified their allegiance by bending to kiss the padishah's skirt. First strode the representative of the descendants of the Prophet, who chanted a prayer, and then the son or sons of the Crimean khan to signify Crimea's vassalage to the Ottoman Empire, and the *ağas* of the stirrup who were intimates of the sultan, the viziers, the judges of the army, and all those in high position, each in his turn. Finally came the grand vizier and the *şeyhülislâm*, for whom and the judge advocates the sultan rose from his throne. Each took his place in an arc around the throne until the whole portico and the space in front of it were alive with an endless variety of color. At the end of the ceremony the master of ceremonies kissed the padishah's skirt, the new ruler rose, turned his head in greeting to all, and walked back through the gate to his private quarters. But before he left there arose from the throats of the heralds the cry, "May you live a thousand years, my padishah!" This was the *alkış* or cheer. In today's Turkey the word means applause.

Yearly ceremonies held at the Gate of Felicity were the congratulations tendered to the sovereign on the Sweets and Sacrifice Holidays (Şeker and Kurban Bayramıs). These began on the eve of the festive day when the palace service people gathered and the palace band played facing the Tower of Justice. At this ceremony the horses of the Privy Stable were on display, glittering with jeweled gear from the Harness Treasury, each horse mounted by a stable attendant to calm him down when the band started.

The ceremony began after afternoon prayer with a reading of the first chapter of the Koran, after which the band played and the heralds cheered.

[8 3]

NECATI ORBAY

Selim III accepting the bayram *congratulations of his dignitaries on the* bayram *throne under the portico of the Gate of Felicity.*

A similar ceremony took place in the Third Court where the Eve Throne
(Arife Tahtı) was set up in front of the Throne Room, and apparently the
padishah went from one to the other. If the sultan was too worn out to make
this second ceremony—it is said Ahmet II didn't come out because his feet
hurt—his turban was set on the throne to symbolize his presence.

On the actual day of the *bayram* the gold throne was used in the usual
place before the Gate of Felicity. It is in fact called the *bayram* throne. The
sultan performed morning prayer with his personal suite in the Room of
the Blessed Mantle and then was dressed in ceremonial garments. In the
seventeenth and eighteenth centuries he wore the robe described for the
enthronement, in the sixteenth a long-sleeved silk one. Several of these are
displayed in the sultans' clothes section in the Third Court. In the sixteenth
century he probably did not wear the Yusufî but a bulky, rounded turban
called *horasanî*. He was perfumed with aloeswood and incense and received
the congratulations of the chief Inner Palace attendants in one of his private
rooms. He was then escorted to the throne by ranks of attendants who
selamed and kissed his skirt.

[8 4]

The ceremony was very much like that of the accession. As each man's turn came he separated himself from the throng in the Second Court and stepped forward, escorted by the chief herald wielding his silver baton. The grand vizier came from the left and passed on to stand at the sultan's right shoulder. For him the sultan got to his feet. Other administrative officers followed, and then came the turn of the important men of religion, the *ulema* (literally the learned). They were headed by the *şeyhülislâm* for whom the sultan not only rose from the throne but walked two steps forward and shook his hand. After a short prayer the *şeyhülislâm* retired to stand at the sultan's left. For certain others the sultan also stood, and no chance was taken on imperial memory. According to the requirement the heralds cried out, "Imperial action, my padishah!" or "Imperial rest, my padishah!" All during this the band played and from time to time cannon sounded from the port, but there was no sound of voices in the court except for the prayers and cheers. All the cheers wished the sultan good fortune and long life but one that reminded him that he too was mortal. Then the throats cried out, "Be not proud, my padishah, God is greater than you."

Finally the heralds gave one last cheer, and the Ağa of the House of Felicity and the grand vizier escorted the sultan back to the Inner Palace. Yet his duties for the day were not completed. He must go to one of the great mosques in procession for the *bayram* prayer, usually Santa Sophia or the Mosque of Sultan Ahmet. For this he changed clothes, mounted a handsomely saddled horse and rode out the Middle Gate where the grand vizier met him. Stirrup *ağas* followed him on foot, and in the square outside the Imperial Gate crowds waited to see him.

At times it turned out that the populace and the military of Istanbul, if not greater, at least were temporarily more powerful than the padishah. This was when a council on foot (*ayak divanı*) was called in the presence of the sultan. It might be convened wherever the sultan happened to be but was most frequently held in front of the Gate of Felicity.

The seventeenth-century sultan, Murat IV, was forced to hold several of these councils. The cause of the first one, when Murat was twenty-one, was complex. On the one hand there was the venality of officials, which became an open scandal. On the other there was the enmity between two high dignitaries, Hafız Ahmet Pasha, who was grand vizier, and Recep (Rejep) Pasha, who wanted to become grand vizier. Using the widespread bribe-taking as a pretext, Recep stirred up the cavalry, and the Janissaries, ever ready for trouble, joined them. They terrorized the city, demanding the heads of seventeen of the sultan's favorites, including Hafız Ahmet. That day the shops closed in terror. The next day the mob came as far as the Imperial Gate, where it was placated by the promise that amends would be made for their grievances the following day. But their patience did not last that long. By morning the rebels had pushed their way through the Imperial Gate and stood and squatted in fierce groups in the First Court.

The grand vizier was about to leave his own palace for the Hall of the Divan when a friend warned him that the mob was in the palace crying for his head. To this Hafiz Ahmet replied: "I have seen my fate in a dream. I am not afraid to die," and he rode out his gate and up the hill and into the palace grounds. Curiously, the mob made a lane for him as if out of respect, but suddenly the mood changed and they threw stones. He was struck from his horse, but still his attendants managed to get him into the Inner Palace, although one was killed and one wounded in the attempt. Murat, who was devoted to his grand vizier, commanded that he flee across the Bosphorus to Üsküdar, and Hafiz Ahmet made his way through the palace gardens to a water-gate and got away.

By now the rebels had forced the Middle Gate and were in the Second Court amid the cypresses and the gazelles, calling for the sultan to come before them and hold a council on foot.

Reluctantly Murat IV emerged from the Gate of Felicity and asked, "What is it you want, my slaves?"

"Give us these men, these seventeen heads," they cried, "or it will fare worse with you!" And they pressed forward until they were all but touching the sacrosanct person of the sultan.

Murat tried to reason with them, but they were in no mood to listen. Angry now, he said, "Why then have you called me here? You do not listen to my words." Surrounded by his pages, he withdrew through the Gate of Felicity into the Third Court. The rebels tried to flood in after him, but the white eunuchs managed to shut the gate and only the tumult penetrated to the House of Felicity. The words were frightening enough: "The seventeen heads or abdicate!"

Recep Pasha had been waiting for this moment. "It is the custom in time of danger," he told the young sultan, "to give up the men the military demand. Better the head of the grand vizier than the head of the sultan."

However little he may have liked it, Murat saw the point, and sadly he gave the order to call Hafiz Ahmet back to his death. Sadly he waited for him at the water-gate and accompanied him up the hill, through the private gardens, bare now in the winter time. With Hafiz Ahmet on hand, the Gate of Felicity was thrown open. A throne was put in place, and Murat

The Hünername *miniature of the enthronement of Selim I. Three pages of the Privy Chamber stand beside him. One man kisses his skirt. Most of the others stand with hands folded in respect.*

NECATI ORBAY

ascended it. Two representatives of the cavalry and two of the Janissaries came up to the portico before him. He tried to plead with them for clemency for the grand vizier, but his words had no effect. "The seventeen heads," came the call repeatedly, sometimes shrill, sometimes gutteral, but always terrifying.

Hafız Ahmet came forward. He had made his final ablutions, the ritual ablutions of Islam. Standing under the domed portico before his ruler, he said, "My padishah, let a thousand slaves like Hafız Ahmet perish for your sake. I ask only that you do not yourself have me put to death, but give me up to those men so that I may die a martyr and that my innocent blood may be upon their heads. Let my body be buried in Üsküdar." He knelt and kissed the ground in front of the sultan, and saying, "In the name of God, the Merciful, the Compassionate. There is no power or might save God, the Most High, the Almighty. His we are, and unto Him we return," he stepped out into the Second Court where he had so often been the central figure.

The sultan, the viziers, the pages all sobbed as the rebels rushed at the long-robed, stately figure. A brave man to the last, he struck his first assailant down, but the others swarmed upon him, daggers out, and when they laid him low he was pierced with seventeen wounds. A Janissary knelt on his chest and severed his head from his body. It was done. The pages performed the only service they could for him. They came forward and spread a cloth over his body. The Gate of Felicity had betrayed its name.

The young sultan, moved and angry at the bloody scene he had witnessed, told the rebels, "God's will be done! But in His appointed time you shall meet with vengeance, you men of blood who have neither the fear of God before your eyes nor respect for the law of the Prophet." The words were portentous. Murat never forgot this day. All he could do now was turn and walk inside, but the time came when he made them pay dearly, Recep Pasha, the instigator of it all, with his life.

Another council on foot was held before the Gate of Felicity to prove that Murat had not killed his brothers. In the past fratricide had been a practice of newly enthroned sultans to eliminate rivals for the head of the state. Horrible as it may seem now, it was a practice shared by other states, Christian and Muslim, although like everything else Ottoman it had been institutionalized. There had actually been a law of fratricide, although by Murat's day it had been repealed and the Cage or incarceration of the princes substituted. However, this was no proof against the sudden whim of a sultan, and the people were anxious for the princes. They were also angry over the killing of a popular vizier, Hüsrev Pasha. "The princes are the son of our lord," the people said, meaning Murat's father, Ahmet I. "We have no confidence in you. You unjustly killed Hüsrev Pasha; you may slaughter the princes too. Bring them out, show them to us!"

Murat tried to assure them the princes were still alive, but finding the people unbelieving, he ordered them brought forth, and Bayezit, Süleyman, Kasım and İbrahim were all escorted from the Cage and shown to the crowd pressing forward toward the gate.

Still not satisfied, the Janissaries demanded, "Give us assurance you will not harm them!" and so the religious head and Recep Pasha, who was now grand vizier, gave that assurance. It turned out to be worthless, for Murat grew bloodthirsty with the years and eventually killed all his brothers except İbrahim, who succeeded him.

Thus was history, as well as ceremony, made before the Gate of Felicity.

THE THIRD COURT

EMERGING from the Gate of Felicity, one finds one's view of the Third Court blocked by the wide Throne Room that immediately faces the inner portico. Since the Throne Room is currently closed to visitors, we shall pass it up for the moment and walk around it and down a bit to take in the vista of the court, square and sunny, sloping slightly away from us, and lined with buildings that appear much lighter than those of the Second Court. They look less aged than the Second Court structures because in most cases they are. No part of the palace except the harem has been so frequently made over as the Third Court, and its present face is largely the result of reconstruction after a fire in 1856/7 plus some restoration by the museum. To trace all its alterations would only be confusing. We shall therefore introduce the court as it is today and then try to bring alive something of the flavor of its imperial days.

The surrounding buildings are of various heights and sizes, some domed, some flat-roofed. Yet one is struck not by their differences but rather by their unity, which comes partly from the fact that they are all of stone or concrete but largely from the colonnade with its series of small domes that runs around most of three sides. Only on the west is the seeming regularity broken, and we shall get to that.

The court was formerly the home of the young pages, to use the Turkish term *iç oğlan* (inside boy), of the Palace School which trained them to serve the Empire. Here with them were the white eunuchs who were in charge of them and who also guarded the Gate of Felicity. Today several of the Palace School halls or dormitories are given over to the display of the museum's unique collections.

The first of these is to be found on the right, tall and fronted with a narrow colonnaded porch. Because it has changed less than some of the others, it will give some idea of what the old halls looked like. It used to be the Expeditionary or Campaign Hall (Seferli Koğuşu), the quarters of the pages who accompanied the sultan on campaign. At present it consists of two rooms. The first is tall and vaulted, its vaults supported by two rows of square stone pillars, and looks very much as it must always have looked with the difference that the gallery, which was standard for all halls of the Palace School, has been removed. The inner room is smaller, lower, flat-roofed, and has a view of the Marmara.

Yet even the Campaign Hall, which has stood here since the early seventeenth century, has had some variety in its history. In the sixteenth century at least part of its site belonged to a dazzling imperial bath built by Selim II but which included baths for the pages and their officers. At some point, probably in the same century, was added the Small Hall (Küçük Oda) for the novice pages, and this was probably entirely rebuilt into the Campaign Hall. It missed destruction by the fire of 1856/7 but was nevertheless some-what altered in the general reconstruction. Its façade was pushed back twenty feet so that today its columns are aligned with those of the Treasury contiguous to it. By then it was no longer used by the Expeditionary Pages, who had been abolished in 1831. Their quarters were assigned to pages connected with the Treasury.

The hall is now furnished with glass cases in which lie or are hung clothing of the sultans, beginning with the Conqueror and continuing into the nineteenth century. On the death of a sultan his clothes, especially his ceremonial robes, were put away in a bag and tagged with his name. Thus the collection is a large one, and the items change from time to time. Those on display now range over the entire Empire period. The robes or kaftans of the days before Mahmut II introduced Western dress are much the more interesting, and one is always sure to see rich examples. The collection has, for example, at least two handsome kaftans of the Conqueror, either of which may be on display. One is a buff or pale gold velvet on which is woven in red a design of three discs interspersed with pairs of wavy lines looking much like lips. It was packed away with the label, "Honored gar-ment of His Majesty the late Sultan Mehmet II, Conqueror of Conquerors,

to whom all sins are forgiven." The other has a motif of tulips and pome-
granates embroidered in gold thread on red velvet, the groups of flowers
separated by the same wavy lines. In a case at the moment of writing is a
black moiré, ermine-lined kaftan that the Conqueror was wearing at his
death. There are also a simple and handsome robe of red velvet tulips on
gold that belonged to Murat III and a kaftan of a gold three-ball design on
black that was worn by Selim I. One of the handsomest is an early, very
elaborate kaftan that belonged to Korkut, son of Bayezit II (1470–1513),
again red velvet with a gold design but lined with a blue silk that protrudes
to make a collar. Ahmet III had a quilted robe of pale gold, Selim III one of
red moiré. Some robes are fur-lined for wintertime. Some are for children:
a little gold suit of Prince Mehmet, son of Murat IV, and a small red robe
belonging to Heybetullah, daughter of Abdülhamit I. These are in the back
room along with other items of apparel such as the light, decorated slippers
the sultans wore indoors, some of leather, some of velvet, and the pearl- and
coral-embroidered slippers of the kadıns. Here also hang embroidered prayer
rugs and examples of old Ottoman fabrics. Most dramatic, however, are the
rich kaftans. Nowhere else can they be seen, for only the Ottomans wore
them.

Directly next to the Campaign Hall, their columned porches connected
by a few steps, is the most beautiful building of the Third Court and perhaps
even of the palace. It is the Imperial Treasury, which attracts more visitors
than any other part of the museum. It is worth examining both for the building itself and for the glitter of jeweled objects it contains, and we shall
take it up separately. It extends to the end of the court; its porch is the only
one that lacks domes.

The court's north end is bordered by two buildings with no architectural significance, except that the same domed colonnade graces them. The
originals were, on the right, the Hall of the Pages of the Commissariat (Kiler
Koğuşu) and on the left the Hall of the Pages of the Treasury (Hazine
Koğuşu). Both burned in the fire. The Commissariat was replaced by a
wooden, two-story building for the Treasury Steward and is now concreted
and the office of the director of the museum and his staff. The other has
become the painting section.

In its rooms on the first floor the latter displays miniatures from Topkapı's collection which is respected by authorities on the subject as the finest
collection of Islamic paintings in the world. It owns all periods, including
some fine Byzantine works, but its store of two genre is unmatched: Ottoman painting and that of the Timurid school established by Tamerlane in

NECATI ORBAY

A portrait of Süleyman the Magnificent in his old age, accompanied by his sword-bearer and the head of the Privy Chamber.

Samarkand and continued by his descendants in Herat. This too is a rotating collection, so that it is impossible to say just what is out at any given time, though one can safely assume an outstanding display.

Ottoman painting is particularly worth one's attention here because there is not much of it to be seen anywhere else. It is different from other Islamic painting, being on the whole less romantic, stronger in color, and more given to realism in details. There developed in Istanbul, for example, a school of portrait painters who painted people as they actually looked without the exaggerated grace or idealization of other Islamic schools. Some of these portraits are sure to be shown, such as the one of the sixteenth-century corsair-admiral, Barbarossa, in his old age, dagger in hand, still sharp-eyed, and not even the carnation he sniffs detracting from the impression that he is still ready to make another raid on the Mediterranean coast. It is the work of one of the most famous Ottoman painters, Nigâri. Most impressive of the portraits, in my opinion, is a full length of Süleyman in his old age, dressed in an ermine-bordered blue robe, simple and stately and a little lonely, followed at a respectful distance by his sword-bearer and another attendant from the Privy Chamber. It too is Nigâri's work.

[9 2]

Some *Hümername* miniatures are sure to be in the main room, for they belong to the best period of Ottoman miniature painting, the latter part of the sixteenth century. At present one can see a double-page painting of the sultan on a hunting expedition accompanied by his hawkers and on the left-hand page drawing his decorated gilt bow on a wild boar. We have seen such a bow in the Arms Section. At another time the pages may be turned to a scene of Murat II shooting an arrow at a target on a high pole while foreign ambassadors look on from behind a hill. At this writing many battle scenes, of which the Ottomans were very fond, are being shown in bright if overwhelming detail. There is much to choose from.

The famous *Surname (Book of Festivals)* made to commemorate the fifty-two-day circumcision festivities of a son of Murat III may well be represented. The sultan sits on a throne in a grandstand put up on the Hip-

Sultan Süleyman I receiving a Western ambassador. This is one of 20 miniatures from a book on the Szeged campaign in Hungary. Note that he is accompanied by his sword-bearer and the head of the Privy Chamber and that all the Ottomans have their hands folded in respect.

[9 3]

podrome while the various guilds of tradesmen from taxidermists to weavers of cloth pass by, thus giving the modern viewer some insight into the variety of trades of old Istanbul.

A favorite of mine is the *Nüzhet (el-esrar) ül-Ahbar der Sefer-i Sigetvar*, a book on the events of Süleyman's Szeged campaign in Hungary on which he died. The miniature from it, reproduced here in black and white, shows Süleyman on a throne under a canopy accepting the obeisance of a Western ambassador. His sword-bearer and the chief of the Privy Chamber stand at his side, two other attendants in front of them. The throne is gold, the canopy of dark colors in floral medallions but lined with gold-decorated red. The sultan's turban and those of the attendants in front are white contrasting, one with a red gown, the other with a black one. Those wearing the high headpieces of the Privy Chamber wear blue and red respectively. The foreign ambassador's outfit is a dull blue except for the white ruff around his neck, his red sleeves and yellow shoes. He is carrying a case in which is probably a document he is about to present to Süleyman. The faces are all realistic and the colors clean. One can get an idea of these resplendent scenes by viewing the canopy in a section of the Third Court to be described shortly.

We also reproduce a portrait of the Conqueror, Mehmet II, which is ascribed to Contanza da Ferrara, an Italian who was in Istanbul in the Conqueror's time and who may have painted it from life.

The Ottomans were fond of albums of the life of the Prophet, and scenes from these, with the Prophet's face blank so as not to indulge in idolatry, are likely to be there. At present a *Falname* or *Book of Fortune-Telling* of the sixteenth or seventeenth century shows a large page with half naked figures, upside down, looking upwards while half figures, some with snake headdresses no doubt indicating demons, glance down on them. Pages from Levni, an eighteenth-century artist, are now hung and are well worth looking at because they depict women who are seldom present in Ottoman miniatures. Though the faces represent a type present in Islamic painting over the centuries, the clothes are realistic and give a clear idea of what the upper-class Ottoman woman wore.

One can count on there being on display some of the paintings from a remarkable book called the *Fatih (Conqueror) Album*, something of a scrapbook of scenes of Central Asian origin, quite different from the elegance of the other miniatures. It contains scenes of nomadic life, animal and demon scenes, and one of a shaman or Central Asiatic religious leader dancing about in religious ecstasy. In them rather squat figures clothed in heavy folds go

A portrait of the Conqueror, Mehmet II, believed to have been painted, perhaps from life, by Contanza da Ferrara, an Italian artist living in Istanbul at the time.

NECATI ORBAY

about the business of nomadic camp life. Even the coloring is unusual, muted greys and brownish reds, and somehow a little sinister. One, however, is particularly appealing and quite modern in feeling, a curled-up, very satisfied looking cat. These are signed by Mehmet Siyah Kalem which means simply Mehmet of the Black Pen or illustrator.

For the visitor already interested in Islamic painting this exhibit is a treasure house. For anyone else it is an introduction to a world of art that is becoming more and more appreciated in the West.

On the second floor of the building a series of modern oils of the sultans is hung, all painted in the nineteenth century, tending to make most of them look alike, and scarcely worth climbing the stairs to see. Yet there are one or two exceptions, a copy of Bellini's famous portrait of the Conqueror and, at the far end, a *bayram* scene of the time of Selim III, with the sultan sitting on the gold throne under the portico of the Gate of Felicity, his courtiers and dignitaries about him. It not only shows the old costumes but illustrates what such a scene must have been like. We reproduce a part of the painting here.

After a passageway to the Fourth Court we come to a small room that was at one time the Treasury of the Sword-Bearer and later the Treasury of the Sacred Relics. Access to it used to be had via the Pavilion of the Blessed Mantle, at which time it stored old coverings of the Kaaba, the sacred shrine at Mecca, that had been replaced by new ones—we shall see one in the Pavilion of the Blessed Mantle—and some of the pavilion's library of religious books. A huge canopy, red on the outside and floral embroidery on tan on the inside, fills it now, hovering over a black and gold throne that sits on crimson silk. This is the sort of thing that was erected to shelter the sultan on campaign. At one side is a mounting block sheathed entirely with silver.

Here one turns to the left to the Pavilion of the Blessed Mantle which deserves and will get a section of its own. From it there has recently been installed a broad marble way that leads to the Throne Room, it having been discovered that one such existed in the early days. Then the Pavilion of the Holy Mantle was the Has Oda, and an old chronicler has related that orders were given to clean the marble way from the Has Oda to the Arz Odası with a light solution of lemon and water.

Beyond the Pavilion of the Blessed Mantle lies the dormitory of the Privy Chamber (Has Oda), the hall of the personal attendants of the sultan, who numbered forty. The present dormitory dates only from the fire and used to consist, like all the halls of the Palace School, of a ground floor and gallery. Now minus the gallery, it is a tall, long room that displays calligraphy and bookbinding. Its entrance is almost hidden by the Ağas' Mosque, and it is easy to miss. Yet to do so would be a mistake, for it introduces the visitor to an important element of Ottoman and particularly court culture.

Dominating the room on the far wall is a huge *tuğra* of Murat III drawn in deep blue against a background of a myriad small flowers. Seeing its infinite complexity and detail, one can well understand that composing the sultan's signature was a special art. The room also invites a view of books in old scripts and of the leather covers, usually decorated with medallions, sometimes gold-filled, that enclose them. In cases there are old Korans going back to the eighth century; Korans written in letters so tiny the whole book could be attached to a battle standard; a Koran of 620 pages all written on one sheet of paper; examples of old marbled Ottoman paper; and a case of old writing instruments. Again the museum has many more examples than can be shown. Among its treasures is a beautifully written Koran belonging to Süleyman with chapter headings and borders illuminated in gold and blue against a background of tiny flowers.

Just outside the dormitory, in a small, long room in which seals were until recently displayed, is a new collection of calligraphy given to the museum and containing works of the finest Persian and Turkish calligraphers from the sixteenth century on up. There are beautifully written copies of the Poem of the Mantle (Kasida-ı Burda) which we shall explain when we come to the Pavilion of the Blessed Mantle, and pages from a collection of fine penmanship called *murekka*.

These two rooms were only part of the Privy Chamber, which once included not only the present Pavilion of the Blessed Mantle but various small in-between places. The original Privy Chamber or Has Oda, now as we have said the Pavilion of the Blessed Mantle, was built by the Conqueror. His foundations still remain beneath it and are connected with the upper floor by an old staircase that debouches into the Room of the Blessed Mantle. In the seventeenth century the Privy Chamber must have been a place of grandeur. A former page, Evliya Çelebi, describes it then as "a large room with a cupola, in each corner there are raised seats or thrones; numerous windows and balconies, fountains and water-basins, and the floor paved with stones of various colors, like a Chinese gallery of pictures." A door led to the harem.

The latest Privy Chamber included a refectory whose walls were covered with tiles interspersed with painted or engraved inscriptions which, since Abdurrahman Şeref found them there, must have survived the fire. Many extolled sultans who had repaired the premises or given it funds. Even Mustafa IV, of whom little else good can be said, allotted sums to the attendants and arranged for the reading of the Koran in memory of his father, Abdülhamit I. The reading was to emphasize the thirty-sixth chapter, the Yâ Sîn, which promises life after death to believers. It was to take place every Friday night, Friday being the Muslim holy day, and every Kandil Gecesi. Kandil Gecesi, the Night of Illumination, comes four times a year, commemorating the conception of the Prophet, his birth, the time when his mission was revealed to him, and his ascent into heaven. Other inscriptions speak of other sultans: Murat who "renovated the Privy Chamber. It is like an exalted sphere in which the golden ring of the door is the sun"; Mahmut II, the Just, "who preferred the comfort of his people to his own comfort and strove to establish peace in his realm."

Other smaller rooms attached to the Privy Chamber included at one time an infirmary, and as long as the sultans lived in Topkapı an office for the ruler's confidential secretary (*sır kâtibi*, secret scribe). We shall profit from the records of some of these when we come to later rooms.

To the end of the Privy Chamber the structures of the Third Court, whatever their individual differences, have been held together by the colonnade which, being what hits the eye first, has given the court unity. Here the unity stops, and what interrupts it is the New Library (Yeni Kütüphane). Formerly the Ağas' Mosque, it is built into the court at an angle so that its prayer niche (mihrap) might indicate the direction of Mecca toward which all Muslims pray. Before the museum's restoration peeling plaster covered it and gave it the look of a rundown, late construction. When the plaster was removed it turned out to be made up of layers of rough stone very much like the Imperial Stable and the Finance Treasury. It is therefore one of the oldest buildings, perhaps dating from the Conqueror. Its old name comes from the fact that the ağas, which the pages were called after their period of novitiate, came here to pray. The inner side of it, at a height a little up from the floor, has three windows which connect it to a room of the harem. This was the harem mosque, the windows of course latticed, by which the harem women could join in the prayer services. The area is now storage space for books.

To the original rectangular structure with its two rows of windows and vaulted roof small low rooms were added at either end. The front addition is now the reading room of the library, converted from a chapel. It is lined with charming seventeenth-century tiles in blues and greens with floral medallions and leafy scrolls. It has been thought that they predated the chapel and were transferred from elsewhere, but on close inspection the tile panels seem definitely designed for the space, so that the chapel itself must be seventeenth century. The reading room is not open to the general public but may be used by those interested in serious research. Surrounded by the brilliant old tiles may be found people of all nations delving into the library's books. They are in many languages, although Ottoman Turkish, Arabic and Persian predominate. It is something of an experience, as I have done, to sit here with a centuries-old, gold-illuminated collection of the poems of Süleyman the Magnificent, a few in his own hand, and glimpse out the windows the throngs of tourists come to take in the once forbidden territory of the House of Felicity.

Books from all the old palace libraries are now in the New Library, and to these have been added a collection put together by Mehmet V, the next to the last sultan, and one of his wives, and some that have been presented.

Back of the New Library, in a corner, is a pinkish building with a balcony and a tall chimney. It was the kitchen that cooked for the sultan, the Kuşhane, which means either saucepan or aviary depending on how you translate it. Beside it a gateway, the Kuşhane Kapısı, leads to the harem via the Court of the Black Eunuchs, and we shall talk about it in connection with that court.

We are now virtually back at the court entrance, on either side of which, in the last centuries of the Empire, were the quarters of the white eunuchs. Those straight ahead of us, which belonged to the chief white eunuch, exhibit palace embroideries, another collection so numerous that much of it has to be stored. The exhibition runs the gamut from very fine work on very fine material to heavy gold and pearl embroidery on velvet. There are cushion covers and belts and many of the squares called *bohças* which were used to wrap up articles. One of blue satin with a sunburst of gold and pearl embroidery in its center once embraced a princess's engagement gifts. Usually on display is a flower-bordered handkerchief belonging to Roxelana, towels and napkins worked in very fine separate stitches or a delicate chain-like stitch. There are *yazma*, which means writing, and which has a painted design washed in sea water to fix the colors. Later *yazma* was printed from wooden blocks. Many of the smaller pieces are edged with *oya*, a tatting-like lace made in floral shapes. There are embroidered prayer rugs and *nihale*, usually round pieces placed under the food dishes on a tray. There are also great round covers that went over the dishes, so heavily worked with gold and pearls they must have added pounds to the bearer's load. At the moment the embroidery section is being redesigned.

Next to it is what is perhaps the only ladies' toilet in existence tiled with two centuries old tiles. Italian tiles of the eighteenth century and a fountain line its back wall. It too was part of the chief white eunuch's suite and probably a room of his bath.

Back in the seventeenth century, at least before the palace fire of 1664/5, the white eunuchs' quarters were elsewhere and the sites to the left and right of the Gate of Felicity were occupied by the Great and Small Halls. It is said colored tiles shone down from their vaulted roofs and their walls blazed with gems in arabesques of gold and silver. At that time the Great Hall had a door called the Sand Door because just outside it stood a pile of sand for the pages to use in scouring clean the metal dishes from which they ate.

On every Şeker Bayramı eve the sultan went to the Great Hall to listen to the pages speak on subjects they had studied. There is a rather touching story told about the boy sultan, Mehmet IV, who was endeavoring to emulate his ancestors on *bayram* eve when his mother, deciding he was too young, sent the chief black eunuch to bring him forcibly back to the harem.

The only extant building in the court so far unmentioned is the Library of Ahmet III, free standing behind the Throne Room in about the center of the area. It occupies the site of what was once the Kiosk in the Pond (Havuzlu Köşk) which Ahmet III tore down. Eight of its green marble columns are now integrated into the arcade of the Campaign Hall. It is undergoing repairs and is therefore not open, but since it does not appear to be in bad shape, it may be possible to see its interior soon.

In the spring of 1719 Ahmet III made the first stroke for its foundation using the same gold pickax his great grandfather, Ahmet I, had employed a century earlier in the founding of the Mosque of Sultan Ahmet. The pickax is now in the Treasury. The library is a graceful building of white marble, quadrangular, domed, and fronted by a covered pillared porch approached by stairs on either side. The porch has a lovely fountain on its outside wall, one part of it spouting water into a trough on the porch, and another reaching to the ground on the outside wall. At some recent period the porch had been enclosed with glass which put it at odds with the character of the building, but the glass has happily been removed.

The Ahmet III Library.

Columns separate its interior into three sections; a fourth, a recess, is a reading area. The sides are lined with book cupboards. A soft light comes from many windows of which there are two tiers, the upper ones partly clear glass and partly stained glass panels separated by white plaster scrollwork, a time-honored Ottoman type of fenestration. Both upper and lower walls are lined with old blue and white tiles confiscated from a private house on the Bosphorus. The old factories at Iznik and Kütahya that had produced the matchless Ottoman tiles had closed down by now, and the new ones Ahmet and Nevşehirli tried to start were not yet in operation.

This was the first building in the palace whose sole purpose was to be a library. Ahmet III stipulated in his founding deed that it was to be for the use of all members of the Inner Palace, and so it was often called the Inner Palace Library (Enderun Kütüphanesi). To it were transferred some of the books from other palace libraries. In bookcases with elaborately inlaid doors it eventually housed 4,364 books in Arabic, Greek, Hebrew, Latin, Persian, Turkish, and some of the Slavonic languages. Those in Western languages were largely from the collection of the Conqueror, of which, however, only a fraction remained, since later Ottoman scholars, up to the eighteenth century, had little interest in the writings of the West. In Eastern languages the Ahmet III Library collection ran from arithmetic to zoology, taking in on the way such subjects as geography, land and sea tactics, and veterinary medicine. As in all the palace libraries, commentaries on the Koran and on the traditions of the Prophet were well represented. Just a couple of years ago the Ahmet III collection was moved to the New Library.

The rest of the Third Court is open, graced with a few shrubs, a marble fountain which was the gift of a stewardess of the harem as late as 1811, and a sundial on a porphyry base. The base is pre-Ottoman, perhaps Byzantine, perhaps going back to pagan Constantinople.

The collections and buildings of the Third Court have revived something of the old life of the palace. But what actually went on in the Third Court?

Privacy and silence reigned here, since it was the hub of the House of Felicity. Outsiders might enter only on the invitation of the sultan, a condition that put it off limits for all but a few high officials. Nevertheless it was a busy place. We have seen that around it were domiciled two groups who were mainstays of the Ottoman Empire, the pages in training for Empire posts and the white eunuchs in charge of them. The latter were largely

Caucasians, never men from Islamic countries, it being against the Holy Law to emasculate a Muslim. Deprived of their sex functions at an early age, they grew up beardless and soon wizened. They were the drillmasters of the pages, one to every ten pages.

Their quarters were rebuilt by Abdülmecit and therefore tell us little of what they were like in the old days. One section, however, apparently escaped destruction, a courtyard that was the eunuchs' recreation center. Abdurrahman Şeref found there many old inscriptions, one from the seventeenth century telling how a certain grand vizier had made the place an endowment of soap because one day, when he was a palace page, he had wanted to wash his hands at the white eunuchs' fountain and found it soapless. This was to the left of the Gate of Felicity. The little court is still there but not the fountain. This side of the Gate of Felicity, plus the corner building, is now devoted to museum activities.

The head of the white eunuchs' service, the chief white eunuch, was an important palace personage. He was head keeper of the Gate of Felicity, chief of the Inner Palace service, and had the duty of overseeing the Palace School. Under him were the eunuchs in charge of the halls, and four others whose duties ranged from responsibility for the safety of the House of Felicity to marching beside the sultan's horse. Farther down the line were the Seniors of the Table (Sofra Eskicis) who were the pages' taskmasters.

One of these was responsible for an attempt to eliminate eunuchs from the palace entirely. When a certain grand vizier, Çorlu Ali Pasha, was a page he reached for food out of turn one day and was rapped across the knuckles with a wooden spoon by the eunuch in charge of his table. It was a humiliation that haunted Çorlu Ali. Years later, possessed of the highest post of the Empire, he made an effort to end the use of eunuchs, both black and white, but he was one against many, the use of eunuchs had been hallowed by time, and his attempt failed.

With the years the white eunuchs lost some of their influence, and in the eighteenth century supervision of the halls was handed over to senior pages. By this time the method of promoting pages out of the school at an early age was no longer systematically pursued, and senior pages could be as much as sixty years old.

The Palace School of the Empire had no prototype as far as historians have learned. Some think it resembled the ideal academy proposed by Plato, and indeed the Conqueror, who established it, knew Greek and may have been influenced by him. Still, it did not completely follow Plato since its students did not come from a hereditary aristocracy but from the conquered people. It trained men for the sultan's personal service, for the palace service, for the elite military, and for the high posts of Empire. It was a great honor and not at all easy to enter. The applicant had to have a perfect body and a high degree of intelligence.

The curriculum was much more inclusive than that of any educational institution of the time and seems to have been devised by Mehmet the Conqueror, a man with a well-trained, wide-ranging mind. From distinguished teachers brought in from outside the palace the pages learned Arabic in order to be able to read the Koran. In their dormitories were found some Korans with Turkish interpolations between the Arabic lines, teaching aids, no doubt. They learned Persian in order to appreciate its poetry. They read the Ottoman writers to add elegance to their speech. In due time came lessons in warfare, to shoot with the bow, to throw the mace and pike, to handle firearms. The strength of their bodies was built up with wrestling and running. They were trained in horsemanship. These physical activities took place in certain areas of the Fifth Court.

Like all Turks they learned a trade in case fortune should cease to favor them. They became skilled at making bows and arrows, at gunsmithing, leather work, goldsmithing and other crafts. Even the sultans as princes learned crafts. Mehmet the Conqueror was a knowledgeable gardener, Selim I and his son Süleyman goldsmiths, Ahmet III a calligrapher, Selim III a musician. Beyond this the pages were trained in the direction in which their talents lay. Many became men of letters, artists, masters of calligraphy. Since the aim was to turn out a well-rounded man, acquaintance with the precise and elaborate Ottoman etiquette was demanded. And always there was emphasis on the doctrines and duties of Islam.

Certain pages were trained in miniature painting in a Lesson House (Meşkhane) of which there seem to have been two, one just off the Third Court next to the Campaign Hall and the other near the black eunuchs' quarters. Many of the artists were specialists, and unsigned works are apt to be a collective enterprise. One man designed the painting, another drew in black and white, a third did portraits of people. There was a category that created from the imagination, one that specialized in groups of people, another that illuminated manuscripts. Some painted in backgrounds and landscapes; others colored figures. Beginners drew only straight lines.

The school produced many famous artists such as Nigâri who did the portrait of Barbarossa we have mentioned, and Nakkaş (the Painter) Osman who painted the miniatures of the *Hünername*. Although the sixteenth century was the great period for painters, as it was for all the arts, there were court artists throughout the Empire. The palace payroll lists 521 over a period of 270 years.

In the heyday of the Palace School, which lasted from the time of its founding in the fifteenth century until the late seventeenth century, the boys entered it somewhere between the ages of twelve and fourteen and spent in it a varying number of years depending on how far up they chose to go. The school consisted of two general halls, the Great and Small Halls, from which the students matriculated to the vocational halls: the Hall of the Commissariat, the Hall of the Treasury, the Campaign Hall, and the Hall of the Falconers. Highest of all, to which only graduates of the vocational schools were admitted and only a picked number of those, was the Privy Chamber.

The pages of the Hall of the Commissariat served the sultan's meals. They were also in charge of his drinks: sherbets and water which they kept in six flagons of twenty ounces each, always ready for his use. Giving the sultan a drink was as hedged with ceremony as any other royal proceeding. The French traveler, Jean Baptiste Tavernier, described it in the seventeenth century:

> It is an old custom that when the Grand Seigneur asks for water to drink outside of a meal, each time that he drinks it costs him ten gold pieces. Here is the ceremony that brings it to him. In the chamber called Has Oda (Privy Chamber), which is the apartment of the forty pages who are always near the person of the Grand Seigneur, there is always one of them on guard at the entrance who watches the door of the Commissariat where two pages of this quarter are likewise on sentinel duty. When the Grand Seigneur is thirsty and asks for water, the page of the Has Oda immediately makes a sign to the two of the Kiler (Commissariat) of whom one advances toward the *kilerbaşı* (chief of the Commissariat) or grand cup-bearer crying *su* which means water, to inform him that the prince asks to drink; and the other runs to the door of the Has Oda where the older of the forty pages give him ten gold pieces. . . . The water is carried sometimes in a cup of gold, sometimes in a cup of porcelain, placed on a large saucer of gold about two paces in diameter and enriched with precious stones within and without. It

is one of the richest pieces of the *saray*. The grand cup-bearer, who is a white eunuch, carries it in ceremony following the hundred pages of the Kiler who are usually under his charge and held underneath the arms by the two at the entrance who walk at his sides. For it is necessary that he hold it higher than the head so that he can see his way under it. When he is at the door of the Has Oda, the pages of the Kiler who have accompanied him do not pass further, except the two who hold his arms, and the pages of the chamber go with him up to the presence of the Grand Seigneur. But when they are at the door of the room, two older pages take the place of the two pages of the Kiler and finish by conducting the *kilerbaşı* under the arms to offer the cup to the prince.

In addition to this duty the Commissariat kept on hand the various sherbets (sherbet is a liquid in Turkey) made of such fruits as peaches, cherries and raspberries that the sultan fancied. It held drugs, including antidotes for poisons the palace always feared, spices, perfumes, jams, syrups, and ambergris from the Yemen which went into a special sherbet. Stored here too were the enormous candles imported from Wallachia in Central Europe to serve *selâmlık*, harem, and palace mosques. The pages of this hall made sweets for the sultan and prepared for him certain aphrodisiacs that were highly treasured.

The pages of the Hall of the Treasury had the care of the Imperial Treasury in the Third Court. They were in attendance whenever it was opened, always a ceremonial occasion, and made its payments and kept its accounts.

The third vocational school was the Campaign Hall, which changed over the years. Its pages started out by accompanying the sultan to war and doing his laundry in the field. When they were in the palace only the laundering of his turbans was in their hands. This took place every Tuesday to the accompaniment of music while the first officer of the hall washed the muslin turban cover in a silver basin. It was dried in front of the hall and then folded and sprinkled with scent. Like anything connected with the sultan, the duty was a great honor.

As time went on they were trained in a variety of pursuits, becoming musicians, singers, poets and scholars on the one hand, and archers, wrestlers, bath attendants and barbers on the other.

About the pages of the Hall of the Falconers, which stood out in the court near where the Kiosk in the Pond must have been, we know almost nothing. Presumably they trained the sultan's falcons and accompanied him on the hunt. They numbered forty and lasted only until the mid-seventeenth century.

The pages of the Privy Chamber, also limited to about forty, were the ruler's personal attendants. They dressed in cloth of gold and silver, and their allowances were greater than those of the pages of the other halls. Their chief officers, as we have seen in the Friday prayer procession, accompanied the sultan about Istanbul. We shall find them in the service of the Pavilion of the Blessed Mantle.

Each hall had a head whose job it was to inspect the pages' chests for forbidden sweets, spices and love letters which, in view of their being completely cut off from women, could have been written only to each other. The incidence of homosexuality in the Palace School has been thought high despite the surveillance of the white eunuchs, and certainly, what with the lack of heterosexual outlets, it would have been remarkable if it had not existed. For sultans who were inclined to such pleasures, it must have been a happy hunting ground.

All was quiet in these halls. Conversation was permitted only at certain times. The page's day was devoted to study, which he did in his dormitory, using his small chest as a desk, to physical exercise which took place on the playing fields of the Fifth Court, and to prayer, for which he marched across the Third Court to the Ağas' Mosque, head down and hands folded in due humility. Only on the two *bayrams* was this discipline relaxed. Then the pages joined in the general congratulations of the sultan that went on in the Third Court and were allowed four days and four nights of entertainment. The only other time this rigorous life could be interrupted was when a page spent time in the infirmary, and this, as we have seen, could be experienced only with the permission of the sultan.

After their novitiate the pages graduated from wearing a garment called *dolman*, the front of its slit skirt tucked into a girdle, to the traditional but apparently not very long kaftan. Thomas Dallam, the Englishman who was in the palace in the late sixteenth century setting up an organ that was a present to Murat III from Elizabeth of England, has described their dress in Elizabethan prose:

> 200 of his principal padgis apparaled in ritche clothe of goulde to mid-legg, upon thier heads littel caps; great saches of silk about thier

waistes; on their legges red cordovan buckskins. Their heads were all shaven saving behind their eares a locke of hare like a squirrels taile.

They were clean-shaven, it being forbidden to a slave to grow a beard. As further reminder of their slave status their headdresses were outfitted with tassels hanging in front of their ears. Cleanliness was a must. Each page bathed and had a manicure and a pedicure once a week, shaved twice a week, and had his hair cut monthly. Each day he must have a clean handkerchief, an important item of Ottoman apparel.

The number of pages differed at different times, but from the end of the sixteenth century to the beginning of the nineteenth there were eight or nine hundred in Topkapı. The mind boggles at the thought of that number of persons living in the not overly great area of the Third Court. Only strict organization and a minimum of space allotted to each person made it possible.

When a page finished his course of training and was ready to leave the palace a great occasion was made of it. He first went to the Throne Room where he kissed his sovereign's hand and listened intently while the sultan charged him to perform with zeal the new duties that awaited him, to be loyal to his ruler, to keep to himself what he had seen and heard within the palace, and always to be faithful to the religion of Islam. To each he gave a robe of honor, a number of horses, and a sum of money tied up in a handkerchief. Other presents of money, slaves and clothes came the page's way from the *valide sultan*, the grand vizier and other officials.

Now two palace officials accompanied the graduates to the Imperial Gate where they were seen off by the chief white eunuch and the Ağa of the Janissaries, among others. They rode down Divan Yolu to the palace of the grand vizier, in their new role of personages scattering money as they went. Once they had paid their respects to him they had a few days to themselves before starting their new duties. It was then they began to let their beards grow to lend them the dignity proper to an Ottoman official.

The posts to which they were appointed depended on how far up in the Palace School they had progressed. To the graduates of the Privy Chamber went the highest. They became governors of provinces from which several of them rose to the two highest positions of the Empire—admiral of the fleet and grand vizier. The greatest grand vizier of them all, Sokullu Mehmet Pasha, a conscript from Bosnia, was a Palace School product. Sokullu served three sultans, beginning late in Süleyman's reign after having successfully led the army against an insurrection of one of Süleyman's sons. On this sultan's death during the siege of the Hungarian citadel of Szeged Sokullu carried on in Süleyman's name until the stronghold fell. He continued as grand vizier during the eight-year reign of Selim II during which his judgement and courage offset the degeneracy of Selim and kept the Empire intact. Grand vizier until the last, he died in 1579 in the reign of Murat III, stabbed as he was leaving the Hall of the Divan by a crazy man seeking alms.

An entirely different, later product of the school was the traveler and writer, Evliya Çelebi. As conscription of Christians came to be abandoned in the seventeenth century it became possible for Muslim Turks to enter, and many strings were pulled by families to enroll them. Evliya's entry was stage-managed by a relative who was sword-bearer. This person managed to get him into Murat IV's presence to read the Koran, at which he was adept. Impressed, the sultan commanded that he be admitted to the school, although he was fairly advanced in age. He became a page of the Hall of the Commissariat where he studied Arabic grammar, calligraphy, music for which he had a talent, and *tevcit*, the art of reciting the Koran. He had wit and a fine voice, qualities that recommended him to Murat who from time to time sent for Evliya to entertain him. Though graduated into the elite cavalry, he found a wider field and soon began the journeys that engaged his life. He visited a long list of near and far places which he described in his ten-volume *Book of Travels (Seyahatname)* on which his fame is based. Though its accuracy can at times be doubted, it is a celebrated work.

Unlike Sokullu, who as both grand vizier and husband of a princess had access to the House of Felicity, Evliya probably never saw it again after he was graduated. However, several copies of his book found their way into the libraries of the Revan and Baghdad Kiosks.

Though the pages were generally loyal to the throne and certainly without the turbulence of the Janissaries, they got out of hand occasionally, but only once do they seem to have been involved in a real tragedy, and that was when they supported the young *valide*, Mehmet IV's mother Turhan, against the old *valide*, his grandmother, Mahpeyker Kösem, in the struggle that brought about Kösem's death. But this story properly belongs to the harem.

At this time, the seventeenth century, and probably later, the Third Court encompassed several small buildings that must have deprived it of its present airiness. Part of the way down on the right side was the Music Conservatory (Meşkhane, Lesson House), which in the seventeenth century stood next to the Campaign Hall whose pages were the most rigorously trained in music. They played two kinds, chamber and military music. For chamber music they practiced on a variety of instruments, the most usual being the violin, the psaltery, a kind of bagpipe, a wooden flute, and the lute. What they produced from these was quite alien to Western ears, being based on a scale of quarter tones which gave it a wailing quality. For military music they used drum, trumpet, and cymbals. All played from memory since there was no system of notation. Those whose forte was chamber music entertained the sultan each Tuesday while his hair was being trimmed. They put on performances in his private rooms and occasionally in the harem, at which times they would be blindfolded and guarded by eunuchs.

The duties of the hundred and fifty members of the military band (Mehterhane-i hassa) seem to have been more onerous. It played at the palace during the third prayer of the day (ikindi) which takes place in the afternoon. It awakened the palace people two hours before sunrise and closed their day two hours after sunset. For the sultan it played a half-hour before sunrise and an hour and a half after sunset. It played for Şeker Bayramı, the holidays that close the holy month of Ramazan, and again for Kurban Bayramı a month later. It honored foreign embassies on their festive days. It played for the pages when they were being graduated. It escorted the sultan on all his public appearances.

The military band goes back a long way with the Turks, probably to Central Asia where they took it over from the Chinese. The Turks in turn introduced it into Central Europe during the years of their domination. Besides martial music, the band played music in three-quarter time which is thought to have had an influence on the development of the Viennese waltz. A vogue for Turkish music sprang up in Europe in the eighteenth and early nineteenth centuries; witness Mozart's and Beethoven's Turkish marches.

Farther down on the right side of the Third Court in the corner near the Treasury but unattached was the small kiosk of the Master Artisans of the Wardrobe and of the Silverware. Here the Steward of the Treasury parceled out to painters, goldsmiths, silversmiths, tailors, furriers, sword-makers and other artisans the highly skilled work needed for the palace. In a like detached position on the left, outside the Pavilion of the Blessed Mantle, was the two-room office of the Steward of the Commissariat where were stored the plate, porcelain and glassware used in harem and selâmlık.

The old Third Court had several other small buildings which have disappeared, including a place attached to the Campaign Hall which was reserved for the palace mutes, the dilsiz or tongueless ones. Since they could not give away any information, they were used as messengers and were in

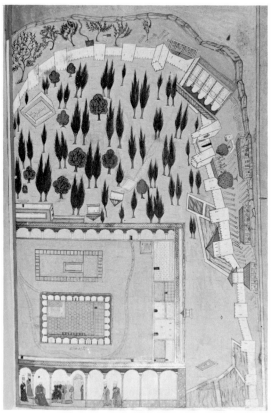

Hünername *Miniature No. 4, showing the east side of the palace from the Third Court to the sea. The entrance to the Third Court does not yet have its portico, although it appears in Miniature No. 3. Since the* Hünername *was in progress between 1579 and 1584, the portico may have been added between the time Miniatures No. 3 and 4 were painted. The entrance says Bab-ı Âli, Sublime Porte, instead of Gate of Felicity. Note the Throne Room just inside the gate and the Kiosk in the Pond behind it.*

NECATI ORBAY

attendance during the sultan's interviews. When a prince or sultan was executed, theirs was the grisly duty of strangling him.

The small buildings on the right-hand side of the court must have been seventeenth-century additions since they do not show up in the *Hünername* miniature of the eastern section of the court. The buildings along here do not even have their colonnade yet or their porches, although a colonnade appears on the north end. In the miniature showing the west side of the court the colonnade follows around in front of the Pavilion of the Blessed Mantle, easy to detect because of its domes. The building that abuts it may well be the Ağas' Mosque, but the rest is harder to figure out. The long structures between the mosque and the wall are presumably the buildings of the harem, which apparently had much more regularity then than now. The Gate of Felicity at the foot of the painting of the eastern side is labeled Sublime Port (Bab-ı Âli), so perhaps it was once called that. Behind it is the

[1 1 0]

Throne Room, where we see it today, the throne indicated in one corner. It is here marked Petition or Presentation Council Hall (Arz Divanhanesi). To the rear of it are the pool and kiosk Ahmet III replaced with his library. Thus the Third Court, like the Empire, seems to have become more complicated with time and to have been simplified again only after the desertion of the palace.

As for the Palace School, Mahmut much reduced it and in 1908 the Young Turks abolished all but the pages serving the Pavilion of the Blessed Mantle. One rather pathetic lesson room of the nineteenth century remained to the end, not very large but big enough for the number of pages left. The museum found it falling to pieces and restored it for the use of museum personnel. One passes without noticing it in the southeast corner of the court on the way to the exhibit of sultans' clothes.

NECATI ORBAY

Hünername *Miniature No. 5: the west side of the palace from the Third Court to the sea. Some of the buildings on the right are presumably the harem of the late 16th century.*

THE THRONE ROOM

THE THRONE ROOM (Arz Odası, Presentation Room) was built for ceremony. Dignified, with a wide, columned porch and the oft-encountered deep
eaves extending out over the Third Court, it has the appearance of a matriarch waiting to greet suppliants. Only, as one views it coming in from the
Gate of Felicity, the matriarch seems not to sit but to squat. I always feel
one needs first to walk down into the court to see the building in its entirety,
and then come back and take in the details of its gateward face.

Since the ground slopes down the court, one is able to look up at it, a
quadrangular building set apart from the others in both site and character.
Its yellowish walls, interrupted by two rows of windows, the lower large,
the upper small, form a background for the twenty-two white marble pillars that edge its porch on all four sides, supporting arches lined with the
alternating light and dark stone so often a feature of Islamic architecture. A
pierced marble rail connects the pillars, and a marble style-type staircase
takes one up to the porch past a white foundation. Viewed thus, the building has the majesty that befits a throne room. There is a door on this side.
Just what it was used for we do not know, since the sultan must have followed the marble way to the front. The door carries the *tuğra* of Mustafa IV
and an inscription of 1807 stating that the Arz Odası was renewed by him.

The main entrance, the one through which Ottoman dignitaries and
foreign envoys were admitted, is on the side of the Gate of Felicity and set

[1 1 2]

about with considerable decoration to give it importance. It is framed in
contrasting marble, topped by an inscription, and all of this enclosed in an
oblong of simple moldings. The inscription is the *besmele*, the prayer for
beginnings, written in the hand of Ahmet son of Mehmet. The date given,
1136 of the hegira, converts into 1722/3, which makes the calligrapher
Ahmet III. Affixed to the wall on either side of the door are charming tile
panels of a formal pattern, of green, yellow and white flowers on a blue
ground. A mate to them will be found just outside the Circumcision Room
farther into the palace. Centuries later plaques with gilt headpieces were
placed above them bearing the *tuğra* of Abdülmecit over a line of writing
that skips the doorway to say: "The munificent sovereign, Abdülmecit
Khan, victorious forever."

Farther to the right a wall fountain with one spigot is set in the same
simple moldings as the door. Its water flowed into a large marble trough that
still rests on a tile inset in the porch floor. Above it there used to be one of
the landscapes of foreign introduction with which the later sultans felt they
were adorning the palace. The museum has removed this intrusive element.
According to its partly Turkish, partly Persian inscription, the fountain was
"commanded to be brought to life when Sultan Süleyman was keeper of the
world" to provide "the water of life for the people of the Divan." This fits
in with the Throne Room being called the Presentation Hall of the Divan in
the *Hünername* miniature.

The building has a subsidiary door to the left, the Gift Door, past which
gifts to the sultan were carried for him to view. Apparently it was repaired
by Mahmut II since over it is a verse signed by him.

It must already be clear that the Throne Room represents many periods.
Its foundation goes back to the Conqueror, and the building we see, or at
least its fundamental structure, was constructed by Selim I (1512–1520), but
it has obviously had many alterations. The last came under Abdülmecit after
the fire of 1856/7 when the inside was pretty well burned out except for the
fireplace, a fountain and the throne.

Although the exterior has been restored by the museum, the interior
is still in the process and the Throne Room is therefore at present closed.
Once the restoration is complete and the scaffolding removed you will see a
medium-sized room, not the tiled one of early times but a room decorated
on walls and domed ceiling with painted Ottoman motifs. Its old fireplace
hood is newly gilded and the ornate ceiling of its throne baldequin freshened,
even to the gilt that edges its top in a fringe and ball design. The fountain,

The main door to the Throne Room. The tile panels beside it are probably the oldest in the palace, though the tuğras *above them belong to Sultan Abdülmecit of the nineteenth century. The fountain dates from Süleyman's time.*

which is on the wall beside the court-side door, is a series of basins which pour forth water from little brass spouts. This is the fountain it is said was turned on when the sultan was speaking so that his words could not be heard without. Evidence of nineteenth-century restoration are its parquet floor and glass-paneled inside doors; but the windows are deep in marble frames as in old buildings.

[114]

*Peacock Panel from the Room
of the Blessed Mantle*

HALUK DOGANBEY

HALUK DOGANBEY

*Sultans' Costumes in
the Treasury*

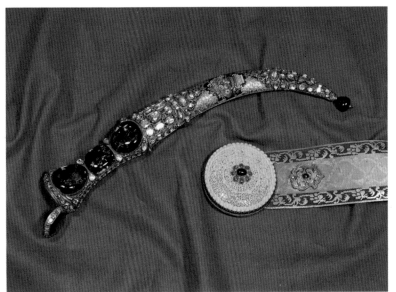

The Topkapi Dagger and Belt

Porcelains

There is an additional much smaller room, once a place that shimmered with precious metal but now a washroom and toilet. As one investigates Topkapı one gets the impression that it had more baths and toilets than any place of comparable size. One cannot fault the Ottomans on sanitation.

When the Throne Room was still brilliant with tiled walls and richly carpeted floor it was seen by a succession of Westerners, some of whom have left descriptions. Ottaviano Bon, the Venetian envoy to Istanbul in the early seventeenth century, as translated by Robert Withers, wrote of it:

> This Roome standeth in a fine little Court adorned with many very delicate Fountaines, and hath within it a Sofa spread with very sumptuous Carpets of Gold, and of crimson Velvet embroydered with very costly Pearles, upon which the Grand Signior sitteth; and about the Chamber in stead of hangings, the walls are covered with very fine white stones, which having divers sorts of leaves and flowers artificially wrought upon them, doe make a glorious shew. There is also a little Roome adjoyning unto it, the whole inside whereof is covered with Silver plate hatcht with Gold, and the ground is spread with very rich Persian Carpets of Silke and Gold.

The throne, made in 1596 and, to judge from its pictures, looking very much like a four-poster bed except for its dome, always sat in the far left corner between the fireplace and the back wall, where the baldequin still is. However, no four-poster was ever so gorgeously arrayed. Its posts and the interior of its dome were then jeweled. When the sultan was enthroned there globes signifying his power over the world were suspended above him. Some of these are on display in the Treasury. Low attachments along the left and back, which are against the walls, formed rests which supported heavily embroidered cushions. An equally ornamented skirt hung to the floor on the right and front, and the seat was covered with appropriately rich fabric.

Jean Baptiste Tavernier, the French traveler and gem expert, also saw the Throne Room in the first half of the seventeenth century, but he was so impressed with the throne's sumptuous coverings he scarcely commented on the room itself, except to note that it was paved with marble on which lay rugs threaded with gold. When not in use the throne coverings were kept in the Treasury, where some of them still are, and Tavernier, whose own observations were augmented by information from a former Treasury page, tells about them in detail. The Treasury held eight of varying degrees of magnificence, the richest being black velvet embroidered with large pearls, others of white velvet worked with diamonds and rubies set in bezels and of a deep violet sewn with turquoises and pearls. The lesser ones were gold-embroidered or gold brocade without jewels. Which of these lavish coverings the sultan chose depended on the importance he gave to the sovereign whose envoy he was receiving.

An audience here was the climax to the pomp and circumstance that went into an ambassador's visitation to the palace. Envoys of the powers brought along to Istanbul a large suite in order to impress the Ottomans with the grandeur of their king, and to this the Porte added a guard of Janissaries. European embassies were set up in the foreign section of the city, Pera, across the Golden Horn from the palace. On the day he was to be received the ambassador, accompanied by his train, rode from his lodging to Tophane, the neighborhood of the arsenal founded by the Conqueror, crossed the Horn by boat, and landed at the Vizier's Dock. In a palace kiosk down on the water he was served sweets and coffee while his procession re-formed and a horse for his use was brought around from the Great Stable. Mounted and with the chief herald before him, he climbed the hill as far as the Procession Kiosk where the grand vizier met him, honored him with a glance of salutation, and passed on. They would meet again in the Divanhane.

The envoy's procession dismounted at the Middle Gate, there to admire the imperial horses that stood nearby, sometimes as many as thirty-two, decked in jeweled harnesses and silver shields. With them was the Master of the Stables in sable-trimmed robe and tall turban. Duly impressed with this display, the ambassador was taken to the head gatekeepers' room of the Middle Gate where he met the interpreter of the Divan who would accompany him throughout the audience. Until the latter days of the Empire the interpreters were Christians, first Europeans in the service of the Porte and later Greeks of a small number of families who became the exclusive possessors of these posts.

Before he could be accepted into the imperial presence the ambassador had first to go to the Hall of the Divan. We have said that his reception was usually on the Janissaries' payday when the number of people in the *saray* swelled from five to ten thousand, all the dignitaries were present in their most resplendent clothes, and everything was calculated to impress the foreigner.

[1 1 6]

Once the grand vizier had taken his place in the Divanhane the visiting ambassador kissed his skirt and seated himself on the backless stool. Then, via the interpreter, both men gravely inquired after each other's health, and the ambassador asked permission to present himself to the sultan. These formalities met, they ate the elaborate meal that has been described. Rose water and incense were sprinkled on them, and those to be admitted to the presence were clothed with long robes of honor, de rigueur for entering the sultan's presence. The run-of-the-mill robe was white camel's hair or Angora, but those given to high officials and ambassadors were sable-trimmed cloth of gold or a brocade of silver and gold.

The number of robes handed out to an ambassador varied according to the dignity which the Porte accorded him. The ambassador of France was allowed the most, twenty-four. When de Marcheville was France's ambassador to the Porte sometime between 1629 and 1637 he was offered only

The Throne Room as seen from the Third Court.

NECATI ORBAY

[1 1 7]

sixteen robes for an imperial audience. Says Tavernier, who was in his suite, "Immediately he had the grand vizier told that he lacked eight vestments and that he would not go to the audience without the number that they had been accustomed to give to the ambassador of France. There was some dispute that delayed the audience almost an hour; but finally, Monsieur de Marcheville remaining firm in his resolution, the grand vizier sent him the other eight vestments."

While the ambassador and his suite were being robed the sultan had proceeded to the Throne Room. If it was to be the audience of a new ambassador, the sultan had been there the previous day to view the presents sent ahead, not personally examining them, but, as we have noted, merely watching them pass the Gift Door. They were invariably a costly array. In the year 1700 the Austrian ambassador, Öttingen, presented a tray, fireplace grates, coolers, watering pots, cases, coffee cups and sherbet vessels of silver, flagons and censors of gold, candlesticks hung with cut glass, watches, a silver warming dish, and an artificial fountain. These were all carried past the Gift Door, entered in a register, and put away in the Imperial Treasury. In addition Öttingen gave presents to the sultan's mother, his favorite concubine, the grand vizier, and the head of the religious establishment, those he felt had the greatest influence with the sultan.

For the ceremony of presentation the most important members of the Inner Service stood close to the sultan—the chief black eunuch, the sword-bearer, the master of the wardrobe, the chief stirrup-holder, and the head of the Privy Chamber, all still as statues, their hands folded in front of them. The sultan wore one of his handsomest robes and topped his turban with an aigrette. First to enter was the Janissary Ağa, and after him in succession the judges of the army, the grand vizier and the admiral of the navy. Only then came the ambassador's turn. He was held under the arms by head door-keepers, a mark of honor and also protection to the padishah. He bowed low to the sultan in three different places, kissed his skirt, and stood back against the wall. His deposition was translated by the interpreter. Then his letter of credentials made its way to the throne, being passed by the official who had been guarding it to the admiral of the navy who in turn handed it to the grand vizier who placed it on the left side of the throne. What with the envoy's suite and the Ottoman officials the room by now held a good number of people, but it is said never to have seemed crowded since everyone had his special place and due space was left in front of the sultan.

Tavernier says the sultan made a speech of welcome but Bon declares the grand vizier spoke for him. Personally I accept Bon, for sometimes Tavernier's imagination ran away with him. There is also disagreement as to whether the ambassador and his suite kissed the sultan's skirt or his hand. At any rate Bon and Tavernier agree that the interview, as short as it was formal, was soon over. The grand vizier gave the word of dismissal, and the envoy walked out backwards, it being impermissible to turn one's back on the padishah.

On Sundays and Tuesdays, when the members of the Divan were received by the sultan, the procedure was much the same. First the judge advocates reported to him and departed. Next the treasurers had their turn, and finally the viziers, the grand vizier first. As Bon-Withers have put it:

> And being come before the presence of the Grand Signior, they stand with their hands before them, holding downe their heads, in token of Humilitie; and so none but the Chief Vizir speaketh, and he gives an account of what hee thinketh fit, delivering his Memorials or Arzes one by one, the which the King having read, the Vizier taketh them, and having put them into a little crimson Sattin bagge, hee most humbly layeth them downe againe before His Majestie.

They too departed backwards, which must have been a neat trick in those long robes.

Later accounts differ a bit, so there were undoubtedly small changes over the years but no real departure from the strict formality of a Throne Room audience until the time of Mahmut II.

It was one of the rules of the Ottoman court that no one could enter the sultan's presence bearing arms. In 1700, the same year Öttingen was received, a new French ambassador, Ferriol, was sent out from Paris. He was already garbed in his robe of honor and about to be presented in the Throne Room when the chief herald, whose duty it was to keep an eye out for arms, noticed that Ferriol was wearing a sword under his robe. The interpreter explained to him that no one, whatever his rank, might go armed into the imperial presence. Ferriol laid his hand on his sword and announced that he would give it up to no one save his king. The grand vizier explained that it was impossible for him to have an audience wearing a sword. The Ağa of the Janissaries tried to persuade him in his turn. Ferriol told them all, "You are subjects, while I am the representative of a great king." The viziers of the dome and the judges of the army gave him their best arguments, in vain. The gatekeepers, who already had him under the arms to escort him to the Throne Room, tried to slip off his sword without his noticing it, but he struck out at them with elbows and knees.

Angry now, Ferriol cried out, "Is it thus they violate the rights of people in this country? Are we then friends or enemies?"

"Friends," replied the interpreter, "but you cannot appear at an audience with your sword."

"In that case I shall not appear at all," and Ferriol took off his robe of honor and left the palace. The next day the Porte sent all the presents from the French king back to him. Ferriol spent ten years in Istanbul without ever being presented at court.

Of all the sultans who sat in state in the Throne Room my favorite is Selim III who reigned from 1789 to 1807. Not for centuries had the Ottoman Empire had a sultan with a mind as enlightened as his. For that very reason he is the most tragic.

As the visitor stands before the door to the Throne Room he is sure to be shown a circle of porphyry inserted into the stone floor. It is here that the body of Selim III was flung after he was murdered in 1808.

Old portraits show Selim III as a man with a long, serious face and deep, brooding eyes, and they do not lie. All his life he struggled to pull the Ottoman Empire out of the backwater into which it had slid, and the struggle cost him his life. The defeats of the Ottoman armies over the past centuries had taught him that they needed to learn European tactics, and he imported French instructors to teach them. It was not to be easy. The army, especially the Janissaries, resented the new training, whereupon Selim recruited a new army, the Nizam-ı Cedit, the New Order, to be drilled on European lines. He also introduced reforms into the administration of the state, and these too were resented. The innovations were castigated as instruments of the *gavûr*, the unbeliever, and contrary to the tenets of Islam.

Nevertheless the troops of the New Order showed their superiority by defending Acre in the war Napoleon started with his invasion of Egypt. Encouraged by its success, Selim ordered the strongest and the best of the Janissaries to serve in the New Order army. At this 10,000 of them rebelled and for the moment had their way.

By 1807 the grand vizier, his assistant the *kaymakam*, the *şeyhülislâm*, and even the Istanbul judge or *kadı* were all determined to liquidate the New Order. Their opportunity came when in May Selim tried to put the Janissaries of a fort at the mouth of the Black Sea in Nizam-ı Cedit uniforms. They called them the uniforms of unbelievers and would have nothing to do with them. Under their chosen leader, one Kabakçı (Pumpkin-Seller) Mustafa they marched on Istanbul and joined up with the Janissaries at the latters' barracks in the Et Meydanı (Meat Square) near Aksaray. There they held a meeting and called for the skin of all those who, as they put it, "had ruined the country." Selim could perhaps have broken the back of the rebellion had he straightway sent for his New Order troops. Unfortunately his highest officials were secretly in league with the rebels and advised appeasement, which didn't work. The *şeyhülislâm* gave a *fetva*, permission according to Islamic law, to depose the sultan.

The insurgents gathered at the palace and sent the *fetva* of deposition in to Selim. The accusations against him were actions contrary to Islamic law and, curiously, his inability to have children. Despite a number of concubines, he had produced no offspring. Selim could only honor the *fetva;* it represented the Holy Law. Quietly he retired to a room in the harem, and his cousin, Mustafa IV who had none of Selim's capacity, ascended the throne of the Ottomans.

Selim lived within the harem for a year, apparently with considerable freedom to move about, all the while passing on his wisdom, his understanding of modern military tactics, and the pitfalls that faced the reformer to his young cousin, Prince Mahmut, who was now heir to the throne. At the end of that time an admirer of Selim, Alemdar (the Standard-Bearer) Mustafa Pasha of the Danube country, gathered his followers and marched on Istanbul. His purpose, which he had kept hidden, was to reinstate Selim on the throne. He arrived with 16,000 loyal soldiers, camped on the Plain of Davutpaşa where he pretended obeisance to Mustafa IV, and then on the twenty-eighth of July, 1808, took 15,000 of his men to Bab-ı Âli and demanded the seal of state from the grand vizier. From there he marched on the palace, entering the Gate of the Fountain of Fresh Water and climbing to the Middle Gate. The gatekeepers could not keep him out, and so, with numerous men, he crossed the Second Court to the Gate of Felicity. There he sent for the chief black eunuch, and while he waited he rested under one of the cypress trees. He was dressed differently from the dignitaries of Istanbul and must have been a strange sight to the members of the palace service. On his head he wore a green conical headpiece with a turban wrapped around it. On his back was a short jacket of dark blue cloth. His shoes were heavy yellow Morocco leather. Twin revolvers hung in holsters at his sides, and a dagger that had been a present from Sultan Selim was thrust in his belt. Added to this accoutrement was a long curved sword with which he played as he sat crosslegged on the ground.

Finally the chief black eunuch came out the Carriage Gate. With him was the *şeyhülislâm* of the time, Arabzade Arif Efendi. In their long robes they walked over to Alemdar.

"I have come to inform you," Alemdar said, "that the *ulema*, the statesmen, and the influential men of Rumelia and the families of Anatolia want Sultan Selim put back on the throne. Tell this to Sultan Mustafa!"

Both went back into the Inner Palace. Arabzade Arif sought out Mustafa IV and repeated Alemdar's words. Upset and fearful, Mustafa turned on the man and accused him of wanting to dethrone him. Arif Efendi left him cursing and returned to Alemdar, who also accused him of double dealing and pulled his sword. Terrified, Arif Efendi ran for the Gate of Felicity, but it swung shut in front of him. Without a haven, he simply collapsed, and Alemdar was now too concerned over the fate of his mission to bother with him.

Meanwhile Mustafa was asking the advice of his courtiers. They pointed out that, besides him, the only living members of the Osmanlı dynasty were Selim and Mustafa's younger brother, Mahmut. If both were killed the throne would be safe for him. The solution appealed to Mustafa's small and cruel mind, and he gave the order for their execution.

Out in the Second Court Alemdar was getting restless. There had been ample time for Selim to have been brought forth. Then when he saw the Gate of Felicity being shut he understood Mustafa was putting up resistance. It had been respect for the sacred character of the House of Felicity that had made him stop in the Second Court. This, he realized, had been a mistake. He should have forced his way through and found Selim himself. Now he and his men stormed the doors and broke into the Third Court, calling out, "We want Sultan Selim."

"There is your sultan," someone told them and pointed to the body that lay wrapped in a quilt on the stone in front of the Throne Room door.

After this bitter sign of the need for change Mahmut II, who acceded to the throne, abolished the Janissaries as soon as he could build up a loyal army. He adopted Western dress and forced it on his officials. He changed the Divan members into a cabinet on Western lines and permitted the ministers not only to sit in his presence but also to discuss with him affairs of state. Without the long robes and the groups of men standing in rigid silence with folded hands, the Throne Room lost its imperial character. In the next reign it would not be used at all. Ceremony would move to the new palace of Dolmabahçe.

THE IMPERIAL TREASURY

THE IMPERIAL TREASURY (Hazine-i Hümayun) or Privy Treasury (Hazine-i Hassa) perhaps belonged personally to the sultan. Although it used to
contain great chests of coins, it was primarily a treasury for gems and valuable objects. Much of its contents has been dissipated over the years, yet
more than enough remains to make the collection an eye-dazzling display.

The dazzle is all within. The exterior of the building, filling in the
northeast corner of the Third Court, is suggestive of serenity rather than
glitter. Like most of the court, it has its colonnade, largely of vari-colored
marble pillars. They support pointed arches of sandstone and introduce a
wide, equally white porch that tempts one to linger to examine the cut stone
of the building, the broad frames of the carved wooden doors, and the stalactite niche on the right-hand wall of the porch where it lies up against the
Campaign Hall. They announce that one is in the presence of early classic
Ottoman, and indeed the restoration of the Treasury, undertaken in the
early 1940's, has carried it back to its past.

The Treasury consists of four rooms—two with domes, two flat-roofed
—two porches, one facing the Marmara and the other the court, and two
basements to which stairs descend in the thick walls between the rooms.
Though often called the Conqueror's Kiosk (Fatih Köşkü), no one really
knows when it was built. Signs uncovered during the restoration point to a
very early period, yet there is nothing to prove that its builder was the

Conqueror. The museum administration now believes that the three east rooms overlooking the Marmara belonged to the bath known as the Bath of Selim II, that there may have been a building in the Conqueror's time extending from the present end or north room farther into the Third Court, and that one of the Conqueror's seven defense towers rose on the site of the present outer porch. That the porches are a later addition is attested by the *Hünername* miniature of this part of the palace, which shows that in the latter part of the sixteenth century there was a continuous building without porches along the Marmara side of the Third Court.

The rooms of the Treasury are worth examining for themselves as well as for their contents. If one goes in the farthest door to the right, one finds oneself in the cool room *(soğukluk)* of Selim II's bath. We know there was a building here along before the time of Selim II, for there are records of its destruction in the time of Bayezit II by an earthquake in 1509 so frightful it sent waves pouring over the city walls. At that time the room seems to have been Bayezit's bedroom which he had fortunately left an hour earlier. The palace people fled to the gardens where a tent was put up for the sultan. When the quakes continued, as they did for forty-five days, Bayezit moved to Edirne. Topkapı and the rest of the damaged buildings in Istanbul and its vicinity were repaired the next year. We know from the evidence of old writers that this area became a handsome bath usually believed to have been constructed for Selim II by Sinan. He may have completely rebuilt or he may have done over old rooms. Sinan himself gives little help in deciding this. He says simply that he built three baths in the New Palace of the Ruler, but since Selim II's reign lies within the period when Sinan was chief architect, it seems safe to assume the bath was his work. It not only extended into the present Treasury but also took in a part of what is now the Campaign Hall. Personally I am quite willing to concede the three east Treasury rooms to Sinan. They have the restful, satisfying proportions associated with his work and his happy combination of decorated and plane surfaces.

In the cool room the corner vaults supporting the drum of the dome form a sunburst of ribs, and in between the drum's small-paned windows stalactites hang frozen. The lower windows, which face the Sea of Marmara, are deep-set in pointed arches. Into the left wall as one enters are inserted niches, large ones vaulted like the ceiling in sunbursts of ribs. In the opposite wall in a dignified frame from which more stalactites pend is set a smallish door now hidden by a case of jade objects; it once led to a part of Selim's bath. The walls of this room, as well as of the others, are pure white so that they do not compete with the objects displayed.

It is not my purpose here to list all the treasures in the cases of these rooms, a great variety of things that range from pre-Ottoman to late Ottoman. They will be found identified in the guide one can buy at the Middle Gate. Many are objects of intrinsic beauty; most have a history. Others are simply elaborate and useless, especially the gifts sent from Europe in the eighteenth and nineteenth centuries. However, certain of them I find of special interest.

Each of the Treasury rooms has a throne, and in the cool room is the ebony throne inlaid with ivory and mother-of-pearl that belonged to Murat IV. It supposedly accompanied him on the campaign in which he recaptured Baghdad for the Empire, and he had it on hand from which to accept the obeisance of the reconquered people. Other objects interesting to Westerners because of the insight they offer into Ottoman life are the *nargiles* or water pipes the Ottomans liked to smoke. Their mouthpieces are set with diamonds and connected by long tubes to cut crystal bases which held the water through which the smoke passed. Another tube led from the base to the little pan where the tobacco burned. These particular water pipes date from the seventeenth to the nineteenth century. Also typically Ottoman are some little coffee-cup holders, one set ostentatiously inlaid with small rose diamonds. The room also contains the brilliant enameled gold pen-box encrusted with gems which was part of the Art of Turkey exhibit that traveled in America in 1967 and '68. It is a glittering example of Turkish goldsmithing of the seventeenth century.

When the place was a cool room it was here that Selim II slipped and fell, inflicting on himself the injury that brought on his death.

The next room to the left is also vaulted and domed and so close to the cool room in dimensions and decorations that I think it was perhaps the dressing room (*camekân*) to the bath. It was probably transferred to the use of the Treasury at an early date. It is, I suspect, what Evliya Çelebi was referring to when he said that the cupola of the Privy Treasury lay to the left of the bath.

Among its treasures is a bejeweled cradle of gold on silver which is one of the Treasury's showpieces. It is seventeenth-century Turkish work made for an imperial infant. When a child was born to one of the sultan's women it was the custom to present it with three cradles, one, the least elaborate, made by the mint and on hand for the birth, and two others, vying in magnificence, gifts of the *valide sultan* and the grand vizier. Such a cradle was brought to the palace in procession, the *beşik alayı* or cradle procession, which entered the Imperial Gate and passed through the First and Second Courts. At the Carriage Gate the cradle went to the chief black eunuch. He took it to the sultan to be admired and then gave it to the stewardess of the harem who carried it to the mother's room. There the most important women of the court had gathered for the occasion, and they rose to their feet to greet it. While the midwife offered a prayer, the baby was placed in the cradle. The Treasury's cradle, handsome as it is, must be one of those presented by the *valide* or the grand vizier.

The throne in this room is quite different from the others. It is narrow and covered with a dome supported by four slender columns. All of it is inlaid with tortoise-shell and mother-of-pearl set with great and small gems. Especially worth notice are the back of the seat and the dome on which leaf and floral branches flow out from a vase, all of it inlay and gems. From the dome a globe descends suspending a very large emerald. It first belonged to

The imperial jeweled cradle from the Treasury.

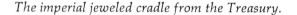

NECATI ORBAY

[126]

Ahmet I of the early seventeenth century and is known as the Eve Throne (Arife Tahtı) because, as we have seen, it was used for the ceremonies on the eve of a *bayram*. It was made by one of the Empire's master craftsmen of the time, a specialist in mother-of-pearl inlay, who later rose to become an architect and designed the Sultan Ahmet or Blue Mosque.

Here too is a case showing the robes, turbans and aigrettes of various sultans. Over them are suspended the small jeweled and gilded globes with gold tassels that formerly hung over thrones. The globes represented the world, the tassles signifying the ruling of it, and all therefore within the sultan's grasp. We have said that Süleyman the Magnificent was an accomplished goldsmith, and here in a wall case on the right, in the center, is an aigrette-holder of his workmanship set with two huge emeralds and a good-sized ruby. Two inlaid chests of the seventeenth and eighteenth centuries in which the sultans used to keep jewels are of particular interest, for we shall find Tavernier mentioning some like them when we come to describe the old Treasury. Finally we must mention the fact that the famous Topkapı dagger that caused all the turmoil in the James Bond movie, "Topkapı," is on display here. Its hilt is set with enormous emeralds, and its top hides a watch. The dagger was sent as a present to Nadir Shah, ruler of Persia, by Mahmut I in 1747. Arriving after Nadir Shah had been killed in a revolution, it was brought back by the Ottoman envoy and added to the treasure. You can tell it from the other daggers in the same case because it has the three great emeralds on the side and one on the top which opens to reveal the watch.

The third room has a flat roof that was once made of wood, but when the museum undertook to restore the pavilion it changed the wooden roofs to concrete for fire prevention. In the back wall is a fireplace, a tall, narrow, typically Ottoman *ocak*, this one of cut stone. On the Marmara side a balcony juts out over the wall of the palace, held up by very large marble supports, but the door to it is closed. However, the windows offer a view of the Marmara and, like those in the second room, are furnished with old carved wooden shutters.

The throne here was until recently known as Shah Ismail's, supposed to have been part of the booty Selim I brought back from his war with Persia. An elaborate oval plated with gold and set with myriad emeralds, rubies and pearls in an enamel base, it is raised on rather fat, equally bejeweled legs. It is of Mogul workmanship—which means it has a Turkic element since the Moguls were Turks who came down from the north to

The Eve Throne of Ahmet I.

conquer India. Recent investigation by the museum staff has discovered that no such throne is listed in the register in which Selim's Persian booty was noted, and it is now believed to have been a present to Mahmut I by Nadir Shah of Persia in 1764. Nadir Shah is known to have carried on a successful campaign against India and very likely carried off the throne then. He and Mahmut I were courting each other's favor at the time, as we have seen from the history of the Topkapı dagger. Among other notable exhibits here are a Koran case belonging to Mehmet III with a floral design in diamonds and a tooled-leather, gem-encrusted bookbinding made by the chief palace jeweler for the poems of Murat III.

Some of the booty of Selim I's Persian campaign is still in the Treasury in this room: Shah Ismail's belt, armlet and goblet. The belt and armlet are similar, plates of gold on iron held together with fabric, each bearing an

On the left a gold-ornamented pitcher set with rubies and emeralds on a jade base, 16th-century Turkish work; on the right a 16th-century Turkish water vessel set all over with rubies and emeralds in high relief, its side plaques jewels on jade, its basic material gold, and ornamented with snake heads, including the spout.

COURTESY TURKISH PRESS DEPARTMENT

inscription that clearly says it belonged to Shah Ismail. The goblet is black amber, its round body encircled with flowers of gold and on it the words: "Shah Ismail's property." In another case on the other side of the room are some of the furnishings that were used on the throne in the Throne Room: the cover, the pillow, the curtain, all embroidered in pearls and other gems, and other appurtenances such as the side and back of the throne. Even the thread is gold.

This room gives access to the covered porch that overlooks the water. In its center is an exquisite little pool and fountain carved from a single piece of marble in large flutes. The south wall has a graceful stalactite niche, a reproduction but carved by hand. The two open sides of the porch offer a wide panorama of the Anatolian shore across the Marmara, of the Bosphorus in the distance, and, close in, of the old outer wall of the palace along the sea. Better than anywhere else the view from here shows how the railroad, running close to the wall, brought an end to the kiosks that once rose from it. At one time this porch was enclosed with a grille and glass, but the museum has opened it up and freed its columns and arches.

There is an entrance here to the fourth room of the Treasury, once called the Ambassador's Treasury because from Mahmut II's time on it stored the precious articles used during receptions of foreign ambassadors and those that were to go out as presents, via Ottoman ambassadors, to foreign sovereigns. Like the third room, it has a flat roof, now concrete, and a tall fireplace. It is lighted by six windows, but since two of them are to the covered porch just described and two to the porch flanking the Third Court, it is only dimly lit, except of course for the modern spot lights that illumine the displays. The room has some of the most valuable objects of the Treasury, many of them once a part of the *sürre*, the gifts that were sent yearly by the sultan to the Arabian holy cities of Mecca and Medina. Selim I began the custom when he conquered Arabia, and it was continued as long as the Arabian lands were a part of the Ottoman Empire, until World War I. These particular objects had been sent to ornament the Prophet's tomb in Medina. They were returned to Istanbul during World War I by the Ottoman governor of the Hijaz to keep them from falling into enemy hands. Among them are three very impressive emerald and pearl pendants, the emeralds truly huge. The room also has the ruby ring Sultan Abdülaziz was wearing when he committed suicide. It was stolen from him by one of his female attendants and purchased from her for the Treasury by Abdülhamit II.

The Gold Bayram *Throne*

The İftariye

The room too has its throne, the famous gold *bayram* throne that some-times sat under the portico of the Gate of Felicity. It was made by melting down 80,000 gold ducats and has already been described. Here also is the huge Kaşıkcı Elması, the Spoonmaker's Diamond. How this got into the Treasury is not known, but there are two stories concerning its provenance. The favorite and the more romantic has it that a fisherman found it in a rubbish heap near the Istanbul gate of Eğrikapı in 1669 and that the fisher-man, having no idea of the value of his find, bartered it to a spoonmaker for three wooden spoons. The spoonmaker in turn sold it to a jeweler for ten silver coins. The jeweler, however, suspected he might have something of value here and sought the advice of another jeweler, who immediately wanted to be cut in on any deal having to do with it. This led to a quarrel, and the whole affair reached the ear of the head jeweler of the state, who purchased the stone from them both. Then the grand vizier got wind of it and from him its fame spread to the sultan, Mehmet IV, who had it pur-chased for the palace.

The alternative story relates that it was bought from the Maharajah of Madras in India in 1774 by a French officer, one Pigot, and that it passed from hand to hand until it was auctioned off to Napoleon's mother. After Napoleon's fall she sold her jewels, and it was then purchased by one of the officers of the Ottoman governor of Janina, Tepedelenli Ali Pasha, for 150,000 goldpieces and went into Tepedelenli Ali's treasury. At that time he had succeeded in making himself the almost independent ruler of the terri-tory he was supposed to administer for the Porte. Considered a rebel, he was shorn of his realm by Mahmut II. His treasury was taken over by the central government, and with it went the Spoonmaker's Diamond.

The diamond is shaped like a teardrop—or, some say, like the bowl of a spoon and took its name from its shape—is of eighty-six carats, the fifth biggest in the world, and at some time has been set with forty-nine smaller but clear diamonds which surround it in two rows. The Treasury records give no data on the stone, so one is free to believe either story. The one fact we have on it is that, after it was acquired, it was used in the aigrette the sultan wore on his accession.

In the storerooms down in the vaults, unseen by the public, are even today still more treasures: watches, Korans, bags of diamonds and other precious stones, and a host of objects for which there is no room upstairs.

From any of the Treasury's rooms one can return to the court-side porch where one started. The north end of it had been enclosed in concrete in the mid-eighteenth century, thus making an additional room. The museum pulled the concrete out from between the pillars and returned the porch to its original length and beauty. Before leaving it, one should study the handsome doors. Handsomest is the one that leads to the third room. It is placed in a marble frame edged with moldings; a sunburst vault graces the doorway, which is so deeply set there is room for niches at right angles to the door on either side. The lintel is contrasting stone, its keystone carved in a lamp. What is unusual for the palace, there is no inscription over it, only flat stone.

The door itself is one of the finest examples of the woodwork style of the Conqueror's period, and I wonder where it originally was, for this doorway had been blocked up. It is divided into three surfaces which further divide into rectangles and squares of concentric moldings. These enclose decorations in plant forms, except for the top rectangles which are carved with calligraphic inscriptions saying, "O, Forgiver of sins, O, Concealer of faults." Another door, carved with stars, was transferred here from a theological school of the old city.

When the structure became a treasury is as much of a mystery as its origin. It was formerly thought that Selim I first put it to that use, but a document has turned up that extends the time back to his father, Bayezit II, and Kemal Çiğ thinks the Conqueror himself stored treasure in the portion of it he built. Tradition may have fastened on Selim I because he piled up more wealth than it had known before.

In 1514 he defeated Shah Ismail of Persia in a high valley of the mountains of eastern Anatolia and captured a huge amount of booty, including the personal effects of Ismail on display and his favorite wife, Taclı Hanım. She became the slave of a highly placed Ottoman, and her fortune in jewels went with her. The rest of the booty was sent to Istanbul. Only a few years later, in 1517, Selim brought another Middle Eastern ruler to his knees, the Mameluke sultan of Egypt, and reduced Egypt to an Ottoman dominion. The booty from this campaign exceeded even that from Persia. Selim sent the most valuable part of it home by fleet, but still had a thousand camels loaded with gold and silver to accompany him to Istanbul. The vast amount of booty from these campaigns not only filled the Imperial Treasury and the Finance Treasury but overflowed into a harem treasury and the strong rooms of the Fortress of Seven Towers.

So proud was Selim of the riches he had added to the Treasury that he had the door sealed with his imperial seal and said, "I have filled the Treasury with gold. If any of my successors fills it with copper, let the Treasury

The Nadir Shah throne in the Treasury.

be sealed with his seal; if not, let them continue to seal it with my seal." His seal was still being used when Topkapı became a museum. Even now in the museum's possession, it bears the words "Sultan Selim Shah" in the center and around the edge in Arabic, "Who puts his trust in God, the Sublime, the Creator."

At the beginning of each reign the new sultan inspected the Imperial Treasury in which he inherited all that his predecessors had accumulated and to which he would add wealth of his own. There went into it, in addition to war booty, some of which was destined for the Finance Treasury in the Second Court, the annual revenue from Egypt, estimated by the Venetian envoy in the early seventeenth century at six hundred thousand crowns a year, and the effects of deceased statesmen who, being the sultan's slaves, had their wealth confiscated by his treasury on their death, even to the jeweled bridles for their horses and their robes of honor. Also kept here were presents brought by foreign ambassadors or carried home by Turkish ambassadors to foreign countries, and the gifts it was the custom of state dignitaries to present to the sultan on the occasions of weddings of princesses, the circumcision of princes, *bayrams*, the accession of a new sultan, or the erection of a new palace or pavilion. Finally a certain number of valuable objects were purchased for this treasury. From it the sultan sent presents

[133]

to foreign rulers, and on those same occasions when presents were given to him, he passed out large numbers of gifts to his officials. At times, as we have seen, it loaned money to the Finance Treasury. When times grew bad for the Empire, some of its objects were melted down for coinage. The Imperial Treasury was a place of passage, of constant accretion and decretion, although certain fabricated objects have stayed forever.

The most precise account we have of the contents of the old Treasury comes from Tavernier who gleaned his information from former Treasury officials of the seventeenth century. The Treasury then, as today, consisted of four rooms and basement, though not all of them the present four rooms. He says of it:

The first [room] contains a great quantity of bows, arrows, crossbows, muskets, guns, sabers, and other arms of that nature which are all so many masterpieces which have been presented to the Turkish emperor. All those arms are either hung from the ceiling or attached to the wall;

Jewel-embroidered satin and velvet quivers from the Treasury.

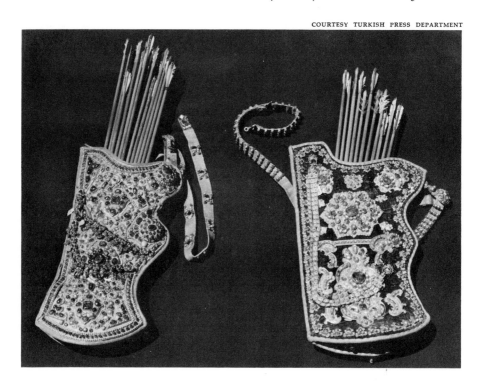

[1 3 4]

but in a pitiable state, all rusted and covered with dust, and the Grand Seigneur suffers that they be neglected because there are presented to him every day very well made arms of a newness that makes him forget the old ones. . . .

The second room has a large dome of the same height and architecture as that of the bath. . . . This one contains six large coffers, each twelve feet long on six of width and height . . . and two men have the care of lifting them, they are so heavy. These coffers called *ambar* [storage places] are full of all sort of clothes which belong to the Grand Seigneur, vestments, rich furs, magnificent turbans, and cushions embroidered with pearls. Besides these six coffers there are eight others eight feet long and four wide where are kept pieces of scarlet, the fine cloth of Holland and England, pieces of velvet, brocades of gold and silver, embroidered bed coverlets, and other riches of that nature. As for the bridles and saddles of horses covered with precious stones, they repose on arms which come out from the wall, and all that chamber is very well maintained and with much neatness.

The third room is large and rather resembles a hall. One discovers there first a large coffer of which the inside is divided into three parts, and is like three coffers one on the other, which are open in front . . . so that one can search the lowest without moving that above. The coffer at the bottom contains the rich coverings of the throne of which I have talked in the description of the Hall of Audience. That in the middle holds all the horsecloths enriched with pearls and precious stones which serve in the great solemnities. In the coffer at the top are kept the bridles, breastpieces, cruppers, and stirrups of which diamonds, rubies, emeralds and pearls are the riches; but the greatest part is covered with turquoises which they know perfectly well how to apply. . . .

There are also in that same room many other coffers of different size which enclose quantities of very precious things. Some are filled with rich swords garnished with precious stones and with sabers which are also covered. . . . The sides and the hilts of the maces of arms that they carry on parade are also covered with precious stones, and all the equipage of the Turks are superb and do not spare silver. When the Grand Seigneur wants to honor a pasha he sends him one of these swords or one of these sabers with a robe of gold brocade lined with some rich fur; but these rich pieces only come and go for by the death of the pashas . . . they are retrieved by the Treasury. . . .

The other coffers are filled with ambergris, musk, aloeswood and sandalwood. . . . It is the custom to present a pipe of aloeswood [to a guest]. They take this wood according as it is oily, of the body of a pea or of a small bean, and after having moistened it put it on a few embers in a kind of perfume pan which they present to the company. It has a strong smoke with which each perfumes his beard and his head and even the inside of his turban, after which he washes his hands crying out *Elhamdullah* which is to say thanks to God. . . .

There is also in these coffers a quantity of aromatic and precious drugs, stones of bezoar [an antidote for poison] and much mastic with which the *sultanes* and the other girls of the *saray* are ordinarily amused. They keep it always in the mouth, and this mastic makes the breath good and the teeth clean, which they like.

One sees in that same room and in other coffers a quantity of gold and silver vessels which are never used, the Grand Seigneur having others for his ordinary use in the Kiler and is served at his table only with porcelain. There are among other pieces several basins and ewers of gold, of which some are enriched with divers precious stones. . . .

They keep in one of the coffers large candlesticks of more than two feet, made of some very dear composition of greyish color which resembles wax and which comes from Ethiopia, each candle costing almost a hundred crowns. They are used only when the Grand Seigneur goes to visit the *sultanes*, and then they light two of these candles in two large candlesticks enriched with precious stones. When they are little more than half burned the black eunuchs who serve in the harem light others and out of courtesy present the ends which remain to the principal women who are close to the *sultanes*.

There are moreover in one of these coffers a quantity of clocks and watches of German make, and many Turkish daggers and ink-stands, all the pieces being masterpieces of master craftsmen and garnished with precious stones. One sees finally against the wall covered with material of scarlet many Turkish arms carefully preserved, bows, arrows, shields, and hammered arms of very beautiful workmanship, and most of the pieces are very valuable.

But what is most precious in that room is a coffer strong and all of iron which contains another of a foot and a half or thereabouts, square, where are found the great riches. When this coffer is opened, one sees a kind of goldsmith's ring casket in which are ranged all sorts

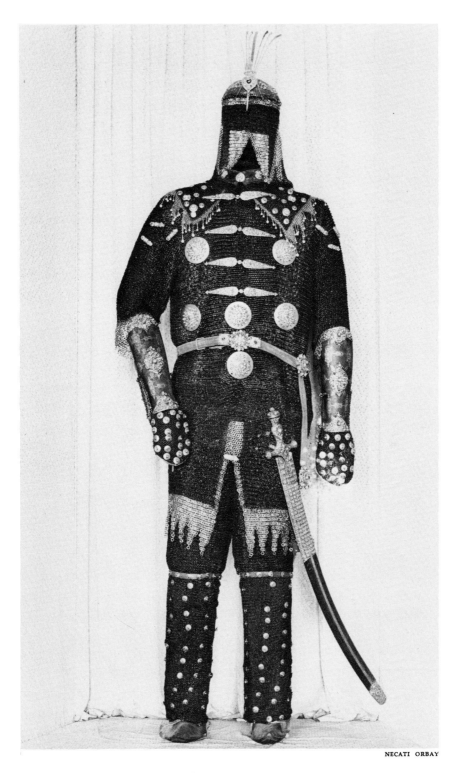

The jeweled chain mail armor and the jeweled sword of Murat IV, the conqueror of Erivan and Baghdad, now displayed in the Treasury.

of rings of very great price, diamonds, rubies, emeralds, a great number of beautiful topazes, and four cat's eyes which one can scarcely estimate for their beauty. The first layer raised, one discovers small drawers of divers jewels and great rose diamonds and earrings and other rose rubies and emeralds, towers and chains of pearls and bracelets. There is apart a chest where are the *sorguç* or aigrette-holders which are attached to the turban of the Grand Seigneur. These are very like small handles in the fashion of tulips covered with the most beautiful precious stones of the *saray*, and this is where the aigrette, that rich plume, enters. . . .

The middle [of the third room] is occupied by a stand . . . covered and surrounded with a tapestry of gold and silk, and on it one sees there in relief the Emperor Charles V seated on a throne, holding in one hand the world, in the other a sword, with all the great of the empire around him who give him homage. At the foot of the tapestry one reads certain verses in Gothic characters; and the upper part of the stand is full of books in Latin, French, Italian, German, English and other languages of our Europe. They are for navigation and they are accompanied by two celestial and terrestrial globes and some geographic maps designed on vellum, which makes one judge that all this has been taken on the sea by some Turkish corsair and sent as a present to the Grand Seigneur. . . .

The fourth room of the Treasury is very dark and only in the day does it receive a little light from a lantern which is on the court and which has three strong grilles one above the other. Above the door one sees the words engraved in the Turkish language: "Money acquired by the diligence of Rüstem [a grand vizier of Süleyman]. . . .

[The fourth room] is filled with coffers two feet long, wide and high in proportion, reinforced with bands of iron and each closed with two padlocks. The number is not always equal, because the money goes and comes in that chamber and because the coffers are transported according to the need. . . . [The grand vizier] has the key to this fourth room of the Treasury, and the first *defterdar* [treasurer] another, and outside of that it is always sealed with the seal of the Grand Seigneur. It is ordinarily opened only on the days when the Divan meets or to put money into it or to take it out of it. . . .

Although Tavernier does not say so, the Treasury was the repository for a great number of books. Many of the best of these came into the possession of the Treasury, like the other articles, as gifts, by confiscation of pashas' belongings, as war booty, and by purchase. When they were transferred to the New Library 841 Turkish books alone were catalogued, in addition to those in Persian and Arabic, more than in any other palace collection. Among them is a *Velâdetname (Book of Birth Rejoicing)* written in 1775/6 for Hatice Sultan, a daughter of Abdülhamit I, to celebrate her birth. It was a gift of the sword-bearer of the time. Here too was kept the *Hünername* with its famous miniatures.

The basement vaults which Turks call the Bodrum (cellar) Tavernier calls the Secret Treasury. He gives an account of this too:

> In the fourth room of the Treasury one sees a door furnished with sheets of metal and bars of iron which opens into the first passage of the place where the Secret Treasury of the Grand Seigneur is kept . . . where one sees several coffers ranged of the same size as those of the room one has just left.
>
> It is in these coffers that there has been enclosed for a long time all the savings of the Ottoman monarchs; and there enters there only gold, all the silver being taken to the other treasury for ordinary needs. . . .
>
> All the gold that is entered under that vault is in sacks of leather . . . and it is by his own hand that the Grand Seigneur applies to them his own seal, which is the same his predecessors used with the reservation of the name which ought to be that of the reigning monarch. The seal of Murat [IV] carries the engraved words, "The help of God be upon His servant Emperor Murat."
>
> This is then the manner in which the sacks of gold enter the Secret Treasury. All the gold and silver which enters the *saray* is carried first to a chamber of the Treasury, and each is put apart in the coffers which are designated for it. When there is enough gold to go into two hundred *keses* [purses or sacks] which makes eighteen million pounds, the grand vizier immediately notifies the Grand Seigneur who specifies the day to go to take them to the Secret Treasury. The day having come, the grand vizier, conducted under the arms by the *haznedarbaşi* [head of the Treasury] who is on the left, the most honorable [position] among the Turks, and by the *silâhtar* [sword-bearer] *ağa* who is on the right, goes to the chamber of the Treasury where the sixty pages awaiting him range in rows at [one] side and the other, hands crossed on their stomachs. The Grand Seigneur having traversed the chamber

and having had the first door of the Secret Treasury opened, preceded by several candlesticks of white wax, the pages follow him two by two until under the vault, where they carry the sacks tied with a piece of silk. They place on the knot a piece of soft red wax where the Grand Seigneur applies his own seal, which is a ring of gold where are engraved the words which I have mentioned . . . after which they put the sacks into the coffers which are double padlocked each one.

Before leaving the vault the Chief of the Treasury ordinarily makes this compliment to the Grand Seigneur: "My felicitous padishah, we hope you will make your liberality seen toward your slaves." According to the humor of the Grand Seigneur then, he orders there be distributed twenty or thirty purses, each purse, as I have said, five hundred crowns. . . . The grand vizier and the other great of the Porte . . . wait in the fourth room for him to leave the vault, and then he has them open the coffer of his jewels to show them what are the most precious. As his favorites are always there and certain other persons whom the prince esteems for their merit, there is scarcely anyone there to whom he does not make some present, and he does not have to make it of great value. The Treasury closed, the Grand Seigneur returns to his quarters where the great accompany him as far as the door.

When the Treasury was opened there was always great ceremony. Whether the sultan himself was to enter it, or the grand vizier, or only the chief of the Treasury, the Treasury pages lined the way to the door. First the protective covering had to be taken off the padlock, and then the chief of the Treasury examined the seal—Selim I's seal—which had been placed over the lock. Finding it intact, he had the master of the keys break it and open the lock. Whatever was put in or taken out was noted in a register, and the place was locked and sealed as before. At such times as the chief of the Treasury went in without the grand vizier or the sultan—which was to get some article the sultan wanted—he sometimes took the opportunity to carry off something for himself on the pretext that it was to go to the sultan. Its absence should have been noted in the register, but usually the clerk whose duty this was was so anxious to keep on good terms with the Treasury head, whose recommendation he needed for promotion, that he overlooked the theft. This did not happen often, however, because if the pilfering was discovered punishment was swift and severe.

When Tavernier wrote there were sixty Treasury pages, dressed in kaftans and special headdresses. Treasury pages survived Mahmut II's demotion of the Palace School, and in the reign of one of the last sultans we still find them, fewer in number and dressed in dark jacket and trousers and fez, standing in ranks for a Treasury opening.

Since the Treasury continued to hold wealth, it was not allowed to fall to pieces as were the stable and kitchens. Yet the more it was repaired the farther it departed from the old Treasury. When the museum began the work of reconditioning it, it was not a simple matter of strengthening and repairing the old structure, but of looking for signs of the original construction and decoration and following the style they indicated. Whatever was added was patterned after early extant work. There were, for example, no remnants of the plaster window decoration characteristic of its era, and so the museum looked for a suitable specimen to copy. They found it in the tomb of Cem (Jem), the Conqueror's son, in Bursa.

On Mehmet II's death Cem, his favorite son and some say about to be designated his successor, set himself up as rival to his older brother Bayezit, complete with court and literary circle in the old Ottoman capital of Bursa. Bayezit won the conflict, and Cem fled west into exile. Being in the nature of a hot potato, he was passed from one Western ruler to the other until he finally died of poison in Naples in 1495. His body in death wandered almost as much as it had in life, but finally found a resting place in one of the beautifully decorated tombs of the peaceful garden of the Muradiye Mosque in Bursa. His books, his horses, his jewels, his parrot and his monkey, which must have traveled with the body, were presented to his rival. It took four and a half centuries for Cem to influence the palace he had hoped to occupy.

As long as the Empire lasted no subject of the sultan, except those whose duty it was, ever set foot inside the Imperial Treasury. Though late nineteenth-century sultans had three rooms arranged for the display of treasure, this was done to impress foreigners. The rooms could be viewed only by ambassadors and certain other privileged foreigners, on occasion, and with the sultan's permission. Only when the palace became a museum were the Turks able to see their own treasure. Now Turks of all ages flock to it, finding in it a reminder, as I heard one Turk say, of "the days when we were rich."

THE PAVILION OF
THE BLESSED MANTLE

THE PAVILION of the Blessed Mantle (Hırka-ı Saadet Dairesi, literally the Apartment of the Felicitous Mantle) is the most sacred section of the *saray*, housing as it does the most sacred relics of Islam which, despite Muslim aversion to anything smacking of idolatry, have been venerated for centuries. From the outside, until one reaches the porch, nothing indicates its sacred character. It is a rather low building of four domes in the northwest corner of the Third Court directly opposite the Treasury, carrying its share of the court colonnade. Just outside its porch one passes a well, now closed, into which the sweepings from the rooms were poured and on the porch a marble mortar in which incense was ground with which to scent the pavilion. A large marble mounting block for the sultan is contiguous to the porch, and beside it begins the wide marble way to the Throne Room.

The ornate doorway informs one that this is a place of some importance. Over it is inscribed the Declaration of Faith in the hand of Ahmet III. On either side, beside crystal globe lanterns, are more inscriptions, these in the shape of a *tuğra*, saying, on the right, "The king of the world, the illustrious ruler," and on the left, "Sultan Ahmet who follows the Holy Law." They are set in tiled panels of his time, coarse tiles in which the colors have sometimes run, which illustrate the degradation of the Ottoman tile industry by

[1 4 2]

the eighteenth century. The door itself is a solid affair called the Fountain Door (Şadırvan Kapısı) from the jetting fountain just within. Nearby on the porch a notice in several languages is set up, pointing out that this building has religious significance and asking the public to behave accordingly. I have never heard any but hushed voices within it.

It is hardly necessary to point out that the pavilion was not accessible to the public—or even to the general run of palace personnel—during the Empire. In fact so wrapped in mystery were the relics that not even the color of the mantle was generally known, and many colors were ascribed to it. Actually it is black. Even after Topkapı became a museum the area remained off limits for visitors. It was not until August 31, 1962, that the pavilion was opened to the public and many of its holy objects displayed where people could see them. The Blessed Mantle itself, however, still rests in its gold box as it did under the sultans.

One enters a long room tiled with a variety of patterns, some floral, some of the three disc design, some medallions, and one that looks like scattered flower petals, all but the last predominantly blue and white. The jetting fountain that gives the room its name takes up most of the forepart, and beyond it a showcase displays swords of the first four caliphs, the straight swords in use before the curved Turkic sword reached the Middle East, and a bow and sheath said to have belonged to the Prophet. On a dais at the far end there are a Koran stand of carved wood, rather like a large X, many old prayer rugs, a door called the Repentance Door that once was a part of the Kaaba, and a hanging of gold-embroidered green, the holy color of Islam, that at some time hung from the Kaaba wall. In this section too is a famous inlaid door, a modern work of mother-of-pearl made to replace a rococo one ill-suited to the suite, from the time of Mahmut II. All these rooms are dimly lit in a twilight of respect.

At the far left is the door to the Room of the Kerchief (Destimal Odası), named for the pieces of muslin handed to visitors to the pavilion on the fifteenth day of Ramazan. It too is completely tiled in blue and white. From the ceiling hang gold-covered gutter-pipes from the Kaaba presented by sultans, and in cases along the wall are shown some of the ornamental gold boxes that were made to contain the Blessed Mantle. There are also small, jeweled gold cases that fit on the standard to carry the tiny Korans we have seen in the Calligraphy Section and some of the Korans they carried. Elsewhere I have been able to examine one of these closely and found the writing so infinitesimal, it must have strained the eyesight of the scribe who

[1 4 3]

The entrance to the Pavilion of the Blessed Mantle. What looks like a tuğra *to the left of the door is in reality a verse of poetry.*

wrote it. The room also has a gold case fabricated for the Kaaba's blackstone that was held sacred by the Arabs even back in their pagan days.

In a case in the center is a large Koran on skin which tradition ties to Othman, the third caliph to follow the Prophet. It was he who first had the canonical Koran compiled from the various oral and written sources. This copy is said to be open to the page he was reading when he was killed in his house in Medina. However, the style of calligraphy in which it is written points to a time later than Othman, and the tradition may well be erroneous. It is nevertheless a very old Koran.

To return to the room with the fountain—a door in its right-hand wall opens into the Presentation or Reception Room (Arzhane) where visitors waited on the one day a year when the Blessed Mantle might be seen, and then only by the imperial family and high officials. In the center are now shown some of the most venerated relics: the keys of the Kaaba, hairs of the Prophet's beard and a piece of his tooth in gold covers, a mold of his footprint, his seal, and a gold case with some sacred earth from his grave. There is also in the case a letter purported to be from the Prophet to an Egyptian ruler inviting him to join Islam. Since it has never been decided whether or not the Prophet could write—writing being a rare accomplishment among the Arabs of his day—it was perhaps written for him.

This room came to be popularly called Arslanhane (Lion House) purely in error. Its correct name, Arzhane (Petition House) was given to it because it was here the sultan accepted the summaries sent by the grand vizier, ordered them opened and read, and gave whatever orders they prompted.

To the left is the Room of the Blessed Mantle itself. Its open door, though which one may only look, is guarded by a silver fence. In contrast to the other rooms, it is brilliantly lit.

In the second half of the sixteenth century Murat III had the walls tiled with some of the *saray*'s finest tile work. Particularly arresting is the area known as the peacock panel. Its deep, true colors show a leaf scroll design predominantly blue with red and yellow flowers on a white ground. In the center a white medallion sprays forth plum blossoms in which blue peacocks perch. The panel shows a strong affinity to one on the wall of the Golden Way of the harem. The room was continually embellished by later sultans, so that it has become a place of all periods. The ceiling is domed and patterned with twentieth-century gold work added by the next to the last sultan, Mehmet V. From the ceiling hang oil lamps and golden pendants, the pendant over the Holy Mantle set with precious stones, the gift of the seventeenth-century Murat IV. There are sacred inscriptions about the room. Ahmet III

[1 4 5]

again showed his calligraphic skill with the Declaration of Faith. Mahmut II added a fountain and a fireplace. Over the matting on the floor are spread rare prayer rugs of which the pavilion owns forty.

The climax of the room, however, is the latticed, domed canopy of silver decorated in gold and draped with heavy black curtains embroidered in gold thread. In it in a gold box on a gold-plated table habitually lay the Blessed Mantle. It was given by the Prophet to a poet of his time, Kâab bin Züheyr, a one-time opponent who later became a follower. He came to the Prophet one day, asked his forgiveness, and as proof of his sincerity read one of his poems. One line of it, "The world receives abundance from the light of our Prophet," so delighted Muhammed that he then and there took off his cloak and put it over Kâab's shoulders. The rest of the poem is equally eulogistic and calls Muhammed "the sword whose sparks are scattered in all directions, a sword . . . drawn from the scabbard by God Himself." The Islamic world calls it the Kasida-ı Burda or the Panegyric of the Mantle. Sultans have had it inscribed in many places in the *saray*.

The mantle itself is a simple garment of plain black lined with cream color. Kâab preserved it carefully, refusing to sell it even to the caliph of his time. It was only after Kâab's death that a caliph got possession of it, buying it from the poet's heirs. From him it passed down through the Umayyad and Abbaside caliphs until it reached Selim I on his conquest of Egypt.

In front of the Blessed Mantle's box, on a low stool, is laid the sword of the Prophet (seyf-i Nebeviler). The sword itself is plain but the scabbard, made at the order of Ahmet I, heavily ornamented. Just behind the Blessed Mantle is another box, this one covered with gold-embroidered green cloth, in which is kept the Sancağ-ı Şerif, literally the Noble Banner but generally referred to in English as the Sacred Standard. The sultans and grand viziers carried it with them on campaign. It is so old and fragile that both sides of it have been covered with cloth to preserve it. It too is black wool, but was often thought to be green because green cloth so long protected it.

The relics have come from various sources. Some, the Prophet's cloak, hairs from his beard, the sword of the Caliph Omar, and the keys to Mecca and Medina were brought back from Egypt by Selim I. Others were sent to Istanbul from time to time and added to what the Turks call the *mukaddes emanetler*, the sacred trusts.

There is some disagreement as to where the relics were first housed. Some say in the harem, others in the Mosque of Eyüp which was founded by the Conqueror just outside of Istanbul to commemorate a companion of the

The Room of the Blessed Mantle, showing the gold box of the mantle under its latticed silver canopy, the sword of the Prophet in the foreground, the box containing the Sacred Standard behind the mantle.

Prophet who had fallen trying to take the city from the Byzantines. Some later additions to the relics were stored in the Treasury. Palace authorities now believe they were brought together in the Room of the Blessed Mantle by Murat III near the end of the sixteenth century. Under Mahmut II the whole pavilion was given over to them, although their actual display in cases is the contribution of the museum. Because of its sacred contents the building was not allowed to deteriorate.

The care of the relics was a duty of the forty pages of the Privy Chamber, a role they maintained until the end of the Empire. Four in rotation stayed on duty in the Room of the Blessed Mantle day and night, reading the Koran. Five times a day all forty assembled here for prayer. When the palace became a museum the remaining Privy Chamber pages became curators of the holy relics. By now they must all have retired or died.

This pavilion goes back to the Conqueror, as is witnessed by an inscription over one of its doors: "Es-Sultan Mehmet bin Murat Han (the Sultan Mehmet, son of Murat Khan)." It must have been simpler then, for its domes were added by Murat III and IV after the mantle had been moved there. Originally, as we have noted, the building was the Privy Chamber (Has Oda) and remained a part of it until Mahmut II's time. The basement rooms, from the type of construction, have been traced to the Conqueror's time. A ramp, of which a part still exists, led from there to a road the Conqueror must have used to reach the Tile Kiosk on a lower level of the hill.

In the days of the sultans the Room of the Blessed Mantle was regularly cleaned at three different intervals by the pages of the Privy Chamber—weekly, every three weeks, and, with great ceremony, once a year. In the weekly cleaning the walls were rubbed down and the floor swept. Once every three weeks the cleaning of the dome was added. Then, yearly, three days before the sultan's annual visit, the ceremonial cleaning took place. Sometime before this new matting had been put down, woven in the First Court as we have seen. Any needed repairs were seen to so that by cleaning day, the twelfth of Ramazan, all was ready.

On that day the pages of the Privy Chamber, at the command of the sultan, temporarily transported the sacred relics out of the pavilion and into the Revan Kiosk just across the Corridor with Pillars. The sultan, as chief servant of the relics, carried his share. Two large bowls of rose water were set on tables in the pavilion, and sixty sponges provided. The sword-bearer wet a few of these in the rose water and presented them to the sultan. That

august individual actually used them, carefully wiping off the silver lattice.
The work of cleaning having been thus begun by the ruler, the pages took
up the other sponges and wiped down the entire room. While this was going
on the room was scented with musk, amber, and aloeswood. At the finish
the sponges were given to the pages as holy mementoes.

On the fifteenth of Ramazan came the state visit of the padishah accompanied by his sons and high officials. Then, after the men, the women
of the imperial harem paid their visit. On this day it was the custom to kiss
the Holy Mantle, but because the cloak was old and torn, pieces of muslin
were put over it, and it was the muslin that was actually kissed. A separate
piece was provided for each person, and these, called *destimal-ı şerif*, noble
kerchief, were prepared beforehand by the Ağa of the Muslin (Tülbent
Ağası), each piece embroidered and inscribed with verse.

First the mantle had to be withdrawn from its case, which was accomplished by the sultan himself. The gold box containing it was taken out from
the latticed canopy and put on a table. The sultan, who alone had the key to
the box, unlocked and opened it. While his hands performed the holy chore,
his voice intoned the *besmele*: "In the name of God, the Merciful, the Compassionate." Opening the box did not mean that the Blessed Mantle was
immediately exposed. It was wrapped in a number of *bohças* or squares of
cloth, in which was a smaller gold box. This in turn the sultan opened, to
reveal several more *bohças*, all elaborately worked, in which the mantle lay.
It is said to have been wrapped in forty in all—that magic number. Many
things were done forty times in the East. On the fortieth day after child-
birth an Ottoman woman had her ceremonial bath at the *hamam* and
ceased thereafter to be the object of special attention. One could mention
many more instances. Remember Ali Baba and the Forty Thieves? Now the
sultan personally untied the forty *bohças* and brought the mantle to light.
It is almost two yards long and, as we have said, made of black wool lined
with a cream-colored fabric. It has wide sleeves, and there are tears at the
skirt and neck. Its simplicity must have made a strong contrast to the gorgeous garb of the people viewing it.

Now the Ağa of the Muslin produced the kerchief, which was put over
the mantle's right shoulder. This the sultan bent and kissed, and, after him,
one by one according to rank, the princes, the statesmen and attendants
kissed a piece of muslin in the same position. Each person's muslin became
his to keep as a sacred souvenir of the day. While this took place the sultan
stood at the head of the mantle, the grand vizier at his right, the Ağa of the

[1 4 9]

House of Felicity (chief black eunuch) at his left. Meanwhile the Privy Chamber pages constantly chanted the Koran, their musical voices rising and falling to the cadence of the lines.

Next came the turn of the imperial women. Ayşe Osmanoğlu has told about her visits to the Blessed Mantle in the late nineteenth century in the book she has written about her father, Adbülhamit II, *Babam Abdülhamit (My Father, Abdülhamit):*

We began to prepare three days before the visit to the Blessed Mantle, on the fifteenth of Ramazan. We got up early that day, wore our most beautiful long-skirted ceremonial dresses, put on our jewels, and went to Topkapı. My grandmother got into a carriage of the sultanate; the drivers wore the embroidered uniforms of the royal stable, like the drivers of the padishah. Halim Efendi, who was the officer in charge of harem outings, was in front with the guards. The harem *ağas*, wearing embroidered uniforms, followed the carriage of my grandmother, which was in front. Thus we left Yıldız and went to Topkapı. There we were met by old female attendants who came from Dolmabahçe, and we went to the room assigned to each of us in Topkapı. All those outside the palace to whom invitations had previously gone, the married *sultans* [the ruler's daughters were called *sultan*] and the wives of the ministers also came. We invited the people we knew personally.

In the room called the Room of the Armchair my grandmother sat under a canopy in her royal costume, and all of us went and kissed her hand. All together we waited for the opening of the Pavilion of the Blessed Mantle. Sultan Abdülmecit's wives [he was a deceased sultan], Serfiraz and Şayeste, were there too and sat beside my grandmother. Usually the *valide paşa* [the mother of the khedive of Egypt] was at the ceremony.

The *baş musahip* [the head harem eunuch in attendance on the sultan] came to the harem when the Blessed Mantle was opened and, with an Oriental salute, gave the news to my grandmother, the *valide sultan*. The *valide sultan* rose, and after her walked the wives of Abdülmecit and then the *sultans* and the *kadın efendis*, all in order of precedence, and we all went to the Pavilion of the Blessed Mantle. Everyone wore a piece of white muslin on her head. We sensed odors, because incense was burning everywhere, and from behind a curtain came the Noble Koran read in an extremely beautiful voice by the muezzin. The hearts of all of us filled with deep and humble reverence, with slow steps, our skirts sweeping the ground, we walked in ranks until we came in front of the padishah who stood at the foot of the throne. [This is the only mention of a throne in connection with the visit to the Blessed Mantle.] With an Oriental salute from the ground . . . we took the noble kerchief which was given into our hands, kissed it, put it over our heads, withdrew backwards, and went and again stood in our ranks according to precedence. . . .

The young princes, the sons of the padishah, stood in rank in uniform at the foot of the throne.

After us the *valide paşa* and the wives of the grand vizier, the other ministers and the *şeyhülislâm* entered. The lady treasurer and the other old female attendants of the palace and the wives of the respected palace servants also participated in the ceremony. At the end of the ceremony the *baş musahip* appeared, gave an Oriental salute from the ground, and we left in ranks as we had entered, the *valide sultan* in front.

Our carriages drew up to the Harem Gate [Carriage Gate] of Topkapı in order of precedence, and we mounted them and returned to Yıldız Palace in the same formation as we had left it. These carriages, which proceeded slowly because of the horses, usually brought us to the palace at the time of the *iftar* cannon [the cannon that announced the end of the day's fast during Ramazan].

At some point during the ceremony a button at the neck of the mantle was dipped into a silver cup of rose water and dried over an amber-scented brazier. A few drops of this were poured into pitchers which were given away to important people. This was the Hırka-ı Saadet Suyu, the Water of the Blessed Mantle, and was supposed to have medicinal properties, being especially efficacious in cases of paralysis. The tradition was discontinued during the reign of Mahmut II when certain sharpsters were found to be selling their own concoction as Water of the Blessed Mantle.

When the entire ceremony was over the sultan himself wrapped the Blessed Mantle in its coverings and put it back into its boxes. Then the Privy Chamber pages replaced it inside the silver lattice where it rested for another year.

The relic second in importance was the Sancağ-ı Şerif, the Sacred Standard, held to have been the standard of Muhammed himself or at least of his time. How it came to be deposited among the sacred trusts is open to argument, but the most likely story is that it was originally in the treasury of Damascus whence it went back and forth to Mecca with the pilgrims. According to this tradition it did not join the Ottomans until 1593 when it was taken by the Damascus Janissaries on the Austrian campaign and became a part of the sacred trusts of the *saray* in 1595.

The following year, 1596, started inauspiciously for the Ottomans. The army was the victim of a series of defeats in Hungary, a state of affairs which, with their concept of the Holy War against unbelievers, suggested to the Ottomans that they were somehow unworthy of victory. An earthquake that hit Istanbul and part of Anatolia further convinced them that they had offended Divine Power and must change their methods. The cry went up for the new sultan, Mehmet III, to lead the troops in person as his ancestors had done. In June, 1596, he set out for the war.

Before he departed he went to the Pavilion of the Blessed Mantle where the Sacred Standard was taken out of its box and affixed to its staff. During this process the Sura of Victory, the forty-eighth chapter of the Koran, was read aloud. This chapter was produced by Muhammed outside the city of Mecca to which he and his followers were endeavoring to make a pilgrimage and which had refused them entry. While the question of whether to fight or not hung in the air, a follower of Muhammed arranged a truce with the Meccans. The sura was obviously intended as encouragement to the lonely little band. It exhorts the followers of Muhammed to fight for the faith, promising them victory, and says in part: "And if those who disbelieve join battle with you, they will take flight." In Ottoman times it was customarily read aloud during battle.

When the reading of the sura was completed the sultan took the Sacred Standard on his shoulder and carried it to the Throne Room. Officials lining his path in their rich robes and varied headgear sobbed as it passed. It was greeted in the Throne Room with cries of "God is great!" and placed against a column of the throne. According to palace tradition, after the ceremony in the Throne Room the standard was moved to just outside the Gate of Felicity and set up in the depression which is still in the floor.

Troops were mustered for war on the Plain of Davutpaşa on the outskirts of Istanbul. There the Sacred Standard was carried in full view of the populace, put into its gold box and placed in a special carriage for its journey to the front. It had its own tent near that of the sultan or, in his absence, of the grand vizier. With it went a special sheikh who was a descendant of the Prophet. It was his job to read the Sura of Victory during battle.

In 1596 the field of battle was in Hungary, northeast of Buda at the town of Egri. In Western sources this is the Battle of Cerestes. Mehmet III, who had gone to the front reluctantly, would have accepted defeat in an early phase of the battle had it not been for the encouragement of one of his advisers, and the daring of the commander Çicalazade who saved the day with a wild sweep of his troops into enemy forces. Mehmet was therefore able to return to Istanbul victorious and doubtless felt that the Sacred Standard had played a part in the success of the battle. That its presence helped inspire the troops there can be little doubt.

Even the redoubtable Çicalazade must have been moved by it. He was born a non-Muslim, but he had the zeal, even the fanaticism of a convert. His mother, a Turk, had been captured during a raid on the coast of the Morea by one of the Knights of Malta, Count Cicala. He had converted her to Christianity and married her, and their son had in turn been captured by Turks off the Turkish coast. This eighteen-year-old, whose name was Scipio, entered the Palace School as a slave, there became a Muslim and an Ottoman, and later rose high in the sultan's service. He eventually married a granddaughter of Süleyman, became *kaptan paşa*, and after the Battle of Cerestes grand vizier. At one point in his career he forced the Spanish viceroy of Sicily to grant him an interview with his mother, who must have found the fact that he had become an Ottoman some satisfaction for her capture. Or perhaps, like him, she had become so thoroughly imbued with her new environment, as completely Western and Christian as he was Eastern and Muslim, that she deplored his fate.

Generally in the seventeenth century and beyond the sultans did not lead the army in war but left that duty to the grand viziers. On such occasions the Sacred Standard was handed to the vizier in the Throne Room from which he carried its staff on his shoulder. Quickly cavalry officers, running beside him, relieved him of it and bore it the few steps to the Gate of Felicity. From there grand vizier and standard proceeded to the Plain of Davutpaşa where the final seeing-off was enacted. Clothed in robes of honor for the occasion, the grand vizier and the *şeyhülislâm* stood at hand while the sultan kissed the Sacred Standard and handed it over with the words, "I entrust the Sacred Standard to you and you to God. May He be your helper!" At Davutpaşa in 1789 Selim III put the standard into the hands of Alemdar Mustafa who eighteen years later would attempt to reinstate him on the throne.

On the grand vizier's return from the theater of war the Sacred Standard was given back to the padishah at Davutpaşa with like ceremony. It reached the plain in its box, and only then was taken out and affixed to its staff. From there it passed into the city through one of the chief gates and along the main avenue that cuts through the city until it becomes Divan Yolu, down which it was borne to Topkapı. There one of the *ağas* carried it from the Imperial to the Middle Gate where the grand vizier picked it up, bore it on his shoulder to the Throne Room, and there once again presented it to the sultan. The final rite returned it to its precious box in the Room of the Blessed Mantle. This took place to the reading of the Koran in an atmosphere perfumed with amber and aloeswood.

In between military campaigns the Sacred Standard stayed in its box except during particularly serious rebellions when it was produced to act as a dampening influence on the rebels. In 1651 when the Janissaries were especially unruly, the Sacred Standard was brought forth from the palace. The veneration in which it was held was actually such that it quieted the rebels.

The city of Istanbul was shaken by another Janissary uprising in 1687, or rather a continuation of the one that had that year unseated Mehmet IV. Joined by the rabble of the city, the Janissaries invaded and plundered the palace of the grand vizier, Siyavuş Pasha, even breaking into the harem, that holy of holies of the Muslim. The grand vizier lost his life defending it. Other horrors followed. His sister and his wife were mutilated and dragged naked through the city streets. These monstrosities stirred up the decent people, and the preacher of the Mosque of Süleymaniye and other members of the religious establishment roused themselves to do something about it. The result was the Sacred Standard flying over the Imperial Gate of Topkapı. The people rallied to it, found the courage to turn against the pillagers, and liquidated the worst of the Janissaries and their friends.

The last time the Sacred Standard was brought out to add its influence to the quelling of the Janissaries was in 1826 when Mahmut II decided their turbulence and tyranny had gone far enough and put an end to them. Then it was set up at the pulpit of the Mosque of Sultan Ahmet on the lower side of the Hippodrome.

Besides guarding the sacred trusts the Pavilion of the Blessed Mantle played a part in the beginning and end of each sultan's life. We have seen that it was here that a new ruler prayed immediately on his accession. And it was here, on the marble floor outside the Fountain Door to the Third Court that a padishah's bier lay to receive the last honors from the people of the Inner Palace, the ceremony known as *tezkiye*, a canonical purification in which the preacher asks the congregation to confirm the good qualities of the deceased.

THE CORRIDOR WITH PILLARS
AND ITS KIOSKS

THE PAVILION of the Blessed Mantle is skirted on two sides by the L-shaped Corridor with Pillars, a wide hallway whose high, vaulted ceiling gives a sense of vastness the palace possesses nowhere else. Arches of contrasting stone span it from the columns to the rooms that flank it and lend an overall unity to the somewhat patchwork decoration of its walls. This patchwork, however, contains some of the most exquisite of Ottoman tiles.

In the corridor outside the Reception Room of the Pavilion of the Blessed Mantle is the fountain where the ritual ablution for dead sultans was performed. It was from here that the body was borne to the porch of the pavilion for the canonical purification. The fountain is obviously a work of European inspiration quite without the charm of earlier fountains where the water rippled over stones carved in floral patterns. Precocious and more than a little out of character with the *saray*, it simulates a golden urn on a marble pedestal in a curtained niche from which water flowed into a marble basin on the floor. It is surrounded by plaques of green and red marble and porphyry which were originally brought from Egypt by Selim I but affixed to the wall in the time of Süleyman. Over the fountain is yet another plaque bearing the *tuğra* of Mahmut II and an inscription dated 1822/3 praising him for having improved the Pavilion of the Blessed Mantle. In my opinion,

[155]

The Corridor with Pillars looking toward the door to the Golden Way and the harem. To the right of the pillars can be seen a wall of the remains of one of the Conqueror's towers.

in which I am sure I am joined by many others, what he did in adding the fountain was exactly the opposite. However, high over the marble and porphyry slabs are some nice tile circles that go back to 1608/9 in which are inscribed the names of Allah, Muhammed, and the four early caliphs in the hand of a famous calligrapher who signed himself Kemankeş. *Kemankeş* means bowman or archer. To the left one sees a rounded section protruding from the building wall. This is the remains of another of the Conqueror's watch towers.

Past the ablution fountain is a window set in a tiled recess, giving a view of the Room of the Blessed Mantle itself. It is the Supplication Window (Hacet Penceresi) where people prayed for a wish to come true—and no doubt still do. Often, for what reason I do not know, the window is closed with blinds.

Mahmut's rather ugly ablution fountain is more than compensated for by the wealth of tiles that surround the door of the Circumcision Room (Sünnet Odası) on the sea side of the corridor. At even a quick glance the brilliance of their glaze and the grace of their designs are arresting, despite some feeling of confusion from the multiplicity of panels. These tiles are worth describing in some detail, for many of them come from the best period of Ottoman tile work and are famous among authorities on Ottoman ceramics. They illustrate the sultans' predilection for rebuilding the palace. Although the Circumcision Room is itself seventeenth century, certain of the tiles are earlier and were obviously transferred from elsewhere in the palace.

Perhaps the most famous as well as the loveliest are the narrow perpendicular panels, two on either side of the door. They are blue on white, of a height that gives scope for design—five feet six inches—and show a jungle of twisting, intertwining leaves, flowers and birds flowing upward from a pair of gazelles at the foot of the panel. The head of the foremost is turned back as if to hasten his companion who is more interested in eating the foliage. These panels—plus those in the Baghdad Kiosk in the same style— can be dated with reasonable certainty to the latter half of the sixteenth century because of their resemblance to an album of drawings in the same style made for Murat III in 1575. Very likely the same artists who drew the leafy pages for the album made the designs for the tiles. This style with its movement of lancet leaves that twist and curl and penetrate one another is very old, probably originating in Central Asia and moving through centers of Turkic art until it came into flower in Istanbul in the mid-sixteenth century.

Between these leafy panels on the left of the door is a formal design, somewhat earlier, in yellow, green and white on a blue ground that is identical to the tile panels flanking the door of the Throne Room. They must have been made in the same workshop at the same time, and this one at least was originally elsewhere in the palace. They are thought to be the oldest tiles in the *saray*. Above hovers a large horizontal panel with blue tiles painted in gold that, from their similarity to some in Bursa and in the Tile Kiosk, can be dated back to the fifteenth century. Farther to the left the wall is lined with seventeenth-century tiles that afford an opportunity to compare the tile work of the various centuries.

To the right of the door is a sixteenth-century tile panel of small sprays of red and white flowers on a dark blue ground, all rising from a common source, that is very like the peacock panel in the Pavilion of the Holy Mantle and one of the panels of the Golden Way of the harem. It is composed of separate sections, and the precision with which the pieces fit is witness to the care with which they must have been made. The blue and white leaf and deer panels, on the other hand, are all one piece.

The Circumcision Room itself is generously adorned with tiles. The ceiling is painted with the same colors as the tiles so that the room is a harmonious whole. Small niches with marble faces pierce the walls. Of its two tiers of windows the lower ones are deeply set, the side walls of their recesses sprouting little fluted fountains that, the tale goes, were installed to amuse the boyish princes after they had been circumcised. The upper windows are mullioned and bordered with a stained glass that softens the light coming in from the fig tree garden.

There are two traditions as to the use of the room: one that the young princes were circumcised here, another that the sultan prayed here. However, a third possibility, bolstered by an account of von Hammer, is that the princes were brought here after the circumcision had been performed elsewhere.

In the reign of Ahmet III there was a gala circumcision festival held for four of his sons. The procession through the city boasted palm branches of such dimensions that houses had to be demolished to make room for them to pass through the streets. Within the palace tents were erected for the doctors and for the ceremony of the circumcision itself, in which a thousand boys were circumcised at the sultan's expense. After the operation at the hands of the chief surgeon the three older princes were brought to the Circumcision Room to rest. Bayezit, the youngest, had already been given back to his nurse. Later the boys, in the sultan's presence, would be entertained by strolling players and acrobatic acts which would take place on a raft off shore and which must have been witnessed from one of the shore kiosks. This entire circumcision festival has been memorialized in a book of miniatures, the *Surname (Book of Festivals)*, the text by Vehbi, an eighteenth-century poet, and the miniatures of its best copies by Levni.

A curious custom at this time was the exhibition to the chief statesmen of, as von Hammer delicately puts it, "The irrefutable indications of the competency of the surgeon, indications which the grand vizier, then the mufti and the viziers covered with heaps of gold."

According to a verse inscription by the *şeyhülislâm* and poet, Yahya Efendi, the room was built by Sultan İbrahim in 1641, perhaps to rival the Revan and Baghdad Kiosks of his predecessor.

The Circumcision Room was a favorite royal salon of Selim III. The records of his confidential secretary tell us that at six o'clock on the evening of Sunday, the twenty-seventh of March, 1791, one Mehmet Mekki Efendi was given the chief religious post of *şeyhülislâm* in this room. Selim III, in audience costume, a jeweled aigrette fastened to his turban and a *kapaniçe* or frogged robe over his shoulders, must have marched with members of his suite through the wide door at one end of the L of the Corridor with Pillars and along it to the Circumcision Room. There, seated on the sofa at the far end, he received Mehmet Mekki and the *kaymakam* (the grand vizier's assistant who took his place in Istanbul when he was out of the city). Here the *kaymakam* was clothed in a robe of honor and Mehmet Mekki handed the imperial decree which made him the most important figure in the Empire after the grand vizier. He was the chief jurist in charge of the Holy Law, and without his sanction no decree of the sultan was lawful.

Before the ceremony both Mehmet Mekki and the *kaymakam* had been perfumed with incense and served by the sword-bearer with coffee in little cups encased in metal holders in the Presentation Room of the Pavilion of the Holy Mantle. Immediately after his investiture the new *şeyhülislâm* visited the Room of the Holy Mantle itself to pray among the sacred relics.

A year later, on March 10, 1792, the Circumcision Room was the scene of another investiture when Küçük (Small) Hüseyin Pasha, husband of one of Abdülhamit I's daughters, was made *kaptan paşa*. Selim's secretary has recorded that the ceremony took place a little after two o'clock and that Küçük Hüseyin was garbed in a robe of honor.

Mustafa IV, as we have seen, was the sultan who came to the throne on the deposition of Selim III and who gave the order for Selim's execution. Toward the end of 1808, four months after Mustafa had been replaced by Mahmut II, his fate was sealed in this room his predecessor had so often

The Circumcision Room. Note the little fountains in the window embrasures.

used. Here Mahmut and Salihzade, the *şeyhülislâm* of the time, the *kaymakam* and other officials gathered. They discussed their worries over the disorder the partisans of Mustafa were creating and came to the conclusion that an end could be put to them only by the execution of the ex-sultan. Salihzade gave a *fetva* or legal permission for the execution. The head gardener and the palace mutes were summoned, and the order for execution handed to them. They then proceeded to the Cage where Mustafa was living and led him out to the boxwood garden nearby. There the mutes strangled him with their shawl-belts.

It was in the Circumcision Room too that in 1826 Mahmut II made the final decision that had long been on his mind to eliminate the Janissaries. They had killed Alemdar early in Mahmut's reign and had never ceased their trouble-making. Moreover it was obvious that they were no longer of any use in the field and that the Empire needed a modern, trained army. Mahmut eventually chose 7,650 of the best Janissaries, gave them the old title of Eşkinci which originally meant irregular cavalryman, and had them secretly trained in modern warfare. Meanwhile he kept changing the Janissary Ağa and other high officials, including the grand vizier and the *şeyhülislâm*, until the important posts were all filled with men who supported him.

Becoming suspicious, the regular Janissaries rioted in the spring of 1826 and announced they were going to kill the grand vizier, the Janissary Ağa, and all who supported the Eşkinci program. When word of this reached the grand vizier he called a meeting of statesmen at the Yalı Kiosk on the shore and sent word to Mahmut, who by then was living in a palace on the Bosphorus at Beşiktaş. At the same time he alerted the officers of the newly trained army to come to Topkapı with their men.

The Janissaries were told they had to accept modern methods but they insisted on retaining the old ones.

At this point a series of meetings was held—the new military in the Reception Room of the Privy Chamber (Arzhane of the Pavilion of the Blessed Mantle), and the statesmen in the Hall of the Divan, until Mahmut arrived and began to call the officials into the Circumcision Room. There the fateful decision was taken. They all agreed that either the Janissaries had to go or the regime would go. The *şeyhülislâm* issued a *fetva* giving the Holy Law's permission to abolish the Janissaries. The Sacred Standard was taken from its box and handed to the grand vizier, and a town-crier sent through Istanbul and its suburbs calling the people of Islam to rally to it. They responded by gathering before the Imperial Gate in the thousands. After a very moving prayer the Sacred Standard was set up at the pulpit of the Sultan Ahmet Mosque near the palace, and weapons were issued to the people. They would march on the Janissaries.

Mahmut wanted to march with them, but he was persuaded to wait in the pavilion of the Imperial Gate so that he might be able to issue new orders should the leaders of the attack fall.

The loyal forces, with the armed populace following them, encircled the Janissaries' barracks in the Et Meydanı. The Janissaries were given a chance to surrender and refused. Then the artillery opened up with its cannons. The shots penetrated the barracks and set them on fire. Now there was panic within. Some of the Janissaries tried to flee but as they had given no mercy they received none. Raiding parties cleaned up other groups about the city, and it was not long before all the Janissaries in the Empire were disbanded. It was on Thursday, June 16, 1826, that the action started. By Saturday the Janissaries of Istanbul no longer existed. Mahmut therefore ordered the Sacred Standard returned to the palace and set up in front of the Gate of Felicity, where incense was burned and the Koran read.

The padishah stayed in Topkapı for a time and had tents erected in the First Court in which the statesmen worked until the city calmed down. The attack on the Janissaries that followed the decision taken in the Circumcision Room has become known in Ottoman history as the Auspicious Event (Vaka-ı hayriye). Straightway Mahmut organized a new army, the Victorious Troops of Muhammed (Asâkir-i Mansure-i Muhammediye) for the defense of the sorely beset Ottoman Empire.

Outside the Circumcision Room the Corridor with Pillars angles to the left. Its sea side looks out onto a court that borders the Room with Mirrors, and it ends with a door to the Golden Way of the harem. At the end near the harem one can make out two sides of one of the old stone towers that go back to the Conqueror. The rest of it is incorporated into an entry-way to the Mirrored Room Abdülhamit I built in the late eighteenth century. It may be in this tower, the museum authorities think, that Sultan İbrahim was killed after his dethronement in the seventeenth century.

The museum has recently removed the windows that were a late addition to the Corridor with Pillars. On this side one can now walk out onto a little terrace and look down onto a garden. The museum architect is soon to delve beneath its earth and expects to find paving. This will indicate that the garden was once a courtyard, perhaps for the building which has left traces in the wall that separates the garden from the harem. A marble doorway that goes nowhere and two tiled niches are set high in the wall, which rises above a ramp that has obviously been broken by the pillars that support the Mirrored Room. Where this ramp originally began the museum has yet to learn, but under it runs the ramp of the Conqueror we have mentioned. All this indicates that there have been many changes in this section of the palace.

The Corridor with Pillars goes back at least to the end of the sixteenth century. It was here in 1599 during the reign of Mehmet III that Thomas Dallam of England installed and played an organ sent as a present to that sultan by Elizabeth of England. Dallam describes the corridor and his experiences in his diary:

> This great house it selfe hathe in it tow rankes of marble pillors; the pettestales of them ar made of brass and double gilte. The wales [walls] on 3 sides of the house are waled but halfe waye to the eaves; the other halfe is open; but yf any storme or great wynde should hapen, they can sodonly Let fale suche hanginges made of cotten wolle for that purpose as will kepe out all kindes of wethere, and sudenly they can open them againe. The fourthe side of the house, which is close and joynethe unto another house, the wale is made of purfeare [porphyry], or suche kinde of stone as when a man walketh by it he maye se him selfe tharin. Upon the grounde, not only in this house, but all other that I se in the Serraliae [Seraglio], we treade upon ritch silke garpites, one of them as muche as four or six men can carrie. Thare weare in this house nether stouls, tables, or formes, only one coutche of estate. Thare is one side of it a fishe ponde, that is full of fishe that be of divers collores.

Dallam went to the *saray* every day for a month to put up the organ and get it working. All this time he was attended by pages of the Palace School who did their best to persuade him to stay in the service of the sultan. The organ could be played mechanically as well as manually, and on its first view by Mehmet III it was arranged that it should be played mechanically and that Dallam should stay out of sight.

> Firste the clocke strouke 22; then The chime of 16 bels went of, and played a songe of 4 partes. That beinge done, tow personagis which stood upon to corners of the seconde storie, houldinge tow silver trumpetes in there handes, did lift them to theire heades, and sounded a

tantarra. Than the muzicke went of, and the orgon played a song of 5 partes twyse over. In the tope of the orgon, being 16 foute hie, did stande a holly bushe full of blacke birds and thrushis, which at the end of the musick did singe and shake theire wynges.

Mehmet was so fascinated he demanded to know who could play the organ's keys, and when told only the man who had set it up, he commanded Dallam to an audience. Dallam had been told by the English ambassador that one must never turn one's back on the sultan, and so he was more than a little worried throughout his performance.

When I came within the Dore, That which I did se was verrie wonderfull unto me. I cam in direcktly upon the Grand Sinyore's ryghte hande, som 16 of my passis from him, but he would not turne his head to louke upon me. He satt in greate state, yeat the sighte of him was nothinge in Comparrison of the traine that stood behinde him, the sighte whearof did make me almoste to thinke that I was in another worlde. The Grand Sinyor satt still, behouldinge the presente which was befor him, and I stood daslinge my eyes with loukinge upon his people that stood be-hinde him, the which was four hundrethe persons in number. Tow hundrethe of them were his princepall padgis, the yongest of them 16 yeares of age, some 20, and some 30. They weare apparled in ritche clothe of goulde made in gowns to the mydlegge. . . . Those 200 weare all verrie proper men [*i.e.*, not eunuchs] and Christians borne.

The third hundrethe weare Dum men, that could nether heare nor speake, and theye weare likwyse in gouns of riche Clothe of gould and Cordivan buskins. . . . Som of them had haukes in theire fistes.

The fourthe hundrethe weare all dwarffs, bige-bodied men, but verrie low of stature. Everie Dwarfe did weare a simmeterrie [scimitar] by his side, and they weare also apareled in gowns of Clothe of gould. . . .

When I had stode almost one quarter of an houre behouldinge this wonder full sighte, I harde the Grand Sinyore speake unto the Coppa-gaw, [*kapıcı* or gatekeeper], who stood near unto him. Than the Cop-pagaw cam unto me, and touke my cloake from aboute me, and laye it Doune upon the Carpites, and bid me go and playe on the organ; but I refused to do so, because the Grand Sinyor satt so neare the place wheare I should playe that I could not com at it, but I muste needes turne my backe Towardes him and touche his Kne with my britchis, which no man, in paine of deathe, myghte dow, savinge only the Coppagaw. So he smyled, and lett me stande a little. Than the Grand Sinyor spoake againe, and the Coppagaw, with a merrie countenance, bid me go with good curridge, and thruste me on. When I cam verrie neare the Grand Sinyor, I bowed my heade as low as my kne, not movinge my cape, and turned my backe righte towardes him, and touched his kne with my britchis.

He satt in a verrie ritche Chaire of estate, upon his thumbe a ringe with a diamon in it halfe an inche square, a faire simeterie by his side, a bow, and a quiver of Arros.

He satt so righte behind me that he could not se what I did; tharfore he stood up, and his Coppagaw removed his Chaire to one side, wher he myghte se my handes; but, in his risinge from his chaire, he gave me a thruste forwardes, which he could not otherwyse dow, he satt so neare me; but I thought he had bene drawinge his sorde to cut of my heade.

I stood thar playinge suche things as I coulde untill the clock strouke, and then I boued my heade as low as I coulde, and wente from him with my back towardes him. . . . Than I saw the Grand Sinyor put his hande behind him full of goulde, which the Coppagaw Received, and brought unto me fortie and five peecis of goulde called chickers [perhaps *şikke*, the Turkish word for coin], and than was I put out againe wheare I came in, beinge not a little joyfull of my good suckses.

In Dallam's day the Corridor with Pillars had neither the Circumcision Room nor the Revan Kiosk, although there seems to have been something else in place of the latter. The Pavilion of the Blessed Mantle, the Conqueror's Privy Chamber, was there however, the other house of which he speaks, to which the "fourthe side . . . joynethe."

Across from the Pavilion of the Blessed Mantle on the highest point of the *saray* hill lies the Revan Kiosk on the site of an older kiosk probably of the time of the Conqueror. In the eighteenth century it began to be called the Sarık Odası (the Room of the Turban) because the padishah's turbans were kept there on stands of silver- and gold-covered boxwood. It is a building of irregular shape, almost a smaller edition of the more famous Baghdad Kiosk. Its outside walls are tiled in light blue in the upper third and set with colored marble below. Inside, tiled walls, mother-of-pearl window-shutters and cabinet doors, bronze fireplace and floral-decorated ceiling all resemble the Baghdad Kiosk, although it does not have anything that can rival the deer and vase panels of the latter. Yet the room has its own charm, enhanced by the little niches tiled with flower and plant forms.

In the early days of this century the Revan Kiosk was in such a sad state of disrepair that Abdurrahman Şeref said of it: "The roof has been leaking for many years; the priceless paintings on the soffits of the projections are deteriorated. The parchment is rotting and hanging down; the mother-of-pearl inlays are falling off the window-shutters. Even the planks of the floor are damaged." So little did the Turks of the late nineteenth and early twentieth centuries value their artistic heritage. The pendulum has fortunately swung back, and the Revan Kiosk is restored and open. Now the light filters through the mullioned windows and shines on the tiles of the wall and on the bronze chimney piece. The inlays are intact again and add their gleam to the iridescence that here and there illuminates a room made dusky by the deep eaves that shadow its windows. Ottoman rooms were particularly notable for their ceilings, and the Revan's does not disappoint one. It is truly Ottoman, a central panel of gold decoration on a blue ground surrounded by colorful floral and leafy borders.

Murat IV had had this kiosk built in 1635 to celebrate his capture of the city of Erivan (Revan) from Persia. He had carefully prepared for this campaign, even confiscating great fortunes to get the money to equip his troops. Finally he marched out to Erzurum in eastern Anatolia where the Sacred Standard had preceded him with the grand vizier who was awaiting him. From there the army marched east and laid siege to Erivan. For a week they besieged it. Then Murat, growing impatient, called each of his generals to him. To one he said: "Here is the day to display all your valiancy"; to another: "Take care that the young cavalry confided to your care does not pull back an inch"; and to the Ağa of the Janissaries: "Listen, Ağa, the night rounds of Istanbul and the bastinadoes given drunks are not works of valor. Here is the place to show a brave heart." To the soldiers he dispensed money—thirty or forty piasters for each enemy head; fifty ducats to each man who lost a horse; twenty-five piasters to each man who was wounded; a ducat each to those who collected the balls of the enemy batteries. Mixing his metaphors but appealing to their courage, he cried, "Do not let up, my wolves! The hour has come to display your wings, my falcons!"

For another week the Ottoman artillery kept up the bombardment, and then on the eighth of August, 1635, the enemy capitulated. Not only the city but the treasure of Erivan became Murat's. The following Friday he

NECATI ORBAY

The Revan Kiosk and the marble pool which usually spouts water.

sent messengers back to Istanbul with orders to have the city illuminated for a week in celebration of the imperial victory.

Murat IV had come to the throne a youth, but as he grew to manhood his capacity for anger grew with him. By this time twenty-six years old, tall, black-eyed, black-bearded and fierce-looking, he had become so cruel he accompanied this order with the command to kill the brothers he had promised a council on foot only a few years ago to protect. Two of them, Bayezit and Süleyman, were strangled. A few years later Kasım, a third brother, would be executed. Until now the feelings of the populace, with whom the princes were popular, had stayed his determination. Now, with a victory to celebrate, he felt the people would pass over the deaths of the princes. In this he deceived himself. It is said that the illumination of the city for the victory was no match for the light of the torches that accompanied the funeral of the princes. It was in the Revan Kiosk, where Murat IV had had his brother Kasım strangled, that he himself died.

The Revan Kiosk was twice the setting for scenes of vengeance. Ahmet III had been put on the throne by the Janissaries who had deposed his brother, Mustafa II, in 1703. Flushed with success, they had attempted to run roughshod over the administration, even inciting the gardeners, one of whose duties was as palace guards, to rebellion. Ahmet III dismissed seven hundred of the gardeners and replaced them with Christian conscripts. This was the last time Christian youths were conscripted. He then set about getting rid of the other trouble-makers. Chief among them was the Ağa of the Janissaries, Çalık, who had arrogated unto himself certain privileges including that of entertaining the sultan, and had even tried to take precedence over the grand vizier. Ahmet invited the viziers, Çalık and the chief members of the *ulema* or religious institution to the Revan Kiosk for a lecture on religious traditions. The men left their horses at the Garden Gate at the foot of the Fourth Court, but once they were inside the kiosk the mounts were moved to the Imperial Gate at the opposite side of the palace. According to von Hammer, "At the moment the assembly congregated the *kaftancı* threw a *kaftan* [robe] over the shoulders of Tschalik [Çalık] while the grand vizier declared that the sultan had named him governor of Cyprus." This meant banishment from court. " 'What is my crime?' cried Tschalik, full of fury, and immediately ran down to the Garden Gate in the hope of finding his horse. Foiled in his attempt he . . . hastened to the Cannon Gate and mounted the galley that awaited him. The chamberlain who accompanied him was at the same time the bearer of his sentence of death, rendered by the sultan. . . . The execution of Tschalik was followed by that of the other chiefs of the rebels."

This took place in 1703. Twenty-seven years later, in 1730, Nevşehirli Ibrahim Pasha prayed in this room with some of the *ulema*, falling to his knees and touching his turbaned head to the floor in the prescribed Muslim ritual, while rebels led by Patrona Halil cried for that head. "I am a dead man," Nevşehirli told the clergy. "It is now your duty to save the sultan." They were able to save his life but not his throne.

That same year a bloodier scene was enacted here. Patrona Halil was summoned to the Revan Kiosk by Mahmut I whom his rebellion had enthroned. Like successful rebels before him he and his intimates had been riding high. Patrona Halil had accompanied Mahmut to the suburb of Eyüp for the traditional ceremony when the sultan was girt with the sword of Osman, the first Ottoman sultan. He had put his men in many high offices, made a Greek butcher prince of Moldavia, an Ottoman tributary in Europe, and even taken part in the deliberations of the Divan. The *valide sultan* had felt constrained to send sherbet to a concubine of his who had given birth. With all this arrogance, a counter force sprang up, put together largely by

The interior of the Revan Kiosk off the Corridor with Pillars.

the chief black eunuch, Beşir Ağa, who enlisted the help of a Janissary officer, Pehlivan Halil. (*Pehlivan* means wrestler and hence strong.) Under Pehlivan's direction a trap was set for Patrona Halil and his cronies. After a Divan meeting Patrona and his principal partisans were invited into the House of Felicity to be clothed in robes of honor by the padishah, an honor

Patrona had long coveted. Meanwhile, the previous night, Pehlivan Halil had secreted thirty armed men in the Circumcision Room and the Revan Kiosk. First Patrona was escorted into the kiosk, where the sultan was seated on a sofa. There, in the sultan's presence, Pehlivan Halil set upon him. Patrona was supposedly unarmed, being in the presence of the padishah, but he had a dagger hidden in his belt and attempted to protect himself with it. It was useless. Pehlivan cut off first his arm and then his head. His immediate followers were put to death in like manner, twenty-six of them, called one by one into the House of Felicity to be overcome by the forces hidden there. Circumcision Room, Revan Kiosk and the Corridor with Pillars outside them must have run with blood.

In the eighteenth century the Revan Kiosk became a library called the Library of the Privy Chamber, its cabinets filled with books at the order of Abdülhamit I and Selim III. Eventually it housed more than a thousand, many of them rare works, all now in the New Library. It had, for example, the collection of the poems by Süleyman which I mentioned examining in the New Library. The book was made only a year before his death. Besides poetry, the Revan Kiosk held books on religion and history. It was not unusual for several copies to be made of a celebrated work, and in the Revan Kiosk were seventeen of the history of Raşit, an official chronicler of the eighteenth century. In it too was a famous map, half of a world map made by Piri Reis in 1513. (*Reis* means head man or commander.) He studied twenty odd maps for it, including one of the western hemisphere drawn by Christopher Columbus in 1489. He probably acquired it during a raid on the coast of Spain. The extant half of the map shows the east coast of America and on its left margin contains a notation of Columbus' discovery.

Piri Reis was a Turk from Gallipoli who first went to sea under his Turkish corsair uncle and later was incorporated into the Ottoman navy, playing his part in the victories that built up Ottoman sea strength in the sixteenth century. It was under Selim I that he drew the world map and presented it to that sultan on his victories in Egypt. The half now in the New Library came to light in 1929 but the other half has never been found.

The Circumcision Room, the Revan Kiosk, and the Corridor with Pillars are today under the roof that extends from the Pavilion of the Blessed Mantle, though each was built at a different time and for a different purpose. From the corridor one can either go through a door in the east wall and down some steps into what used to be the Tulip Garden, or simply step out onto the marble terrace of the Fourth Court.

THE FOURTH COURT

THE FOURTH COURT bears no resemblance to the other courts of the *saray*, which are rectangular, on one level, and surrounded by porticoed buildings. It is instead a collection of gardens and kiosks on various levels extending from the northern end of the Third Court to the far inner wall of the palace. Here the ground begins to slope down toward the water, and so to reach it one steps down from the Third Court either by a stairway between the Painting Section and the Treasury of the Holy Mantle, a passageway that tunnels under the Administration Building, or the stairs from the Corridor with Pillars. Since the Turks called these courts palaces, this was the Dördüncü Yer or Fourth Place. (Also, by beginning to count with the Second Court, it was sometimes called the Third Place.)

If one takes the route under the Administration building one arrives at a terrace with a stunning view up the Bosphorus and down the Marmara and across to the Asiatic shore, but a place where the immediate buildings are of little historical interest. In a corner on the east is the small simple Mosque on the Terrace (Sofa Camii) with a single minaret. Today the word *sofa* means great hall or corridor, but in the old days it also designated a terrace. The mosque was erected by Mahmut II and rebuilt, according to an inscription over the door, by Abdülmecit in 1858/9 for the attendants of the Inner Palace. Until Mahmut's time there had stood here the Kiosk of the Sword-Bearer (Silâhtar Ağa Köşkü) which he had pulled down in 1809 because it had been the scene of the decision to dethrone Selim III. It is a sad-looking little place except for its single minaret which rises sturdily.

Just beyond the Mosque on the Terrace, in a superb location on the edge of a palisade that overlooks the water, stands the Mecidiye (Mejidiyeh), on the site of two former kiosks, the Tent Kiosk (Çadır Köşkü) and the Kiosk of the Third Place (Uçüncü Yer Köşkü). Its style of architecture and furnishings, which are mid-nineteenth century French, have nothing to do with the rest of the palace, and it is not without reason that it is sometimes called the New Kiosk. Abdülmecit built it just before Dolmabahçe, the wedding-cake palace on the European shore of the Bosphorus. Both were the work of an Armenian family of architects named Balyan who long served the sultans. It was a time of Westernization movements in architecture as well as in politics, and also in living habits. European sofas came in to replace the Ottoman divans that had ranged along entire walls. The women of the court and

The Mecidiye Kiosk in the Fourth Court.

[1 7 2]

the elite began to sit on chairs instead of cushions on the floor. The *mangal* or brazier at which most people warmed themselves rose from resting on a large tray on the floor to standing on legs so that its warmth could the more easily reach the level of sofa or chair. And so the Mecidiye is filled with a collection of French furniture of the time of Louis Philippe that bears witness to the changes in Ottoman court life in the mid-nineteenth century. Up close, the ornateness of the building defeats itself, but seen from afar, as from a ferry to Asia, the clumsiness of the stonework fades into the façade, and it stands out on its cliff in noble silhouette. Though the ground floor is not open to the public, the lower floor has been turned into a charming restaurant with a fine view of the Marmara and Bosphorus. It is a branch of the well-known Konyalı Restaurant in Sirkeci.

The main room of the Mecidiye is very large and allowed Abdülmecit to look over a good part of the waterways of Istanbul. The entire building has European fireplaces with mantels instead of the old hooded Ottoman *ocak*s, and over the mantels of the main room huge gilt mirrors hang. Tall curlicue candleholders and chandeliers provided light. The chairs are gilt-framed and many of them upholstered in old Ottoman designs. At present they are being re-upholstered in fabrics especially made to imitate the old ones. Many of the pieces of furniture are handsome for their time, some inlaid with tortoiseshell over which a gold pattern has been laid. A huge standing portrait of Abdülmecit hangs in the room to the right of the grand salon.

The entrances to the kiosk are all at the back, facing a pleasing little garden which contains a voluted marble fountain over which a willow drapes itself. Carved in low relief at the bottom of its basin is a motif rare in Ottoman art. It consists of a fish, a crab, and possibly an eel, an old design used by the Mamelukes of Egypt and the Timurides of Iran. How it came to be used in this pool one does not know. A few fish appear in some of the earliest pieces of Ottoman ceramics excavated in the old tile-making town of Iznik in Anatolia. The fountain must surely antedate the Mecidiye. Perhaps here the earliest and latest Ottoman meet.

A little back of the Mecidiye stands a tiny, equally French kiosk, the Esvap Odası or Wardrobe Room. It has been suggested that officials were clothed here in their ceremonial robes before an audience in the Mecidiye. However, Abdülmecit and his court wore Western dress, which means that the time of the old robes of honor was over. It is more likely that dignitaries left their outer clothing and adjusted their decorations here.

[1 7 3]

Down a few steps from the Mecidiye garden an incline leads to a gate to Gülhane Parki, Rose House Park, now public, which in the old days was the outer garden in the Fifth Place or Fifth Court of the palace. Both sides of the gate, called the Third Gate (Üçüncü Kapı), are flanked by guardhouses in the style of the Mecidiye.

Across the path and up a few steps lie two gardens separated by a small square building and a wall. The building is the Room of the Chief Physician (Hekimbaşı Odası). It was also called the Tower of the Chief Tutor (Baş Lâla Kulesi), because it was under his jurisdiction. Today it is only the remnant of a building that was one of the Conqueror's towers and then probably higher than at present. The chief physician looked after the health of the sultan and the imperial family. Here under his eyes and those of the chief tutor the palace drugs were prepared, mixed and sealed in bottles, jars and boxes. (This pharmacy was in addition to the one in the Commissariat.) Every year at Nevruz, the Persian New Year which falls in the spring, the chief physician sent gifts of aromatic pastes to the sultan, the princesses, the kadıns, the grand vizier, and other important people, in return receiving presents and a robe of honor. From the time of the Conqueror the palace always had a great many physicians in attendance. Under Murat III there were sixty of them, some Turks, some Jews. In later years the doctors tended to be Europeans. The chief physician apparently changed frequently. Although there were twenty-three sultans from the Conqueror through Mahmut II, there were seventy-two chief physicians.

The chief physician was a member of the *ulema*, medicine then being a preserve of the religious establishment, as was all education. This truncated tower remained his headquarters until some time in the late years of the Empire when it was used for the cleaning of palace arms and still later as a music conservatory. Today it is empty.

Extending from this tower between the two gardens as far as the Kiosk on the Terrace is a very old wall. Until late times it was crenellated, but Abdülhamit II had its teeth filled in to obstruct the view from the Tulip Garden to the Palace of Yıldız where he lived. Actually Yıldız is far away on a steep rise up the Bosphorus, but so fearful of assassination was Abdülhamit that he went to great lengths to protect himself. The wall is very thick, and the windows within its arches are barred. It suggests part of an early defense arrangement, along with the tower.

The upper part of the two gardens, a more or less quadrangle that spreads from the Mecidiye terrace to the Revan Kiosk, was the famous

*The tiered marble fountain below the Baghdad Kiosk
in what was once the Tulip Garden.*

Tulip Garden of the early eighteenth century. The tulip was much used in Ottoman decoration, especially in tile work. Because the word Allah, when written in Ottoman letters, was thought to have a shape resembling the tulip, the flower was considered particularly suitable for decoration in mosques, fountains (which have a religious significance since giving water to a wayfarer is a pious act in Islam) and tombs. It developed from a popular motif to a craze, and the years from 1718 to 1730 in the reign of Ahmet III are known as the Tulip Period (Lâle Devri). Rare varieties were grown, fancy names were given them such as Ruby-Colored Dart, and so outrageous did the prices become they had to be regulated.

It was at this time that Ahmet III had this garden planted to tulips, undoubtedly the rarest he and his grand vizier and son-in-law, Nevşehirli İbrahim Pasha, could find in the market. Here on an April evening in the full of the moon Ahmet held the Festival of Tulips, which he added to the court calendar and which became one of the most important fêtes of a period noted for its pleasure gatherings. Vases of tulips interspersed with colored glass lamps sat upon row after row of shelves that had been installed for the festival. Here and there, to add brilliance, stood glass globes of colored liquids. Bird cages swung from the branches of trees, the birds adding their song to the merriment. These entertainments were çırağan (chirahan), which means torch and thus illumination.

On certain evenings of the çırağan the sultan proclaimed *halvet*, a state of privacy when men were banished from the fête. All the garden gates were closed. The Bostancıs or gardeners stood guard outside them and the black eunuchs inside, so that the women might move freely within. There the girls ran among the tulips and competed for the sweets that had been hidden here and there. Laughter rang out. Music and dancing gave gaiety. And all did their best to entertain the only man in their lives, the sultan.

Jean-Claude Flachat, a Frenchman who lived in Istanbul during the reign following Ahmet III's, has left a description of these evenings in which he says the sultan invited the girl of his choice into a temporary kiosk that had been set up in the garden, closed the curtains and presumably made love to her then and there. It makes good copy but reads to me like a Western invention. In the first place Flachat's information was necessarily second hand. Secondly the proceeding seems entirely un-Ottoman, being without the ceremony that surrounded everything in the sultan's life. Although a sultan, especially Ahmet III, was not hesitant about taking to bed whatever girl caught his fancy, it was done privately and almost according to ritual. For him to pick a girl out of a crowd and take her in a tent-like affair around which other women were scattered simply does not fit the *saray* pattern, especially as his *kadıns*, who were often jealous of competition, were among the throng. It may well be, however, that at such a fête the sultan was attracted by a girl whom he later invited into his bed in the seclusion of the harem.

The feast of the tulips was celebrated into the reign of Ahmet's successor, Mahmut I, but thereafter abandoned along with the tulip craze. It is unlikely that the tulip gardens were any longer maintained in quite their former glory. Today their site is planted with roses.

At the end of the wall lies the Kiosk on the Terrace (Sofa Köşkü). It is often attributed to Ahmet III, although an inscription on its doorway credits him only with its renovation—in 1704/5. There seems to have been an earlier kiosk here, and perhaps what happened was that Ahmet had it completely rebuilt. The earlier one is mentioned in old chronicles as the Sofa Köşkü, from which the present one must have taken its name. It is also known as the Kara (Dark) Mustafa Pasha Kiosk, but for that name there is no satisfactory explanation.

The kiosk is a wooden building, the only one of wood outside the harem. The interior is Turkish rococo and very ornate, probably dating from a renovation in 1752/3. Yet it must have been a pleasant place in which to converse or rest on its long divans. Selim III found it so and on April 15, 1797, held an evening of music and "tulip" entertainment here. (Just what "tulip" entertainment was in Selim III's time I have never been able to find out.) It is also a pleasing daytime room. The tall windows that reach from the floor almost to the ceiling look out onto gardens. Its central panels painted in red and gilt liven up its interior. The religious inscriptions without which no Ottoman building was complete run over the panels, and above the inscriptions is hung a description of the personal appearance of the Prophet, a *hilye-i şerif*, by a poet named Hakanî Mehmet. The room is divided into three sections by low walls of gilded, red-painted wood looking something like the sides of a fancy sleigh, and in the center of one division sits a gilt bronze brazier, the gift of Louis XV to Mahmut I in 1742. On each of two walls is hung a *kavukluk*, a stand for a *kavuk* or turban. One of these has a large shelf, presumably for the sultan's turban, and under it two smaller shelves perhaps for the turbans of young princes. The room's ceiling is quite different from earlier ones, being composed of three panels decorated with crisscross lines instead of floral motifs. One finds this type in several

NECATI ORBAY

The interior of the Kiosk on the Terrace looking toward the former Tulip Garden.

rooms with eighteenth-century decoration. At the Marmara side of the kiosk, past a stairway, is a small room which may have been a bedroom, although who slept there no one knows.

In 1710 Ahmet III held a council in this kiosk attended by the grand vizier, pashas, high members of the religious institution and others to decide how to react to the many provocations and violations of the frontier by Russia. The şeyhülislâm gave the word that according to Holy Law war was not only legitimate but necessary, and so war was declared against the Russia of Peter the Great. Thirty thousand Janissaries were enlisted, ten thousand infantrymen, and seven thousand gunners. A fleet of shallow-draft boats was gathered to navigate the Sea of Azov. The Ottoman forces were so overpowering the Russians soon sued for peace, to which the grand vizier acquiesced. It turned out to be a mistake, for it gave the Russians time to mobilize for the next war that broke out soon thereafter. In those days Russians and Ottomans were fighting for control of the Crimea and the Black Sea.

It was in this kiosk that one of the Crimean khans, Devlet Girey, a few years later warned Ahmet III: "My padishah, we must not trust peace with Russia; the Crimea is even now passing out of our hands, and all Turkey in Europe is on its way to being lost. The ultimate goal of the Russians is Constantinople!"

There are two doors to the Kiosk on the Terrace, one on a level with the Tulip Garden, the other down seventeen steps to a lower garden where a pool still lies along the old arched wall that separates the terraces. On the level of the Tulip Garden, just outside the kiosk, there is located the loveliest of the palace's outdoor fountains, a tiered affair surmounted by a pierced marble ball. The water drops musically from layer to layer of carved marble. Its first home was one of the destroyed kiosks on Saray-burnu (Palace Point). As one turns to the right of this fountain and passes on the left the foundation of the Revan Kiosk, one mounts a flight of steps to the marble terrace outside the Corridor with Pillars. Here tucked into a corner beside the Revan Kiosk is a pool enclosed by a low pierced marble balustrade. In it near the wall of the kiosk rises a small square fountain with many jets from which the water spurts to fall into and out of the fountain and into the pool. A graceful balcony protrudes into it from the Corridor with Pillars. This is one of the most restful and charming spots of the *saray*. With the pool on one side, the view of the Marmara ahead, and the exotic Baghdad Kiosk to one's right, one can easily forget the modern city of Istanbul and be carried back to the days when long-robed figures trod this marble floor and the sultan in his splendid costume sat in the little bower of the İftariye at the terrace edge.

In the early seventeenth century before any of the terrace buildings went up, there was a very much larger pool here fed by thirty fountains. The Venetian envoy of the time, Ottaviano Bon, says:

> And in the Lake there was a little Boat, the which (as I was enformed) the Grand Signior did oftentimes goe into with his Mutes and Buffones, to make them row up and downe, and to sport with them, making them leape into the water; and many times as he walked with them above upon the sides of the Lake, he would throw them downe into it, and plunge them head over eares.

[179]

The İftariye is the place of the *iftar*, the breaking of the fast at sundown during Ramazan. It is a small balcony covered with a dome of gilt bronze supported by four slender columns, its sides open, now a favorite resting place for tourists. Two gardens lie below it, on two different levels; the lower one has at one end a gate called, for no known reason, the Elephant Gate (Fiil Kapısı). These are the same gardens that can be seen from the terrace of the Corridor with Pillars. In the distance lie the Marmara and the Asiatic shore. The İftariye was built by Sultan İbrahim who came here to break his fast and to be congratulated by the palace *ağas* after *bayram* prayer while the palace orchestra played and the Cannon Gate sounded off its guns. There are the usual inscriptions in the balcony. They run around the inside roof and consist of a poem with frequent interpolations of short prayers such as: "O Lord, bless him!" and "O Lord, make him mighty!" Abdurrahman Şeref thought these some of the charms made up for İbrahim by Cinci (Jinji) Hüseyin, a religious fanatic who was one of İbrahim's favorites.

Just to the right, beside the terrace, rises the famous Baghdad Kiosk, perhaps the finest example of seventeenth-century Ottoman building to be found. Octagonal in shape and limned against a backdrop of sea and sky, it remains untouched by later Europeanizing hands. Its dome, its broad eaves, its slender columns and rounded arches, its exterior walls half tile and half marble are all reminders that Ottoman architecture had a distinction of its own and that it belonged to the East. The kiosk rests on a foundation in the garden below from which it rises to such a height that the rooms and porch are level with the terrace.

The kiosk is surrounded by a balcony that, like many of the palace porches, for a time was enclosed in glass. From this the main door opens guarded by the prayer, in Persian, "May this door always be open with prosperity." The room has four projections and four recesses, and every inch of them is ornamented. Like most old Ottoman rooms of the palace, its walls are divided by a tile inscription at the point where the arches of the vault rise toward the central dome. Below it are the blue and white lancet-leafed panels. They antedate the kiosk and probably came from the same workshop and the same period as those at the Circumcision Room. The only difference is that these panels are taller, being eight to nine feet high, are composed of several pieces, and in some of them the foliage rises not from gazelles but from a vase. Above the calligraphic band tiles in a variety of floral patterns line the arches and the pendentives and the spaces between the upper windows, all predominantly blue and green and bathed by the blue light that enters through the colored panes in the upper windows. Below the frieze are window-shutters and cabinets with mother-of-pearl inlaid doors in a pattern of discs, and niches framed in squares softened by carved and inlaid front pieces. Their backs are tiled. One intruding wall is commanded by a tall bronze chimney piece. In spite of the extent and variety of its decoration there is repose in this room because of its height, its recesses, and the fact that its decorations are kept to small patterns. The dome is worth craning one's neck to see, for it is painted on gazelle skin in the old floral motifs that make it quite distinct from the ceiling of the Kiosk on the Terrace.

The calligraphic frieze that runs around the room in white on a blue ground is in Arabic, which the sultans could read, having been taught it in

The exterior of the Baghdad Kiosk from the marble terrace.

NECATI ORBAY

their youth in the Princes' School, and repeats some of the most famous verses of the Koran. Among them is the Verse of the Throne, considered the most sacred and recited at the end of each ritual prayer. Because it is central to the religion that was so deeply ingrained in the Ottomans, I quote it here:

> Allah! There is no God save Him, the Alive, the Eternal. Neither slumber nor sleep overtaketh Him. Unto Him belongeth whatsoever is in the heavens and whatsoever is in the earth. Who is he that intercedeth with Him save by His leave? He knoweth that which is in front of them and that which is behind them, while they encompass nothing of His knowledge save what He will. His throne includeth the heavens and the earth, and He is never weary of preserving them. He is the Sublime, the Tremendous.

It was as familiar to the Ottomans as the Twenty-Third Psalm is to us.

The interior of the Baghdad Kiosk is furnished in the sparse Ottoman manner, with divans in the recesses and a brazier, perhaps a museum addition, in the center. At one side stands a screen of intricately carved woodwork with mother-of-pearl inlay handicrafted by Abdülhamit II. He used to come here first whenever he visited the Pavilion of the Blessed Mantle, but instead of resting inside the kiosk, says Abdurrahman Şeref, "He had a part of the portico closed in, a sofa, several armchairs, and a mirror there [the mirror is perhaps significant for viewing what was behind him], and also a vulgar stove installed. He had the window curtains drawn close and stayed there in that dark and narrow place." Why he felt safer there on the narrow portico rather than in the spacious kiosk is a mystery, except that perhaps the kiosk had too many windows to suit him. Such an enclosure remains at the back of the kiosk, out of sight of the visitor. He also had the stone arcade of the foundation filled in, probably so that no one could get underneath the kiosk to plant a bomb there. One was actually placed in his carriage, but he was fortunately out of it when the thing went off.

The kiosk became a library under Abdülhamit I and Selim III, and though it never held as many volumes as the Revan Kiosk it had a variety of books: many literary works, thirty-eight Korans, a collection of the *kanuns* or laws of Süleyman, and a renowned work called the *Asafname* or *Book of Asaf* (Asaf was the wise vizier of Solomon and hence a model for all viziers), a treatise on how a grand vizier should conduct himself, written by Lutfi Pasha, a dismissed grand vizier of Süleyman.

The interior of the Baghdad Kiosk, showing the massive bronze chimney piece and the elaborate decoration of the room.

Apparently people could be as little trusted with books then as now. In 1790 Selim III issued a decree tightening the regulations as to who might have permission to read the books in the Baghdad and Revan Kiosks. Some people had been preempting them and selling them in the bazaar.

Momentous occasions may have taken place in the Baghdad Kiosk, but they have not come down to us. We know only that it was here the sultan sometimes received his officials, where he took his *keyif* (pleasure), probably held discussions on literary or religious matters, a favorite pastime of many sultans, and read or had read to him the books in the cabinets.

It was built as we know to celebrate the retaking of Baghdad by Murat IV in 1639. Baghdad had first been captured by Süleyman but retaken by the Persians. Murat showed great skill and courage in the siege, working with his men in the trenches and even accepting a challenge to personal combat in which Murat killed his opponent. His victory procession in Istanbul on June 10, 1639, was memorable, the historian Creasy points out, "because it was then that Constantinople beheld for the last time the once familiar spectacle of the return of her monarch victorious from a campaign, which he had conducted in person." He rode in steel armor, a leopard skin over one shoulder, and a triple aigrette, "placed obliquely, in the Persian mode," in his turban. "All the vessels of war fired constant salutes, so that the sea seemed in a blaze."

Murat was not given much time to bask in his glory or to enjoy the pavilion he built. One of his weaknesses was an overfondness for alcohol. He was not well when he returned from the Baghdad campaign but recovered somewhat. At the end of Ramazan, which fell early in 1640, he was able to accept the usual *bayram* congratulations and then watched an exhibition of the pages' skills from the Pearl Kiosk down on the shore. Unfortunately he did not stop there but indulged in a little horse racing and went to a banquet at the house of one of his cronies, the swordbearer, on the Hippodrome. There he further challenged fate by drinking too much. The next day he took to his bed and a few days later died.

The Ottomans, who believed so strongly in portents they found a sign for everything, were convinced his death had been foretold in one of the Koranic verses inscribed in the frieze of the Baghdad Kiosk, the one which begins, "And when Abraham and Ishmael were raising the foundation of the House. . . ." Since İbrahim is Turkish for Abraham, it was thought that this was a signal that Murat's last living brother, İbrahim, would soon inherit the House of the Ottomans.

[1 8 4]

THE QUARTERS OF
THE BLACK EUNUCHS

AT TOPKAPI the living space of the black eunuchs stretches in somewhat irregular, elongated form from the Carriage Gate of the Second Court to the Main Gate (Cümle Kapısı) of the harem. It is the introduction to the harem, which is natural since the black eunuchs were its guardians.

The original harem eunuchs were white, but whether they were located at the site of the present harem eunuchs' domain we do not know. The fire of 1574 undoubtedly wiped out their buildings. Nor do we know where their quarters were rebuilt. What we do know is that, after a period of competition between blacks and whites, the black eunuchs permanently secured the harem service in 1594 and that their quarters were in their present location as early as 1606/7. These buildings burned in the second great palace fire, that of 1665/6, and were rebuilt, this time of stone, by Mehmet IV around 1667–1669, to judge from the inscriptions found there. The emphasis on stone suggests that they may formerly have been made of wood. What we see today is Mehmet IV's seventeenth-century work.

The black eunuchs' quarters are arranged around an open court, but before one reaches this one must first go through two anterooms which lie between it and the Carriage Gate. The first, into which the gate opens, is a small, dark and windowless place with the descriptive title of the Dome with

Closets (Dolap Kubbesi), being roofed with a dome and having, along two walls, closets with very fine locks. According to tales told in the *saray* magical happenings went on in these closets. One day the sultan then on the throne became so enraged at a novice eunuch that he chased him, dagger in hand, through the eunuchs' court into this room. Unable to get out, the fellow attempted to hide in one of the closets. Unfortunately the voluminous skirt the black eunuchs wore caught in the door. The sultan, seeing it protruding, yanked the door open—to find no one there. The eunuch had been spirited away. The other closet is supposed to have been a similar vanishing point for a slave girl who disappeared. Both of these individuals are credited with having become saints.

The room has more than mythical history. Here were kept, as an inscription on the inner door says, "the gift of the holy coverings of the windows of the sacred tomb and room of the Prophet (peace and blessing be upon him) at Medina." Here the tradeswomen called *kira* from a famous one whose name was Esther Kira were admitted to leave their wares with the eunuchs who later displayed them to the women and purchased for them their choices. By bribing and cultivating a eunuch a woman of the harem was sometimes able to get messages out of the palace via these tradeswomen.

Esther Kira was a Jewess who led a highly successful life until its tragic end. She was a favorite of Süleyman's mother, Hafise, and for the favors she did that lady she and her progeny were exempted from taxes forever. Hafise died and then Süleyman, and his son Selim and grandson Murat. Still Esther Kira kept her influence through all these reigns and even became a favorite of the next *valide*, Safiye, mother of Mehmet III. Safiye was a rapacious soul who aroused the ire of the populace. Esther Kira's relationship with her then became a hazard rather than an asset. Furthermore the Kira family was suspected of having had a hand in the debasement of money which reduced the value of military pay. As a result of these factors she was slaughtered in public. Nevertheless the profession of *kira* hung on as long as the seclusion of women lasted. In latter years the *kira* was called *bohça kadın* from the *bohças* or squares of cloth in which they wrapped their wares.

This room is also the place where the powerful seventeenth-century *valide*, Kösem Mahpeyker, grandmother of Mehmet IV, was captured when Mehmet's mother and her accomplices carried out their plot to do away with her.

The door opposite the Carriage Gate has leaves of bronze brought from Egypt, another example of how things were imported from all over the

The gate in the Court-yard of the Black Eu-nuchs that leads eventu-ally to the Carriage Gate in the Second Court.

NECATI ORBAY

Empire for Topkapı. On them is found the phrase, in Arabic, "Our God Who openest doors, open for us the best door." It is a favorite inscription in the palace.

Beyond this doorway is the second of the anterooms, larger and with the very long name of the Place of the Attendants' Guard at the Tower Door (Kule Kapısı Hademe-i Nöbet Mahalı). It is in fact the first guard room of the harem and is high and handsome. Its walls are lined with tiles of various periods, some in floral designs, some in formal shapes, some in large circles enclosing calligraphy. A thick frieze of religious inscriptions runs around it part way up, relating the name of God; the Prophet; the Ten Blessed who were the Prophet's companions; Hüseyin and Hasan, the martyred sons of Ali, husband of the Prophet's daughter, Fatma; and the Divine Attributes

[187]

The Courtyard of the Black Eunuchs showing the Cümle Kapısı or Main Gate of the harem at the far end.

or the ninety-nine beautiful names of God which the devout Muslim repeats as he fingers his prayer beads. They include such attributes as the Hearer, the Seer, the Bestower, the Pardoner, the Life-Giver, the Light and the Guide. To the Muslim there is special merit in repeating them. (It must not be supposed, however, that every Turk one sees fingering prayer beads is actually reciting these names. Running one's fingers over the beads has become simply a habit.)

The room is architecturally interesting in that a wide, tiled archway divides it in two, one half being covered with a windowed dome and the other flat-roofed. Along one side stands a stone mounting block for the sultan, very likely often used because it is the one nearest the Imperial Stable and the chief exits from the palace. Grilled windows open from the room to the small mosque or chapel (mescit) of the black eunuchs.

The guard room has many doors which enabled the eunuchs to go from there in various directions: to the tower that rises behind the Divanhane and houses the sultan's lodge; to the small court that gives ingress to their chapel; to the eunuchs' court; and to an Exit Door (Gidiş Kapısı) that leads down a long, uncovered corridor to the Shawl or Curtain Gate (Perde Kapısı). On the right of the corridor, reaching to the end, is a suite of rooms with porch, raised so that it has a view above the wall that separates the eunuchs' quarters from those of the cariyes (jariyes) or women slaves. This was a meşkhane, a conservatory for the arts, either music or miniature painting.

It was along the passage beside this and out the Curtain Gate that a new sultan rode to proceed in magnificent procession to the mosque in the suburb of Eyüp. There he was girt with the sword of Osman and became the latest representative of the long line of Osmanlı sultans. The Curtain Gate gets its name from the custom, on that day, of lining the path of the corridor with Kashmire shawls for the sultan to ride over. His act bestowed on them particular worth, and they were afterwards distributed as favors among the halberdiers, black eunuchs and other attendants.

The guard room suffered from the fire of 1665/6 and was restored by Mehmet IV, as indicated by various inscriptions within it. The most high-flown, which rests over the door to the eunuchs' court, says in part:

> When he (Mehmet IV) was away at war, the capital, deprived of his presence, could not resist the burning grief of his absence, and its very heart flamed. The Sultan ordered skilled architects to rebuild it in stone.

The fire was set by some lower-grade women who had been sent to prepare the harem for the return of the court from Edirne. Somehow they came upon one of the bejeweled imperial cradles and could not resist prying out the best stones. Then they hid the cradle. The theft might not have been discovered for some time had not the valide sultan suddenly sent for the cradle. When it could not be found accusations traveled about the harem

[189]

in whispers and filled the guilty women with fear. They thought a fire would consume the cradle entirely. So they lit the cedar roof of the harem with their candles, and soon the wind had the fire well under way. It did considerable damage in the harem and reached as far as the Hall of the Divan before it was put out by gardeners and halberdiers. The women were found out, transferred to Edirne and strangled there at the sultan's command.

The courtyard beyond the door that commemorates the fire is the center of the black eunuchs' area, long and narrow and open to the sky except for domes at either end. It is sided on left and right by high walls behind which were their living quarters. Though constrained by these walls the courtyard is a cheerful place with almost the feeling of a garden from the lively floral tiles that line it.

The black men were usually gathered in the Sudan or the interior of Africa by Arab slave-traders and castrated somewhere on their way to the coast, before they reached the lands of the Ottoman Empire. There castration was a sin, although conveniently enough it was not a sin to use the services of those castrated elsewhere. Before being admitted to the *saray* each eunuch was examined by a doctor to make sure the castration had been complete. The operation had usually been performed when the man was a boy, and eunuchs were still young when taken into *saray* service. For the most part they were sent as presents to the sultan by the governors of Egypt. They were called *ağas*, as were the white eunuchs and the pages. The title was simply one of respect.

Eunuchs came into their service in the rank or lack of rank called lowest (*en aşağı*) and from there passed successively through the grades of novice (*acem*), members of the guard (*nöbet kalfası*), middle grade (*ortancı*), and the highest rank (*hasıllı*). The chief of the guard and the eunuchs outside the ranks were chosen from the *hasıllı*.

The chief of the guard (*baş kapı gulâmı* or head slave of the gate) was the master of all the lower ranks. His assistant (*yayla baş kapı gulâmı* or summer head slave of the gate) was in charge of the guard when the chief was away with the court. Promotions from rank to rank came as vacancies occurred. Chief of the guard was as high as a eunuch could go via the hierarchy. The other posts were filled by appointment by the Ağa of the House of Felicity or by the sultan—such as the eunuch imam or prayer leader for the harem, the *müsendereci*, an untranslatable word, who saw to it that the others performed their secular and religious duties, including cleanliness. Another independent group were those who waited on the sultan when he was in the harem, the *musahips*, which again cannot be conveniently fitted into an English word but which is usually translated as courtier. (However, not all courtiers were eunuchs.) There were also the black eunuch treasurer (*haznedar ağası*) and his assistant or deputy (*hazine vekili*) who looked after the financial affairs of the harem.

Each prince or *şehzade* old enough to have an apartment of his own had a black eunuch *lâla*, a tutor or adviser who was in fact in charge of him. The *valide sultan* had a chief *ağa* with a staff, as did the married princesses and the *kadıns*. They were all under the command of the Ağa of the House of Felicity, who had a staff of his own. His was headed up by the *oda lâlası*, supervisor of the room, who took charge of the harem in his absence.

The Ağa of the House of Felicity was one of the most important officials of the palace, ranking next to the grand vizier and *şeyhülislâm*. He was appointed by the sultan himself. The text of such an appointment by Selim III has come down to us and shows the extent of the authority of the chief black eunuch:

> You who are my noble Ağa of the House of Felicity, Bilâl Ağa, because you have for some time been my supporting slave and faithful and beloved *lâla* . . . I honor you from all my slaves and appoint you Ağa of the House of Felicity and overseer of the Holy Cities [Mecca and Medina]. I appoint you officer over all the small and great and young and old of all groups of *ağas* of the imperial harem and of the halberdiers of the Old Palace and the Guardians of the Walnut Tree [Koz Bekçileri], and all of the servants of the Holy Cities know you are the master in all matters and affairs, and no one will act except you say so, and they will obey you completely. . . .

We see from this that Selim gave the post to the eunuch who had been his tutor when prince.

All these black eunuchs except those in the entourage of married princesses managed to find living space in the area around the court. Their number has been put as high as six hundred, but personally I do not believe their quarters could have accommodated nearly that many, even allowing for those who lived in the palaces of the princesses and for the Turkish custom of sleeping on mattresses which could be put close together on the floor. The estimate of "some two hundred" by Mouradgea d'Ohsson, who made a study of the Empire in the late eighteenth century, seems nearer the

NECATI ORBAY

The vaulted corridor of the dormitory of the black eunuchs.

mark. Those in the hierarchy, that is, the lowest up through the chief of the guard, were housed in the three-story building to the left as one enters the court. Its entrance is from a colonnaded porch tiled and decorated with the Poem of the Mantle in heavy script baked in the tile. The upper floors, which overhang the porch and are thus wider than the ground floor, were designated for the ranks, whereas the chief of the guard had most of the ground floor for himself. The two rows of rooms for the entire height of the building are divided by a constricted corridor or vaulted court with a hooded fireplace at the end. To one side of it is the eunuchs' sitting room, the *ocak başı*, the place near the hearth.

From here they could watch the punishments being administered in the vaulted court. Of this Abdurrahman Şeref says: "When a novice merited punishment, the chief of the guard sat in this corridor; the culprit was made to lie down on the matting covering the floor and received the *falaka* [striking the soles of the feet] or the *tabanca* [slapping the face] punishment, according to the degree of his guilt." The palace custom of covering the floors with matting must have helped enormously in keeping down the cold and dampness of the paving.

Off this corridor on the ground floor was the guard chief's suite of very small rooms. What has been called his dining room, although it probably wasn't restricted to that purpose, used to have a fountain on which was inscribed a verse from the Koran and the following message, which gives an idea of the cohesiveness of the black eunuchs:

> This is the subject of this notice: to our brethren who have been honored in our time with the service of the Sultan in this Imperial Hall, and to those who will come after us, let it be known that the *ağas* our brethren who were here in the year 1015 (1606/7) decided altogether, seniors and newcomers, old and young, that they all found it advisable that when one of us is freed we should each, to please God, give him our quarterly allowance. But that notice was burned. So in the time of His Excellency the Ağa of the House of Felicity Abas Ağa, the *lâla* Hızır Ağa, the Ağa of the Old Palace Mahmut Ağa, and the chief of the guard the *ağa* Su'eyp Ağa, it was written down again in its original form. Let our brethren who come after us make no objection, and let them not refrain from acting accordingly. In the year 1079 (1668/9).

At the northern end of the dormitory but opening onto the larger court is the black eunuchs' chapel, small and square and lined with seventeenth-century tiles in lovely floral patterns. Two of them, however, depict the holy sites of Islam: the pilgrimage city of Mecca with its many gates, each named, as the Gate for Good People and the Gate for Dirty People, and showing the Kaaba surrounded with lamps; and the city of Medina where Muhammed's tomb is situated. In this little chapel the *şeyhülislâm* was sometimes received by the sultan when appointed to his post. One of them reported having seen here the young princes being taught to chant the Koran. Actually the chapel is so small it became inadequate, and at prayer time the eunuchs overflowed onto the porch of the dormitory. Its high windows, which still have the original glass, look out onto the little court of the *meşkhane* bath.

Past the dormitory the wall protrudes to become even with the edge of the porch for a short distance until one reaches the porch of the *kızlar ağası's* suite. This protrusion encloses a small room which in later times was called the boot room *(papuçluk)* but in earlier times was sometimes a prison for middle-grade eunuchs and sometimes a place where novices waited for promotion. Because of its proximity to the *kızlar ağası's* quarters, it may have housed his attendants, perhaps his slaves, in an upstairs loft.

Next to this and off the harem end of the courtyard is the suite of the chief black eunuch, whose title was Ağa of the House of Felicity (Darüs-saadet Ağası) but who was frequently called *kızlar ağası, ağa* of the girls. I shall frequently refer to him by that name. Despite his importance and the fact that his rooms are highly decorated, they are modest in size. Somehow in these rooms he was served by his corps of eunuch attendants and by his own female slaves. He was the only person in the palace outside the royal family to be allowed slaves. His building, though contiguous to others, was probably separately constructed. It is of stone, two stories high, with the Princes' School which was in his charge on the second floor. His ground-floor apartment has two rooms, plus corridors and bath. One room, though tiled and having a small tiled fireplace, curiously has no light except what comes though the door to the main room. A *dolap* or revolving cupboard also connects the rooms, but when in use could hardly have been a source of light. The place was perhaps the *kızlar ağası's* prayer room.

These rooms now house boxes in which are deposited certain skeletons we shall discuss later, some of which were found in the black eunuchs' area. One day when I was examining the *kızlar ağası's* apartment the guard who was escorting me was called to the telephone. He started off, then turned back and asked, "Are you afraid to stay alone here?"

A staircase lined with coarse Italian tiles in which the colors have run leads in two jumps to a light and beautifully tiled room which was the vestibule to the Princes' School. It too has a tile of the Kaaba, signed by a halberdier of the Imperial Guard, one Ali of Alexandria, and dated 1077 (1666/7). The motif is a popular one and found elsewhere in the palace. Off the side opposite the Princes' School opens a washroom and a room that was perhaps for the *hocas* or teachers. It is perfectly simple except for its tiled fireplace. Of this the border, the hood and the cone are set with multi-color tiles in small patterns. Although it is seventeenth century, one of its designs strongly suggests the twisting leaves of the tile work at the door to the Circumcision Room and in the Baghdad Kiosk.

The principal room on this floor is the domed Princes' School, of good size and showing signs of having been decorated in at least two periods. The upper and lower halves of its walls do not harmonize, the upper being earlier

The Princes' School. Note the early 17th-century tiles of the upper walls and the later baroque paneling and fireplace.

NECATI ORBAY

Ottoman, tiled and pierced with windows set in scrollwork, and the lower rococo, faced with gilt-decorated wooden panels and supplied with a tinted marble baroque fireplace. From a date it bears we know that the woodwork belongs to the eighteenth century, whereas the tiles of floral sprays and medallions belong to the seventeenth. One panel is even reminiscent of the sixteenth. It is likely that the tiling goes all the way down behind the wooden panels and that the room was once all of a piece. Between the tile and wood sections runs a ceramic frieze of calligraphy in the hand of the Younger Beşir Ağa, an Ağa of the House of Felicity for Mahmut I. It lists the attributes of God and gives the well-known Poem of the Mantle. Despite

[195]

these manifestations of piety, Beşir was an evil man whose fate will be described later.

It was in this room that the *hocas* came to instruct the young princes and perhaps the young princesses. They were chosen from among the Empire's most eminent scholars. Religion being an important part of the curriculum, each day when the the princes arrived, they raised their hands to their ears and chanted:

> *Every morning I wake up early*
> *And I say from the heart, "Thanks be to God."*
> *The nightingales in music, the roses in entreaty*
> *And I in prayer say, "Thanks be to God."*

The first day of school was made much of in Ottoman Turkish life. Parents vied in ostentation, and naturally none of these events was grander than a prince's. When in 1766 at age five Selim III was considered ready for school, he was first decked out in a handsome kaftan, a turban placed on his little head, and then led to the Gate of Felicity, accompanied by the Ağa of the House of Felicity and other eunuchs of standing. At the gate the highest members of the religious hierarchy, in their role of heads of the educational system, awaited him and kissed his hand. A tent had been set up in front of the Kiosk of Pearls on the shore, and there these members of the *ulema*, plus dignitaries of the Empire, escorted him, making an impressive procession around the diminutive prince as they marched through the Second and First Courts to the Boot Gate and down to the Marmara sea wall.

After due ceremony at the kiosk the *şeyhülislâm* began the lesson with the classic words, "In the name of God, the Merciful, the Compassionate." The little prince tried to kiss his hand, but the *şeyhülislâm* prevented it by taking the boy in his arms and implanting a kiss on his shoulder. The grand vizier presented him with an embroidered, bejeweled Koran case, such as may be seen in the exhibition in the Treasury. From its Koran he would learn the alphabet, but now he was taught only the first letter, the *elif* which roughly corresponds to our A. The rest of the day was taken up with congratulations and presents. From then on Selim had his lessons in the Princes' School from the teacher appointed for him. As he grew older, added teachers would broaden his knowledge.

To go back to the eunuchs' courtyard, the side opposite the Princes' School is lined with rooms that belonged to the eunuch treasurer and to the *baş musahip* or head courtier to the sultan. The other *musahips* lived on the second floor. The wall angles off here, and in the angle is a raised place filled with earth about which there are two traditions. One has it that the people involved in the murder of the *valide* Kösem, having been put to death, were buried here. Another maintains that the nineteen brothers Mehmet III had strangled when he came to the throne in 1595 were placed here for their funeral ablutions. Neither tradition supplies a reason for the name of the spot which is called the Place of the Forty (Kırk Yeri).

In a small room off the court, now used for the men who guard the harem, there were recently dug up several skeletons. The hands and feet of all were tied and the head of one cut off and placed on his chest. No one knows who they were, but from some silver coins of the time of Mahmut II found beside them it is deduced that they were buried in his reign (1808–1839). They may have been killed for some palace offense and secretly buried here. This suggests they were people of importance, perhaps foreigners whose deaths, had they become known, could have caused complications. Perhaps they had been trying to bribe the eunuchs and were caught at it. In addition to these, several more skeletons were found buried before the Imperial Gate.

A jog on this side takes one into a dark court that is barred by an iron door. On the other side is the Kuşhane Court that leads to the private kitchen where the sultan's meals were prepared. *Kuşhane*, as we have seen, may be translated as either aviary or small saucepan. Barnette Miller thinks there may once have been an aviary here, but it seems to me in this instance small saucepan is the likelier translation. Since the Kuşhane cooked for only one person, it must have used small pots and pans.

At one time the palace pharmacy was off this court and the physicians entered the harem through the Kuşhane Gate. When they reached the patient they were not allowed to give her a physical examination but only to ask about her symptoms. She was of course veiled so that the doctor did not even have the opportunity to see whether she was flushed or pale.

The Carriage and Kuşhane Gates are only two of the five gates that give ingress to the harem, the others being the Curtain Gate, the Funeral or Corpse Gate of the harem, and the Mabeyn Kapısı (the door to the reception room) that opens onto the Corridor with Pillars.

Black eunuchs continued to inhabit their quarters long after the sultan had moved away. It was their *ocak*, their guild to which they could return on retirement. Also there were still women to guard, for Topkapı became the home of the elderly retired slave women. Nine rules were posted for the eunuchs' observations, even in the twentieth century. Since palace customs tended to change but slowly if at all, it is safe to conclude that these rules, posted at the accession of Mehmet V in 1909, are typical of those in reigns long before him and identical with those in Dolmabahge where he lived in 1909. The first rule laid down the law that . . .

> All slaves, of any degree, attached to the Imperial Palace, whether on duty in the palace or on leave or duty outside, must perform their duty and spend their time with perfect courtesy and dignity. They must refrain absolutely from the least infringement pertaining to misconduct, and especially from frequenting places of prostitution and dissipation, from having short or long conversations or relations with persons suspected of vice, and from conduct contrary to the customs and rules of this country.

Rules two, three and four dealt with the harem women, saying that they must "refrain from doing their hair in improper and disgraceful fashion" (which usually meant imitating Western women), that they must cover their faces and not wear "objectionable" clothing. When they went out they had to be attended by a harem *ağa* and have the permission of the Ağa of the House of Felicity. It was the eunuchs' duty to see that the women obeyed these rules, and there were now and then high-spirited women who made the job difficult. Rule five forbade the eunuchs to be in the harem later than a half-hour after sunset. Rules six, seven and eight had to do with locking the harem at night "with strong iron locks," informing the Ağa of the House of Felicity if a woman were taken ill during the night, and forbidding "Christian women such as peddlers, embroiderers and dressmakers" from entering the imperial harem. Rule nine said that an unknown person might be received only on the authorization of the Ağa of the House of Felicity and threatened severe punishment for any infringement of the rules.

The regulations of the eunuchs' guild were also posted, with explanations of ranks and allowances, and of the degrees of punishment and the offenses for which each punishment should be handed out. Such offenses were "conduct contemned by religion, ethics and law, or actions contrary to their tasks and to the recommendations of their superiors," a broad spectrum.

The *kızlar ağası*, whose authority over the women was extensive even at that late date, was always a colorful figure. Until the time of Mahmut II he was garbed in a long, bright robe and tall turban, a dagger protruding from his clothing as a sign of authority. Since he held his post at the pleasure of the sultan, with the advent of a new sultan he often lost it. Such was the case with Yusuf Ağa who, thanks to his popularity with Râbia Gülnuş, the favorite of Mehmet IV, had secured that coveted post. With the death of Mehmet and the accession of Süleyman II, Râbia Gülnuş was banished to the Old Palace and Yusuf, with no one to plead for him, to Egypt. In his day his authority had been all but absolute. It was he who brought about the downfall and execution of Kara Mustafa, the unsuccessful commander of the second siege of Vienna.

Over the centuries there were many powerful *kızlar ağasıs* who grew rich on bribes, saw to it that those who cultivated them received important posts and even in some instances, because of the influence they had with the *valide* and the sultan, controlled the appointment of the grand vizier. As supervisor of the Holy Cities of Mecca and Medina and of the Pious Foundations, they oversaw the distribution of large sums. They made all the arrangements for the sending off of the *sürre*, the yearly gift of the sultan to the Holy Cities. Another of the *kızlar ağası*'s duties or privileges was to represent the imperial bride at the marriage ceremony and to escort her bridegroom to her door at the *zifaf*, the time when the groom first entered the bridal chamber. He was so important that every Wednesday he held a *divan* of his own at the little kiosk near the Stable Gate of the Second Court to examine the affairs of the Pious Foundations. With all this, the most important source of his influence was his closeness to the sultan. He had access to the ruler; he alone transmitted messages between ruler and grand vizier. With so intimate a relationship with the font of power, it is no wonder that he indulged in intrigue, siding first with one faction and then with another to further his own ends.

In the eighteenth century there were two particularly powerful *kızlar ağasıs*, both named Beşir. Beşir the Elder was a fanatically religious man who served both Ahmet III and Mahmut I. He had been a member of Ahmet's suite when that ruler was a prince. Often called Hacı Beşir Ağa because he had made the pilgrimage to Mecca, he was the donor of the Beşir Ağa Mosque near the Imperial Stable. He also put up many useful buildings outside the palace, but not satisfied with good works, he continually interfered in matters of state. Sometimes this was all to the good, as when he organized the plan to rid the country of Patrona Halil and his accomplices. At other times his infringement on the grand vizier's authority brought on dissension. He so infuriated the grand vizier Kabakulak İbrahim Pasha that, though he owed his office to the support of Beşir Ağa, he talked Mahmut I, then new to the throne, into exiling that individual to Egypt. As it happened the plan reached the ear of Beşir who persuaded the *valide sultan* to intercede for him. Mahmut was loathe to change his mind, but finally concluded that "the rights of a mother are greater," and kept Beşir on. Kabakulak İbrahim was dismissed instead.

Beşir Ağa died a natural death at the age of forty-eight, having held the post of Ağa of the House of Felicity for thirty years. Purchased for a mere thirty piasters, he died a rich man. His estate, besides large sums of money, included a hundred and sixty horses and eight hundred watches set with jewels.

Beşir the Younger, who succeeded him and served Mahmut I exclusively, was a different sort. To his predecessor's drive for power he added a strong streak of venality and bribed officials of the state to do his bidding. Yet he had certain qualities. He was a skilled calligrapher as we have noted in the Princes' School, a fine horseman, and a patron of poetry.

Having at one point managed to have his man appointed grand vizier, this Beşir was so bold as to call the highest officer of the Ottoman Empire his personal apprentice. He had no scruples. At another time, when he was at first unsuccessful in bringing about the dismissal of a grand vizier, he had a fire set in Istanbul and the vizier blamed for it, thus gaining his end.

Beşir the Younger eventually became over-arrogant. In 1752 he went so far as to have one of his creatures horsewhip a judge or *kadı*. When the judge complained the *ağa*'s men destroyed his house and the judge with it. So great was the indignation of the *ulema*—a judge was a member of the religious establishment—that the *şeyhülislâm* advised the sultan to get rid of Beşir if he wanted to save his throne. Mahmut then invited Beşir to accompany him to one of the pleasure palaces on the Bosphorus, but when they disembarked handed him over to the head gardener who took him to the Kız Kulesi, the Maiden's Tower (known in the West as the Tower of Leander), out in the waterway. The sultan had planned to exile Beşir to Egypt, but such was the fury of the *ulema* Mahmut was persuaded to have him killed.

In the reign of Osman III in the mid-eighteenth century, when that sultan lay on his death bed, his *kızlar ağası*, Ahmet Abukuf, decided to get rid of the grand vizier while the sultan lay powerless. He sent for the vizier to come to the palace with the purpose of demanding the seal of state and appointing a partisan of his own in his stead. The grand vizier was Ragip Pasha, one of the last great viziers of the Empire. Only because he was informed by the *kızlar ağası*'s secretary did he escape dismissal. He simply hid until Osman died and Mustafa III acceded to the throne, and then appeared at the palace to be confirmed in office by the new sultan.

When the grand vizier was a strong man with ideas of his own he was apt to be at odds with the *kızlar ağası*. We have already seen that Çorlu Ali Pasha tried to do away with eunuchs in the palace. One of his successors, Şehit (the Martyr) Ali Pasha in 1715 ordered the governor of Egypt to cease sending eunuchs to the Porte. If Şehit Ali had lived, this might have been the end of the black eunuchs and hence of the power of the Ağa of the House of Felicity, but he was killed in battle the following year and his order lapsed. The Ağa of the House of Felicity remained a potent figure for a century longer, until in the nineteenth century Mahmut II sheared him of all his functions except supervision of the black eunuchs and the harem.

The use of eunuchs, either black or white, to guard the women's quarters was not picked up from the Byzantine Empire as some think, any more than was the seclusion of women. Eunuchs had already appeared in Anatolia, with the title of *ağa*, long before the Conquest. Moreover the word the Turks used for them, *hadım*, is of Arabic rather than Greek provenance. They were probably not much in use until the Ottomans began to seclude their women, a custom that long antedated them in the Muslim world. The harem in which women were secluded and protected by eunuchs had a firm hold in the Caliphate in the eighth century and was continued by orthodox Islam. The early Ottomans had not practised the custom, but as their state grew and with it the power of the orthodox clergy, seclusion came in. It must have happened gradually. In the early fourteenth century a wife of Orhan, the second Ottoman sultan, could and did receive men in his absence. In the late fifteenth century a granddaughter of the Conqueror publicly gave an oration at her father's funeral in Bursa. However, in the sixteenth century by the time of Süleyman, the tenth sultan, the public appearance of an imperial woman was unthinkable. By then their world was bounded by eunuchs.

These eunuchs, at least the black ones, seem to have been all kinds of people. Some took to learning and literature, some undoubtedly remained ignorant, but all became Muslims and devout. I once met a black eunuch who had been in the service of the last sultan. He was a gentle, soft-spoken man who had become a mystic.

Today the quarters of the black eunuchs in Topkapı are undergoing restoration and may not at present be visited. It is estimated the work will take two years, so that by 1972 the public should be able to see this extraordinary portion of the palace.

THE HAREM

I

ALTHOUGH the imperial harem was inviolable and might be entered by no outsider, man or woman, we know a surprising amount about it, thanks to the researches of Turkish historians and the curiosity of a few Western writers. The latter were able to ferret out information by having their women relatives or friends cultivate *saraylıs*, women who had been brought up in the imperial harem and had married, or the married princesses who had palaces of their own. Some, like Jean Baptiste Flachat, a merchant who supplied the harem with goods and was therefore in contact with the *kızlar ağası*, drew information from present or past palace personnel. The official Ottoman chroniclers, *vakanüvis* (writer of events), recorded the births, deaths and marriages of the princesses and also important decisions influenced by favorites or *valides* during the seventeenth-century period known as the Women's Sultanate. However, of documented information on the harem there is very little, and therefore almost everything said about it, except for the present location of the rooms, must be prefaced by perhaps. These days the imperial harem is being restored, and in the process light is being shed on its involved history. It is expected the restored portions, largely the ground floor, will be opened to the public in the near future. Here, besides endeavoring to describe the harem, we shall people it with some of the women who lived and loved and intrigued here.

The classic upper-class Ottoman household was divided unto three portions—the harem or sacred precinct where the women lived; the *selâmlık* or place of greeting where the master of the household entertained his friends; and the *mabeyn* or place in between which, although outside the women's quarters, could sometimes be used by them.

Topkapı follows the same system, although on a grander scale. Here the term harem covers the area of the black eunuchs, the women's quarters, and the private rooms of the sultan. The *selâmlık* consists of the rooms and kiosks in the Third and Fourth Courts, in the gardens, and on the shore. Some Western writers have called the private apartments of the sultan in the harem the *selâmlık*, but with this I cannot agree. These were rooms for repose, not for receiving men. True, in them he might be waited on by the pages of the Privy Chamber, but the pages were dismissed when he wanted the women with him. The *mabeyn* lies as it should, between harem and *selâmlık*.

Like every institution in the Ottoman Empire, the harem was a hierarchy. The lowest grade of women slaves was at its base and the *valide sultan*, the mother of the sultan, at its apex. Her importance was such that she also had such fancy appellations as Cradle of the Great and Mother-of-Pearl of the Pearl of the Caliphate.

Directly below her ranked the sultan's daughters, also called sultan but with the title coming after the name rather than before it. Thus Mihrimah Sultan was the daughter of Sultan Süleyman. These woman *sultan*s or princesses had privileges not accorded to the sultan's concubines. Once married and in their own homes they were allowed to entertain women from outside the palace, even sometimes Western women such as the wives of ambassadors. They had considerable freedom in moving about the city, properly guarded by their own eunuchs. Their weddings were great spectacles.

Ranking next to them were the ruler's official concubines, the first, second, third and fourth *kadın*s in that order. Except in a few isolated cases they were not, after the early sixteenth century, legal wives. Many reasons for this have been suggested, but it seems to me that the sultans, who had previously married princesses of neighboring states for political reasons, were by now so powerful they had no need of such alliances. Indeed, some of these neighboring states the Empire had by now absorbed.

Kadın is a word that means simply woman, but in the case of the imperial concubines it became a title. The first *kadın* was called *baş* or head *kadın* and ranked well above the others, not because she was necessarily the sultan's favorite but because she was the first woman he had chosen to elevate to that rank after his enthronement, usually the mother of his first child. A *kadın* might not go outside the palace for any reason except when the court moved from place to place. Her only social life was with other palace women. She had the conjugal rights of a wife, and the sultan was supposed to sleep with each in succession. There was even a term for the *kadın*'s turn, *nöbet gecesi* or night turn.

The *kadıns* were not, however, the only women a sultan might take to bed. He was free to choose any of the slave girls in the harem, but in practice usually picked from the *gediklis*, the "privileged ones" who waited on him in the harem. Once the sultan had chosen a girl for his bed she was known as *gözde*, "in the eye" of the sultan, and became an *ikbal* or favored one. The *ikbals* too ranked first, second and so on in the order in which they had been chosen. Unless there was a great number of them, each had a room of her own. In the harem as it is at present these are on the second floor overlooking the court called the Court of the Gözdes.

All these women, except the princesses, entered the harem as slaves. Below them in the hierarchy came the rest of the slave women under the watchful eye of the *kâhya kadın*, the elderly woman stewardess, and her second in command, the *haznedar usta* or mistress of the treasury, also elderly. The *kâhya kadın* was an important person, allowed to carry an imperial seal. The sultan held her in great respect. If his mother was not living he called her mother. If she was, the *kâhya kadın* reported directly to her and in any case was in charge of the training of the women slaves.

In Western sources there has grown up the theory that when the sultan wanted the experience of a new girl, he had the *kâhya kadın* line the girls up in rows, at which time he looked them over and dropped his handkerchief on the shoulder of his choice. This seems to have been copied from one Western source to another so that one frequently encounters it in reading about the palace. Actually, the only first-hand source on this subject, Hafise, who had been the favorite *kadın* of Mustafa II, emphatically denied it. Lady Mary Wortley Montagu visited her in Istanbul after Mustafa's death, at which time Hafise told Lady Mary that no such arrangement existed, but that the sultan sent word by the *kızlar ağası* to a chosen girl. Von Hammer, who probably knew more about the Ottoman court than any other Westerner, having carefully perused the official Ottoman chroniclers, also calls the story untrue and traces it to the custom of an engaged princess sending a

handkerchief to her fiancé as an indication that she had received his engagement presents.

Common sense backs Hafise's story. The most beautiful and charming
girls of the *saray* were appointed to serve the sultan. Why then would he
have to rank girls up to look them over? Hafise also denied the story that
the girl had to enter the bed at the foot and crawl up it. I suspect that the
introduction of a new girl into the sultan's bed took place with something
more formal. It would have been most un-Ottoman otherwise. Probably the
sultan first put her at her ease and, having taken many women to bed for
the first time, would know well how to do it.

All sources agree that she was bathed, perfumed and dressed by other
slaves and, some say, escorted to her destination by music. If she pleased
her lord, her status in the harem immediately rose. She was assigned a
permanent room of her own, though at times the sultan might call her to his.

The routes to the *saray* were well laid down. Many girls came from the
slave market of Istanbul, a well-regulated institution in the heart of the city
where it was the duty of the chief customs officer to keep an eye out for
attractive girls for the palace. Girls arrived by slave ship, usually from the
Caucasus except in time of war when captives from the Aegean islands, the
Balkans, and Eastern Europe added variety to the market. An annual tribute
of girls from the Crimean Khan on the northern shore of the Black Sea
furnished a share. Others were gifts from important officials. Roxelana is
supposed to have been a present to Süleyman from his grand vizier and
brother-in-law, İbrahim. Despite owing her advancement to him, Roxelana
was jealous of İbrahim's influence with the sultan and may have been involved in his execution, although İbrahim's arrogant behavior gave Süleyman plenty of reason. Süleyman had made İbrahim his intimate in every
respect, even sharing his table with him, although it had been the custom
from the time of the Conqueror for the sultan to eat in lonely state. It is also
said that İbrahim shared Süleyman's bed, and there may well have been a
sexual attachment between them. This would have been nothing out of the
ordinary for that time and place, for sexual relations of man with man raised
no eyebrows in the old Middle East. It may be that Roxelana's jealousy had
a sexual component.

Roxelana was a war captive, but as Ottoman victories ebbed, more and
more girls game from the Caucasus. There, especially in Circassia and
Georgia, they grew beautiful women as other countries might grow wheat or
cattle—for sale. The avid demand for them in Istanbul encouraged parents

to preserve their girl children from the disfigurement of the widespread smallpox by inoculation, which started in the Caucasus, spread to Istanbul, and was publicized by Lady Mary Wortley Montagu when she was the wife of the British ambassador at the Porte.

Once in the palace the girls were put through *saray* training. Since they were foreigners and non-Muslim—it being against Islamic law to enslave a Muslim woman—they were all taught the Turkish language and the fundamentals of Islam. Importantly, they were instructed in good manners and the niceties of formal society requisite for *saray* life. They learned to write, even though that ability was not usual among Ottoman women. All learned embroidery, an accomplishment of every Ottoman woman. Many of the embroidered articles on display are the work of *saray* women. Beyond this they were trained as they showed aptitude. Those whose talents lay in such directions learned to play musical instruments, to sing and to dance. Others, as they grew older, became teachers of the younger slaves. Each was in time assigned to a service, as to the coffee service, the ewer service, the bath service, or to the retinues of the *valide*, the princesses and the *kadıns*. Through her service a girl who was not taken to bed by the sultan could rise to become an *usta*, an upper attendant with a suite of girls to do her bidding.

The palace even found husbands for many girls. It was the custom, after a girl had been in Topakı a certain number of years without becoming either *kadın* or *ikbal*, to marry her to one of the state officials. A *saray* woman graced a man's home with her beauty and charm and furthermore gave him a palace connection that could and often did advance his career.

The number of slave women varied with the monarch, at one time reaching as high as eleven or twelve hundred. Though the harem area alloted to the slave women is large, one cannot help wondering how it accommodated such great numbers. The secret may lie in the fact that privacy, except for the *valide*, the *kadıns* and the *ikbals*, was an unheard-of thing.

To return to the harem as a physical entity, it runs from the Carriage Gate of the Second Court to the small, square area that opens onto the Corridor with Pillars, and it spreads out from the walls of the Second and Third Courts to the western edge of the hilltop on which the Inner Palace is built. From here the land drops away abruptly to the outer gardens, on this side now Gühane Parkı. Despite the harem's complexity, on the ground floor, the most important area, it can today be roughly divided into sections. The area of the women slaves lies behind the black eunuchs' quarters; the *valide's* suite is in about the middle of the harem, her court adjoined by the rooms of the first and second *kadıns*; and the rest of the ground floor devoted to the sultan. The apartments of the princes are located on the upper floors at the north end. It has been said that the harem contains 380 rooms, but we cannot be sure of that until the plans of all the floors, newly made by İlban Öz, the present harem architect, have been published. To reach that figure I suspect storerooms and corridors would have to be included.

A fair portion of the harem was partially restored in the early days of the museum and opened to the public. My first sight of it was during those years. In the 1960's it was closed for architectural study and renovation. In the 1970's the several restored rooms will be seen in all the dazzling display of Ottoman decoration. As to the unrepaired rooms, it is only fair to point out that what one writes about them today may not be true tomorrow when the architect turns the searchlight of investigation upon them. Yet observation, inscriptions and sometimes the traditions that revolve around them are revealing. Aside from inscriptions, hard information is difficult to come by. The Ottoman convention that women and women's quarters were too intimate to be discussed has left us with nothing much in the way of written description from the Turks. Certain Westerners—Dallam, an Italian doctor, a French traveler posing as a clockmaker's assistant—caught glimpses of the harem, the Frenchman when the women were away at Edirne, but so brief were their experiences and so changed is the harem, their descriptions are not very meaningful today, except perhaps Dallam who was rather a special case. The women who inhabited the harem wrote nothing that has survived except letters, most of them to the sultan. Although these elucidate the writer's relationship with the ruler, they do nothing to clarify the arrangement of the harem. Tradition, while abundant, is sometimes unreliable.

One of the least reliable is the tradition that has attached the introduction of women into Topakı to Süleyman the Magnificent who, it was believed, moved his favorite, Roxelana, from the Old Palace to Topkapı about 1541. On the contrary the museum authorities now suspect there were occasionally women here as far back as the Conqueror and that Roxelana merely visited Topakı at Süleyman's pleasure. Much of his life was spent on campaign, and it may be that only during his interludes in Istanbul did he bring Roxelana here.

Known in the harem as *Hürrem*, the Joyous One, she was originally second *kadın*. In 1526 she got into a hair-pulling match with the first *kadın*, Gülbahar (Rose of Spring), mother of Süleyman's eldest son. Gülbahar seems to have won, having managed to scratch Roxelana's face. She might better have let herself be worsted. Roxelana excused herself from appearing

NECATI ORBAY

A painting of Roxelana as
a European imagined her.

before Süleyman because of her scratches and thus aroused his sympathy. He was in any event much taken with her. Gülbahar from then on lost imperial favor. Seven years later she left the capital with her son, Mustafa, when he was appointed governor of Manisa, and there she died. After Gülbahar's fall Roxelana had no rivals. Unlike all the other Ottoman sultans down to the last, Süleyman was monogamous most of his life. He may even have legally married Roxelana, although historians disagree on this. Of a bewitching personality, she was also jealous, powerful, and unscrupulous. She lived to see the chief objects of her jealousy, the vizier Ibrahim and Süleyman's eldest son, Mustafa, done away with and to be assured that her own son, Selim, would accede to the throne.

The sultan who is currently credited with having permanently established the imperial harem at Topkapı Sarayı is Süleyman's grandson, Murat III, sometime during his reign (1594–1603). According to the research of Hayrullah Örs, director of the museum, Murat's mother, Nur-u Banu (Lady of Light), did not live in the present harem but in a kiosk, the Valide Yeri (the Place of the Mother), on or near Palace Point. Since with her he brought his *kadıns* and a full retinue of slave girls and eunuchs, he must have built extensively for them in the harem area. What these buildings were we do not know, for apparently not much of them survived the fire a century later.

We left today's harem at the Main Gate (Cümle Kapısı). It is shown at the far end of the picture of the black eunuchs' court, a heavy bronze door with a low-arched lintel of contrasting black and white marble, over it inscribed the Declaration of the Unity of God. The date given is 1078 (1667/8), which puts it after the fire of 1665 and credits it to Mehmet IV. You will recall that that particular fire started in the harem, much of which was destroyed. Thus one frequently encounters the date 1078, proving that considerable rebuilding was done by Mehmet IV.

The Cümle Kapısı, main gate though it is, opens not onto the women's quarters but onto a small dark room called the Place of the Guard (Nöbet Yeri). This is the second guard room, the first being, as we have seen, the second room inside the Carriage Gate. Here waited the eunuchs whose turn it was to guard the harem. Here also the food trays for the harem were laid on a stone table between the Main Door and the Food Door (Aş Kapısı), opening onto a corridor that leads to the slaves' quarters. There were shelves along this corridor to which the eunuchs carried the trays after the door to the women slaves' area had been shut. Then the Food Door was closed and the girls emerged to pick up the trays. All this precaution was to prevent the eunuchs from having contact with the girls, some of whom were inclined to be flirtatious.

Opposite the Main Door is the door to the Golden Way (Altın Yolu), a paved and segmented corridor which abuts the eastern side of the harem, passing on one side the *valide's* court, a set of storerooms, a corridor belonging to the first and second *kadıns*, the rooms of the first and second *kadıns*, one end of the corridor called the Consultation Place of the Jinns (Cin Meşveret Yeri) and the Court of the Gözdes, until it debouches into the small anteroom that gives entrance to both the *mabeyn* and the Corridor with Pillars. On the other side there were once openings to the harem mosque and to the Privy Chamber. It may be one of the oldest parts of the *saray*, at least in its farther section, where it connected with the Conqueror's Privy Chamber.

There appears to be no historical information as to why the corridor is called golden, although there is a tradition that the sultan scattered gold coins here on special occasions for the slaves to pick up. The trouble with this as an explanation is that it was strictly against harem etiquette for the

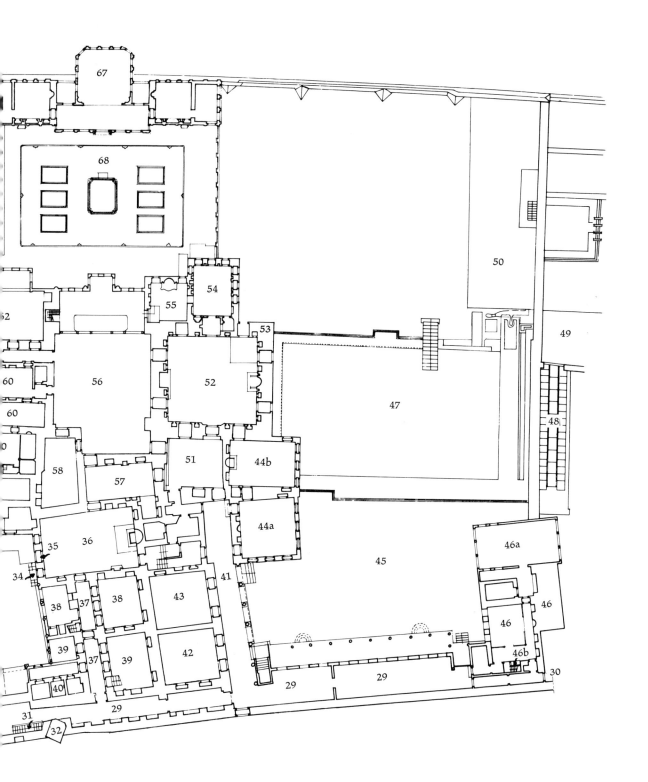

Key to Plan of Ground Floor of THE HAREM OF TOPKAPI PALACE

1. Carriage Gate
2. Dome with Closets
3. Place of the Attendants at the Tower Door
4. Stone mounting block for the sultan
5. Tower behind the Council Hall
6. Way to the Shawl Gate
7. Shawl Gate
8. Porch
9. Conservatory
10. Mosque of the black eunuchs
11. Open courtyard of the black eunuchs
12. Apartment of the black eunuch treasurer
13. Apartment of black eunuchs who waited on the sultan in the harem
14. Place of the Forty
15. Waiting room of the black eunuchs
16. Corridor
17. Kuşhane Gate to the Third Court
18. Kuşhane Court
19. Porch of the black eunuchs' dormitory
20. Black eunuchs' dormitory
21. Area under the Roof, quarters of attendants of the Ağa of the House of Felicity
22. Part of the Princes' School
23. Apartment of the Ağa of the House of Felicity
24. Main Harem Door
25. Place of the Guard
26. Food Door
27. Food Corridor of the women slaves
28. Door to the Golden Way
29. Golden Way
30. Door to the Corridor with Pillars
31. Staircase of Cevri Kalfa
32. Harem Mosque
33. Open courtyard of the *valide sultan*
34. Mounting block for the sultan
35. Throne Door
36. Hall with the Hearth
37. Corridor of the *kadıns*
38. Apartment of the head *kadın*
39. Apartment of the second *kadın*
40. Storerooms
41. Consultation Place of the Jinns
42. Storeroom
43. Harem treasury
44. Double Kiosk
44a. Room with domed ceiling
44b. Room with flat ceiling
45. Courtyard of the Gözdes
46. Mabeyn
46a. Mirrored Room
46b. Secret staircase
47. Open pool
48. Double incline, once used by the sultans as exits from the Inner Palace
49. Garden
50. Elephant House, the ground floor of an old kiosk
51. Vestibule of the Bedroom of Murat III
52. Bedroom of Murat III
53. Part of the room that overlooks the underground pool
54. Kiosk of Ahmet I
55. Room of Ahmet III or the Fruit Room
56. Sultan's Hall
57. Hall with the Fountain
58. Room where Abdülaziz' mother slept
59. Bath Corridor
60. Sultan's Bath
61. *Valide Sultan*'s Bath
62. Bedroom of Abdülhamit I
63. Perhaps at one time a treasury
64. Stairway to the upper-floor suite of Selim III
65. Room of Selim III
66. Corridor of Osman III
67. Kiosk of Osman III
68. Court with the Pond
69. Prayer Room of the *valide sultan*
70. Her bedroom
71. Her sitting room
71a. Raised area for dining
72. Corridor
73. Stairway to the upper-floor suite of the *valide sultan*
74. Her Corridor
75. Storeroom
76. Salon of the *valide sultan*
77. Her Reception Room
78. Corridor to the women slaves' quarters
79. Open courtyard of the women slaves
80. Bath of the women slaves
81. Pantry of the women slaves
82. Stairway to the upper-floor rooms of the women slaves
83. Storeroom
84. Kitchen
85. Laundry of the women slaves
86. Dormitory of the women slaves; its second story continues around to the stairs (No. 82)
87. The Forty Steps to the harem hospital
88. Apartment of the head laundress
89. Apartment of the *kâhya kadın*
90. Apartment of the head nurse
91. Harem hospital
92. Open courtyard of the harem hospital
93. Harem Death Gate

The rooms given no numbers and names are sometimes additional rooms of the suites already numbered, sometimes rooms where water was heated for the baths, and sometimes rooms whose purpose is at present undetermined.

Rendered by Yılmaz Güngör from the plan of İlban Öz, present arctitect in charge of harem restoration.

slaves to appear when the sultan was about. He wore silver hobnails on his shoes to warn of his presence so that the women could withdraw.

What one first sees as one enters the Golden Way is a plain stone staircase famous as the Staircase of Cevri (Jevri) Kalfa, a harem woman. It was here on a Thursday, July 28, 1808, that one of the most important scenes of Ottoman history was enacted when Mahmut II was saved from the assassins sent by his brother, Mustafa IV.

We have already seen that Selim III was dethroned and that when Alemdar Pasha, a noble and general from the Danube country, came to reinstate him, Mustafa IV gave orders that both Selim and Prince Mahmut be executed. He sent a group of men to do the job, including the Master of the Wardrobe called Fettah the Georgian, the Treasury steward, Ebe Selim, and a black eunuch named Nezir. Selim was upstairs in the room he used for prayer. With him was his favorite *kadın*, Refet, and a slave girl or perhaps one of his favorites named Pakize. When he saw men approaching him with drawn swords, he could have had little doubt of what was to be his fate. Standing there with a green turban about his head, a robe of green cloth on his back, and over it a short jacket, very pale but quiet, he asked, "Are you executioners?"

The black eunuch Nezir Ağa said to him, "You are the cause of trouble." (Literally he said, "Trouble breaks out from your head.")

At this terror seized Refet Kadın, who had all along been fearful for the life of her lord. Pakize, in despair, threw herself between the killers and her sultan. A sword came from behind her and cut her in the hand. The blood that flowed must have told Selim that they would stop at nothing. Refet Kadın cried out and tore at her hair. A slave who had come in from the corridor fainted. Selim, knowing his end had come, pronounced the words, "God is great," and proceeded to struggle with his assailants. First a sword cut him in the right cheek. Then other swords came at him, and soon this most enlightened of Ottoman sultans was lying in a heap on the floor. Refet Kadın tried to throw herself on the body, but was prevented. It was wrapped in a quilt and left to lie for the moment on the matting. Selim seems to have been the only sultan to have been killed by the sword rather than by strangling.

Now that this part of the job was done, the killers were determined to perform the other half. The story of the saving of Mahmut has been told many times, and many a teller has added his embellishments. We have therefore turned to the history of Cevdet Pasha, a nineteenth-century official historian. What follows is largely what he has to say.

[2 1 3]

NECATI ORBAY

The Stairway of Cevri Kalfa and the Golden Way.

When the killers first entered the harem the palace people were gripped with fear. They heard Alemdar's blows against the Gate of Felicity. They saw a high official flee to the hoped-for safety of the Campaign Hall. Meanwhile certain people who had been appointed by Selim and were still in palace service climbed out onto the Kuşhane roof and sized up the situation.

[214]

They explained to Anber Ağa who was Mahmut's personal *lâla* and to his companion, Hafız İsa Ağa, that Selim and Mahmut were in danger. Curiously no one seems to have rushed to protect Selim, but Anber and Hafız İsa alerted a Georgian slave named Cevri who was attached to Mahmut's service. When they heard the killers had entered Selim's apartment, they knew Mahmut's turn would come next. The *ağas* got ready to protect him with drawn swords, but Cevri's preparations were different. She went into a *külhane* (ash room) in which was located the stove that heated the water for an adjacent bath at the head of the staircase now named for her. There she filled a bowl with ashes and, to quote Cevdet Pasha, "When the killers attacked this time she immediately threw handfuls of ashes into their eyes. They wiped their eyes, and as they cried, 'Make way!' she kept them busy by throwing ashes again. Anber and İsa Ağas seized the opportunity and hoisted Mahmut above them.

"Meanwhile a dagger thrown by Ebe Selim grazed an arm of Sultan Mahmut in passing. As, partially wounded, he went out in a flurry, he was torn over the right eyebrow by striking his forehead against the doorframe."

Cevdet Pasha doesn't say what door he went out, but others have claimed it was a skylight. They can never have looked at the room at the head of the stairs. The skylight is too high for anyone to climb out even from the shoulders of another person. It is more likely that Mahmut escaped through the window on a nearby staircase to the roof just below it and scraped his forehead on the window-frame. This staircase, to an upper floor, is situated not far from the top of Cevri Kalfa's.

That the killers came to a staircase in their search for Mahmut is a good indication that the heir's apartment was not where it used to be thought, on the ground floor, but somewhere upstairs.

Battered and wounded, Mahmut must have scrambled around several roofs before he reached the Kuşhane roof where he was visible from the Third Court. A group of palace people in the court made a ladder by tying together the sashes from their waists and got Mahmut down. They must have thrown the ladder of sashes up, and Mahmut must have fastened its end to something. Looking at the Kuşhane roof today, one finds nothing to which it could have been affixed except the chimney, and perhaps that is how he managed it. At any rate he was safely landed on the ground.

By this time Selim's body, still wrapped in its quilt, was laid on the stone floor in front of the main door to the Throne Room so that when Alemdar broke through the Gate of Felicity, it was the first thing he saw. Weeping, he said, "Alas, my lord, I traveled here joyfully to enthrone you, and now that I have come my eyes have seen you in this state. Let me take revenge by killing all those the Enderun people say are traitors," and he threw himself upon the "blessed body."

By now the court was filled with Alemdar's men, swords and curved knives in hand. It was not time for weeping, they reminded him, nor yet for revenge. The important thing was to enthrone Prince Mahmut as padishah.

Meanwhile palace people had been taking care of Mahmut. He had lost his footwear in his scramble, and so someone brought him a pair of *mest*, the light-weight slippers the Ottomans wore indoors. Another wiped the blood from his face. Ahmet Efendi, a palace imam or prayer leader, fell at his feet, and then he and another loyal man took Mahmut by the arms and led him out into the Third Court.

Seeing him approach, Alemdar asked, "Who is this?"

Ahmet Efendi answered, "This is our lord, Sultan Mahmut. The reign of the Caliphate is his. I have made obeisance to him. The proper course is for you to complete the auspicious act."

At this Alemdar said to Mahmut, "Ah, my lord, I came to raise your uncle to the throne. Now that my eyes—may they be blind—have seen him in this condition, let me console myself by enthroning you."

The gold throne was brought out from the Treasury, and the twenty-three-year-old Mahmut solemnly seated on it before the Gate of Felicity as the thirtieth Ottoman sultan. Usually the Enderun people were the first to pledge allegiance to a new sultan and the statesmen from outside the palace next. This time, because it was getting late, the outside officials approached the throne first. One by one they signified their allegiance by kissing his skirt. Then he and Alemdar moved to the Throne Room, where, at Alemdar's own request, Mahmut made him grand vizier and clothed him with a furred robe of honor. Then Mahmut passed down the Third Court to pray in the Room of the Blessed Mantle while Alemdar was served sweets and coffee in the Arzhane beside it.

That night Mahmut did not dare return to the harem, not knowing how many of its personnel might be Mustafa's partisans. He spent the night in the Circumcision Room. As for Mustafa, he first took refuge in the *mabeyn*, but when he heard that allegiance had been pledged to his brother, he realized he had lost and allowed himself to be conducted to the Cage. He might have lived out his life in the harem had not some of his partisans hatched a plot to reinstate him. To protect the throne for Mahmut, he was eventually killed.

An old register gives us the details of Mahmut's life the first few days after his enthronement. The following day he went to Friday prayer at Santa Sophia so the people might see him and performed afternoon prayer in the Room of the Blessed Mantle. He rewarded the *aǧa*s who had helped him and had those who had killed Sultan Selim publicly executed. On August first he had his hair cut by the barber who had been cutting it since he was a child. He listened to a reading of the Koran, inspected the *saray* library (probably the Ahmet III Library), had a new seal cut for the grand vizier and gave it to Alemdar with his own hand. Then, in the afternoon, in disguise, he visited the tomb of his father, Abdülhamit I. So began a new reign.

Mahmut was now the only surviving male of the Ottoman dynasty. It was not until 1812 that his first son was born, though by the time of his death his concubines had produced nineteen princes. That the dynasty survived can be laid to Cevri Kalfa and her staircase. For her devotion she was appointed *haznedar* (treasurer) *usta*, the second most important post in the imperial harem.

Farther down the Golden Way three famous tile panels line its wall. One of them bears the date 1574 and the inscription: "This lofty imperial bath was completed in the year 982 of the hegira (1574/5) of the Best of Mankind [Muhammed]." From this it is sometimes concluded that the panel was moved here from the sultan's harem bath at some period when the bath was being done over. Another of the panels appears to come from the Sultan's Hall.

The panels are late sixteenth-century floral, with a very white white, a deep rich blue, and touches of the red that was a mark of the period. They were made in the great tile works of Iznik, old Nicea, where the best tile craftsmen were to be found. Iznik tiles were so famous they were in demand abroad, and so in the year 1592/3 Murat III issued an order that no tiles could be made for foreigners until all the orders for the palace and the religious buildings in the Empire had been filled.

The Turks had a long history of ceramic work. Originally the Uyghurs, sedentary Central Asiatic Turks of the seventh century, had learned the technique from the Chinese and passed it on to their fellow Turks. We will discuss Seljuk and early Ottoman tile-making when we come to the Tile Kiosk. Floral tiles in naturalistic sprays, however, were the special gift of the sixteenth-century Ottomans. Their colors are clear and well-defined. There is no running of the pigments, which were applied under the glaze and baked in. This, according to one expert, was a new technique that resulted in a more brillant glaze. The craftsmen began to use finer brushes which allowed more freedom in the patterns. These were the work of court

[217]

artists made in consultation with the architect. This planning to fit the area is not always noticeable in Topkapı, so many tile panels have been moved about, but it is to be seen in the Bedroom of Murat III and that of the *valide.*

The tile industry in Iznik and its rival city of Kütahya continued into the seventeenth century, but by the end of that century the great period of Ottoman tiles was over. The workshops in both these cities closed down in 1717. Two years later the order was given to reopen them and to send samples of their work to Istanbul, plus two master tile workers. But the great craftsmen had died out, and the effort at tile-making at Tekfur Sarayı, in a corner of Istanbul near the Walls of Manuel, was never really successful. Tiles made there are to be seen at the entrance to the Pavilion of the Blessed Mantle and on the Fountain of Sultan Ahmet just outside the Imperial Gate, but the colors have lost their purity. This workshop soon fell into disuse, and the Ottomans, whose tiles had once been the envy of the world, began to import them from Europe. The year 1756 saw an order to the governor of Belgrade to pass twelve cases of Viennese tiles, at least some of which were to be used in the palace. Italian tiles, which even a quick look shows to be much inferior to the tiles of the Golden Way, also appear on the harem walls.

Across the Golden Way from the Staircase of Cevri Kalfa lies the paved, open Court of the Valide (Valide Taşlığı). It has been called the hub of the harem, and as the harem stands today in a way it is, separating the women slaves' quarters from the sultan's rooms. Yet one must always remember that this may not always have been so. A short corridor connects the court with the slaves' open courtyard off which a two-storied dormitory surrounds the southeast corner and is so arranged, with a gallery overlooking the ground floor, that the *kalfas* could keep an eye on the girls. It is said they were as prone to lesbianism as the pages to homosexuality and were watched accordingly. The Bon-Withers account of the early seventeenth century relates of them:

> Now, it is not lawfull for any one to bring ought in unto them, with which they may commit deeds of beastly uncleannesse; so that if they have a will to eate Cucumbers, Gourds, or such like meates, they are sent in unto them sliced, to deprive them of the meanes of playing the wantons; for, they all being young, lustie, and lascivious Wenches, and wanting the societie of Men (which would better instruct them) are doubtlesse of themselves inclined to that which is naught, and will be possest of unchast thoughts.

[218]

NECATI ORBAY

The Valide's Court.

Off the open women slaves' court are several two-storied, tiled suites for head *kalfas* or *ustas*, and a somewhat larger and more handsome one for the *kâhya kadın*. There is a laundry in one corner, in which at present is stored a little round cubicle with a conical roof that looks as if it came straight out of Hans Christian Andersen. It was the house of a palace dwarf. Lining the open court are baths and a small kitchen which must have been for the concoction of tidbits, since the girls' meals were sent from the palace kitchens. There was apparently one delicacy, dolmas cooked in olive oil, which the palace did not provide for them. A certain document gives an account of these being sent to the harem as presents from outside the palace. The *saray* women returned the trays laden with their cast-off clothing, and these returned trays were called *cevap* or reply. Selim III was greatly exercised that no notes should go outside with these *cevaps* and issued an order to that effect.

Under this section the museum has found construction of the Conqueror's time and a passage from this to the *cariyes'* court that is even now

[219]

being excavated. It suggests that women's quarters on this site may go back to the Conqueror.

From this court a staircase leads down under the westernmost rooms to the harem hospital, which was equipped with its own bath, toilets, and its own laundry. At its south end is the harem Death or Corpse Gate. A wall separates the hospital area from the rest of the *cariyes'* quarters, in addition to which it is removed by being on a lower level. Nothing in this part of the palace has been restored and hence it is not open to the public. From it one can reach the first of a series of gardens, pass between the piers of Osman III's addition and reach the gardens below the Favorites' Court and the Baghdad Kiosk, ending at the Elephant Gate. It is a gateway from the Inner to the Outer Palace.

The only known believable Westerner to catch a glimpse of the slave girls was Thomas Dallam. He was at the palace every day for a month setting up his organ and during that time became friends with the pages of the Privy Chamber who had been appointed to look after him. On one of his last visits he was shown the sultan's private rooms. Though his guide dared not go with him, he was allowed to approach an iron grille beyond which was a court of the women. Since this was about 1600, it was probably a court that does not exist today. Of what he saw he has this to say:

Through [the] grait I did se thirtie of the Grand Sinyor's Concobines [to many Westerners all the girls were thought to be concubines] that weare playinge with a bale in another courte. At the first sighte of them I thoughte they had bene yonge men, but when I saw the hare of their heades hange doone on their backes, platted together with a tasle of smale pearle hanginge in the lower end of it, and by other plaine tokens, I did know them to be women, and verrie prettie ones in deede.

Theie wore upon theire heades nothinge bute a litle capp of clothe of goulde, which did but cover the crowne of her heade; no bandes a boute their neckes, nor anythinge but faire cheans of pearle and a juell hanginge on their breste, and juels in their ears; their coats weare like a souldier's mandilyon, som of reed sattin and som of blew, and som of other collors, and grded like a lace of contraire collor; they wore britchis of scamatie, a fine clothe made of coton woll, as whyte as snow and fine as lane; for I could desarne the skin of their thies throughe it. These britches cam doone to their mydlege; some of them did weare fine cordevan buskins, and som had their leges naked, with a goulde ringe on the smale of her legg; on her foute a velvett panttoble [*pantufla*, a felt slipper] 4 or 5 inches hie. I stood so longe loukinge upon them that he which had showed me all this kindness began to be verrie angrie with me . . . and stamped with his foute to make me give over looking; the which I was verrie lothe to dow, for that sighte did please me wondrous well.

The clothes he describes were probably those the ordinary slave girl wore up to the introduction of Western dress, for style did not change much in the harem.

To get out of their quarters the slave girls must often have passed through the *valide*'s court, off which her suite was located. Its proximity to the sultan's rooms tells us something about her relationship with him. The sultan's mother was the only person on anywhere nearly equal terms with him. She called him my lion (*arslanım*), had access to him, and was one of the most influential—sometimes *the* most influential—person in the palace.

Her court is of good size as harem courts go, about thirty paces by twenty-six, and formerly was larger. It was once surrounded by a portico of twenty-five marble pillars, but at some date three sides of it were filled in so that only on the south is the portico still open. There it covers a fountain. Stones with little depressions pave the court to keep the foot from slipping when it was wet from rain. Such stones also pave the courtyard of the black eunuchs. In the *valide*'s court the walls are tiled where there is room for tiles. It suffered from late redecoration by the introduction of garlands under its second-floor windows and false eaves over them, but has been returned by the museum to its earlier simplicity.

Obliquely across the court runs a path of small round stones which begins at the north door of the court called the Throne Door and continues all the way to both the Carriage Gate and the Curtain Gate. A throne used to be set up beside this door from which the sultan said goodby to his family when he set out for war. The door's outer face bears the *tevhit*, the bearing witness to the oneness of God, and its inner face the lines, "Intercession, O Prophet of God; intercession, O Beloved of God." Beside this door in the court stands the stone mounting block which the sultan used when he started out for the sword-girding ceremony at Eyüp. From the doorway one can enter the sultan's rooms.

The present apartment of the *valide*, off the west side of the court, is composed of several rooms. The possibility is that the ground-floor suite was built in the first half of the seventeenth century for the Valide Kösem. It has no doubt seen many changes, for it gives no impression of having been planned but on the contrary of being the result of a series of personal whims. Directly off the court is the double room known as the Hall of the Valide. The left-hand area is lined with Italian tiles, the right decorated in Turkish rococo replete with embossed ornaments, paintings and gildings, rather like the Sultan's Hall. It was done over in the eighteenth century, probably during Osman III's spate of building. There was no living *valide* after him until we come to Selim III.

This room was used for three nights by Sultan Abdülaziz when he was dethroned in 1876. He had been given no time to take clothing with him, and at Topkapı not even clogs could be found for him to use in the bath. After protesting his plight to his nephew, now Murat V, he was transferred to the Feriye Palace on the Bosphorus. There he committed suicide with a pair of small, sharp-pointed scissors which are still in one of Topkapı's storerooms.

From this room toward the west runs the Corridor of the Valide, at first wide enough to be a room, then narrowing, and lined with quite inferior yellowish Italian tiles. To the left is an area of tiled corridors that turn here and there to reach the court of the slave girls. One of room size was perhaps part of the *valide's* suite. The corridor takes one to a pleasant if not very large room, its dome painted with leaves and branches. Scenes decorate its upper walls, and a high window looks into the *valide's* upper story. It is obviously earlier than much of its decoration. It not only retains its mother-of-pearl inlaid doors, but when the museum first went to work on the room, years back, it found that a *dolap* or revolving cupboard had been made out of an old fireplace. The museum restored the fireplace and the tiles of its hood and surrounding wall. One end of the room is raised, and it was here that the *valide* usually dined at a tray resting on legs. Over this portion is a flat, crisscross ceiling reminiscent of the one of the Kiosk on the Terrace and suggesting the eighteenth century.

Next to this is the *valide's* bedroom, smaller but more interesting since it has not been subject to redecoration. The walls of its bed place are still lined with seventeenth-century tiles, probably put up for either Kösem or Turhan, her daughter-in-law. Blue on a white ground, they are delightful panels of floral sprays that rise from jet fountains. The canopy over the bed place is supported by columns and topped by a shallow balustrade underscored by scrollwork. Very likely some of the *valide's* slaves slept here. It must have been reached by a portable ladder, as were other balconies in the harem. The ceiling of this room is another divided one, partly domed and partly flat. What is unique about it is that the flat section is faced with tiles. The room gets its light only from little windows in arches of the dome. By night it must have had a particular charm when the enormous candles used in the harem cast their glow on the tiles and illuminated the grace of the floral sprays.

Many visitors to the harem have commented on its darkness which comes from the fact that several rooms are lighted only by dome windows and others only by windows that look out onto an inside court. The late rooms, though intrinsically less beautiful, are much brighter. Yet there are some early rooms with outside windows, and there must have been more before the many additions.

Behind the *valide's* bedroom are two small rooms, one of them a prayer room, on its walls the tile panels of Mecca and Medina. The other is just a small, low-ceilinged place that leads to a corridor. I have seen it called Selim's music room or *meşkhane,* but I don't know that I believe it. The

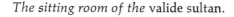

The sitting room of the valide sultan.

NECATI ORBAY

The tiled ceiling and bed place in the bedroom of the valide. The cylinders on the floor are modern fire extinguishers.

NECATI ORBAY

corridor and, in my opinion, this little nondescript room are obvious afterthoughts. They appear to have no function and just because of this raise the question of their origin. Observation of a reproduction of a drawing made in 1660 by a Hollander, Willem van de Velde, reveals a high covered porch here. Probably of wood, it must have been a victim of the harem fire of 1665. It is my own personal theory that when Mehmet IV ordered the reconstruction of the harem after the fire, this porch was changed into an enclosed corridor. This seems clear to me from the drawing of the same

[2 2 4]

face of the harem by Grelot in 1680 (reproduced here). In Grelot the outer wall is continuous under an uninterrupted roof from the Hall of the Sultan all the way to a southern corner near the Divan Tower. If the corridor had not been there in Grelot's time, the façade along the *valide*'s quarters would have been indented. Furthermore a close look at the current harem plan shows the corridor's inside walls to be sturdy enough to have originally formed the outside of the harem.

Grelot indicates two ranges of windows here where today there is only one, so that the ceilings of both corridor and the low rooms contiguous to it must once have been considerably higher. Their ceilings were probably lowered when the second story's *valide* suite was added, resting as it does over the *valide*'s prayer room, the useless room, the corridor, and her dining area. It seems obvious that her dining area was narrowed at this time to provide room for the stairs to the upper suite, and it was probably then that it was given its present eighteenth-century crisscross ceiling.

When the corridor was built the little room was perhaps just a corner of it, and the whole thing may have had a purpose, as to connect the *valide*'s suite with a domed room Mehmet IV had built at its north end. Today it merely comes to a stop, and the only egress at this end is a door on the inner side to a continuation of the old Valide's Corridor. Here, hidden behind another door, a broad and turning staircase takes one immediately into another world, the Europeanized, second-story suite of the *valide*. Even the stairs, with their elaborate wooden corner posts, change the mood. The suite itself is of two rooms. The first lies over the *valide*'s dining area and has the window that looks down into her domed sitting room.

Its decoration is largely scenic—garden scenes framed in gilt over which a narrow calligrapher's frieze has been painted in gold on a dark ground. Here the old Ottoman frieze has become narrower, it is no longer of tile, but it is still present. The principal room is the second, and it extends out a bit from the story below it, so situated that it is a corner room. From its many windows the *valide* could watch the always busy Golden Horn and the boats sailing the Bosphorus and thus see something of the world. It is large enough so that its gilded wall panels surmounted by landscapes, and its elaborately gilded and mirrored fireplace do not overcome one. Around its walls under the windows runs a continuous sofa. It is cheerful and light-flooded and by far the prettiest of the Europeanized rooms of the harem.

For a long time it was thought that Selim III built these rooms for his mother, and many writers on the harem call them Mihrişah's rooms. The present administration of the museum refuses to go along with this. They have found nothing to support a date for their construction, but only for certain decoration. The rooms can therefore be attributed to any time after European taste became the fashion. To me the main room's fireplace and especially the tiles within it suggest the fireplace of the ground-floor room of Selim III built by Osman III, and it is therefore my guess that Osman III built this suite too. The presence of Selim III's *tuğra* shows that it received at least some of its decoration at his command. That Selim's mother, Mihrişah, used it a great deal is likely, for it connects easily with the second-story suite Selim built for himself.

An interesting bit of *saray* jealousy reveals itself here. When Abdurrahman Şeref inspected this area, two lines were missing from an inscription in the first room. Later the museum found them hidden away somewhere. They turned out to refer to Selim's mother, connecting the "exalted building of the *valide sultan*" to "Mihrişah Kadın, a sea of benevolence and a mine of constancy." What probably happened is that these lines were removed by order of the mother of Mustafa IV, who wanted no eulogies to her predecessor.

Back on the ground floor, starting from the Valide's Corridor, runs the Corridor of the Bath (Hamam Koridoru), off which both the *valide*'s and the sultan's baths are located. It connects with the Sultan's Hall (Hünkâr Sofası). Before we consider this area, which will lead us to the sultan's rooms, we had best locate the rest of the women's on the ground floor. Those of the first and second *kadın*s lie off a narrow corridor that runs from the Hall with the Hearth to the Golden Way. Nearer the Hall with the Hearth and therefore handier to the sultan is the suite of the first *kadın*. It is neither very large nor very light, and on this floor consists of two rooms, a toilet, and a stairway to the upper story. The room to the left, called her music room or *meşk odası*, is pretty horrible. Its walls present purple and white European tiles, its fireplace has been turned into a niche where sits a European armoire and over it is a sea scene. That the room was once Ottoman in style is attested by the few old tiles that remain in its niches and its covered-over tall and narrow fireplace. The room on the right of the corridor, though rococo, is more pleasing, with less ugly European tiles and red and gilt panels. The best tiles are in the little hallway, which has never been "modernized." The music room is now used as a storeroom, which serves it right. In it I saw an old large, metal-studded leather saddle bag which perhaps was used in the *sürre* or procession of yearly gifts to the Holy Cities.

The lady who lived in these rooms was certainly sequestered, and one hopes that the sultan invited her out of them often.

A Room of the Valide Sultan

HALUK DOGANBEY

A Room of the Double Kiosk in the Harem

Next to this suite, off the same passage, are the rooms of the second *kadın*, different in details but equally constrained. The only windows either of these suites have are to the Valide's Court. The rooms as yet show no sign of restoration and will probably be closed for some time to come. The other *kadıns* must have lived on the second floor, though their suites cannot now be pinpointed.

Before we leave the area of the Valide's Court it may be interesting to learn something about these women who dominated the harem and at times the sultan. Many were fascinating characters, but we shall concentrate on the most powerful of them, Mahpeyker Kösem, favorite *kadın* of Ahmet I, mother of Murat IV and İbrahim, and grandmother of Mehmet IV. Mehmet's mother, Turhan, became her rival for power.

Kösem was a Greek, said to have been the daughter of a Greek priest of one of the Aegean islands, probably captured during one of the Ottoman-Venetian maritime campaigns. Her name was then Anastasia but was changed after her capture, no doubt on her admission to the palace, to Mahpeyker (Moon-Shaped), and later by Sultan Ahmet to Kösem (Leader of the Flock). She seems to have been first sold to the governor of Bosnia from whose household the fame of her beauty, charm and exquisite manners penetrated to the *kızlar ağası* who either bought her for the palace or persuaded the governor to present her as a gift. She was probably twelve or thirteen at the time, and Ahmet I was not on the throne yet. Nor could he have made her a *kadın* immediately on his accession; it is known that others preceded her. When she did catch his eye, however, she soon outstripped all in his affections.

Kösem gave Ahmet six children: Murat IV, İbrahim, the unfortunate princes Kasım and Süleyman, and two girls, Ayşe and Fatma. Three of the boys died violently. The girls, being luckier as female Ottoman royal children often were, lived out their lives. Each had six husbands. Ayşe died at the age of forty-nine. It is not known when Fatma died, but she married for the last time at the age of sixty-two.

Kösem did not interfere in affairs of state during the life of Ahmet I, nor did she immediately come into her own on his death. Mustafa, born of a different mother, acceded, and Kösem retired to the Old Palace. Nor was Osman II, who came to the throne next, one of her sons, but he paid her the signal honor of visiting her in the Old Palace, so she must have been considered important even then. Finally, after a period of confusion, came the turn of her eldest son, Murat IV. He was only fourteen, and his youth gave Kösem her opportunity. She was a woman of force and intelligence, and she commanded the administration of the state. In order to avoid the interference of harem favorites she encouraged homosexual tendencies in Murat who dallied with the youths of the Palace School and with a Persian companion. When he was twenty-three he took power into his own hands, but his relationship with his mother stayed close. When he was out of the capital she kept him informed.

We have seen that Murat grew into a merciless man and killed all his brothers except Ibrahim. On his deathbed, crazed with cruelty, he gave the order for Ibrahim's execution. Kösem blocked it and thus saved the Ottoman dynasty from annihilation and enabled it to continue for another three hundred years. Thus all subsequent Ottoman sultans were descended from her.

Unfortunately Ibrahim, who succeeded Murat in 1640, was wholly unfit for the task. He was mentally weak and had lived so long in fear of his life that when the *kızlar ağası* came to inform him that he was now sultan, he thought he was being called out to be killed and refused to leave the heir's apartment. Only when Kösem had Murat's body brought into his view did Ibrahim believe he was safe.

In the early years of Ibrahim's reign Kösem was again the supreme power. She concerned herself with policy and appointments and on the whole administered the Empire wisely, with the exception of financial matters. In order to keep the childish Ibrahim amused she plied him with new slaves and gave in to his desires to smother his favorites with luxuries. Yet she had a more statesmanlike reason for tempting him with slave girls. Ibrahim was the last of his line, and on him depended the continuation of the House of Osman. He was subject to fits of impotence, and the country waited two years after his accession for his first child to be born. Eventually, however, his sexual power became so stimulated that he is credited with taking twenty-four girls in twenty-four hours, a rumor that seems a bit extravagant. At any rate between 1642 and 1646 Ibrahim had ten children. More credit for the offspring went to magic than to the mothers. A character named Cinci (Jinji) Hüseyin informed Kösem that he had inherited certain magic formulas and secured her permission to try them on the padishah. It so happened that pronouncement of the formulas and relief from impotence coincided, and Cinci's fortune was made. He was loaded with presents and money and given a high theological post for which he was little fitted. We have noted some of his formulas in the Iftariye of the Fourth Court.

As Ibrahim became used to the position of sultan he became more foolish instead of more stable. One of the women story-tellers who were popular among Ottomans used to entertain the harem women with tales of an Eastern monarch who was so fond of skins he had his garments, cushions, rugs and hangings all made of sable. Ibrahim emulated him by having a room hung with furs and even clothing his cats in sable. So great was the palace demand for scents, furs and women that the price of all three rose in Istanbul. Nor was this the extent of his follies.

Meanwhile his harem favorites had become jealous of Kösem and stirred up her son to resist her. Seeing him behaving so foolishly as to appear with his beard adorned with jewels and watching him squander the resources of the Empire while powerless to stop him, Kösem withdrew from the palace to a country house and later to a house in a garden in Eyüp.

Obviously things could not go on like this. The court and the religious establishment called for the deposition of this frivolous and unheeding sultan. It is evidence of Kösem's dominant position that they felt they had to consult her. In her heart Kösem must have been in favor of Ibrahim's deposition, but because he was her son and very likely because she did not want to see the position of *valide sultan* pass to someone else, she resisted. She was, however, talked down, and Ibrahim's seven-year-old son, who became Mehmet IV, was enthroned before the Gate of Felicity. Von Hammer says: "All the dignitaries could not be admitted to that ceremony for fear of frightening the child by too great a crowd."

Ibrahim was imprisoned in one of the rooms of the Cage, high up under the roof off a balcony that looks down onto the Favorites' Court. Unfortunately for him the usual thing happened. A group of people began to agitate for his return, and he was strangled, it is now thought in the tower that has been swallowed up by the *mabeyn*. How much Kösem had to do with his execution has always been a source of controversy. Von Hammer finds in her favor and thinks that to the extent that she had anything to do with it, she was motivated by concern for the state.

There is no controversy over what happened next. Kösem continued to be the ruling personality, even sitting with the child in the sultan's lodge and tutoring him in the decisions handed down from there. She used the youth of the sultan and his mother as an excuse for refusing to retire to the Old Palace. This situation was not to last. Turhan Valide, a blonde Russian, had a will to match Kösem's and no doubt an eye on the *valide*'s suite. She soon commenced to plot against Kösem, who was now called the Great or Old

Valide, and the people of the court and state took sides. The officers of the Janissaries rallied to Kösem, whereas the black eunuchs favored Turhan. Plot followed plot, and to protect themselves against the machinations of Turhan's eunuchs Kösem and the Janissary officers decided to do away with three of the opposition ringleaders. A night was agreed upon, and Kösem arranged that certain gates of the palace be left open. It must have been hard to keep a secret in the palace, so close were the quarters and so rife the intrigue. The plan must have been betrayed, for that very night Turhan and her black eunuchs went to work.

They were able to persuade the halberdiers with tresses and the pages of the Privy Chamber to join them by convincing them that the young sultan was in danger. Süleyman Ağa, the chief black eunuch, was their leader and guided them to Kösem's apartment. Her eunuchs, who were guarding it, either fell before the pages' swords or fled.

Hearing the commotion, Kösem thought the Janissary officers had arrived and called out, "Have they come?"

"Yes, they have come," Süleyman Ağa answered. "Only come out."

Doing so, she recognized who it was who had come and, a terrified and toothless old woman of sixty-two, fled from her sleeping room down the corridors of the *saray*, along the Golden Way and through the Court of the Black Eunuchs to the Dome with Closets, probably hoping to get out through the Carriage Gate. The gate was closed, and so Kösem attempted to hide in one of the closets of the little room.

Süleyman Ağa led eunuchs, pages and halberdiers after her. A slave interposed herself saying, "I am the *valide sultan*," but the eunuchs cried, "It is not she" and thrust her aside. They raced along and when they did not find her in the last room before the Carriage Gate they took to ransacking the closets. Breaking down the doors, they found the old *valide* and dragged her out. Somewhere in this vicinity one of the halberdiers cut down the cord of a curtain, with which they strangled her. She was a strong woman and fought for her life. The blood that gushed from her nose and ears stained the clothing of her murderers. Thus easily could the furious overturn the powerful in Topkapı.

So Turhan won the battle and became supreme in the harem and strong in the councils of state. She too was a capable woman, if a cruel one. Be it said to her credit that she realized the Empire needed a strong man at the head and had Mehmet Köprülü appointed grand vizier. Thus began the service of the Köprülü family to the Empire and for a period a reversal of the decline of Ottoman fortunes. Their strength of character put an end to harem influence, and although later *valide*s had some power, none ever achieved Kösem's strength.

The only quarters of the *valide* we have not discussed is her bath. Its location next to the sultan's is one more indication of her closeness to her son. Not even the rooms of the *kadın*s were as intimately associated with his as were hers. The *valide*'s bath is a smaller replica of the sultan's, and we shall therefore describe his. There is a tradition that hers was built in 1653, but it may be that it was done over then, in the time of Turhan. There is nothing to date the sultan's unless one accepts the tradition that the tile panel of the Golden Way comes from here. It may be that not only this bath but the entire water system of the palace were the work of Sinan, but at present this cannot be proved.

The bath follows the usual pattern of three rooms: dressing room, cool room, and warm room. It was in the last that the sultan did his bathing; here the fountains are. The most important is a wall cascade from which the water flowed into an oblong tub with a seat added to each end. The sultan did not sit in the tub, since as a Muslim he would wash only in running water, but rather on one of the seats. A bath attendant poured water over him with a basin. This fountain was for hot water which was heated by a boiler in an adjacent room. In the corners on either side wall fountains gave water probably of different temperatures. To the left as one enters from the Bath Corridor is a grill of bronze behind which there is still another fountain. Here the sultan performed his more intimate ablutions.

As in non-royal *hamam*s, the ceiling consists of a myriad of small domes supported by columns, these very slender. The classic Ottoman stalactite capitals on them are evidence of the early origin of the bath. A few European capitals have intruded, probably the result of renovation. All is white marble in this room; all is light.

The sultan was attended in the harem bath by older women until he was dressed, when young ones came to serve him coffee and to entertain him while he relaxed in the sybaritic surroundings of his dressing room with its couch and rich hangings.

The Bath Corridor, which is narrow, is divided architecturally into three sections, perhaps indicating three stages of construction, and is lined with Italian tiles of a late date. Over the doorway of each section is an inscription. The one nearest the Valide's Corridor offers good wishes, the second talks about "this heavenly hall," meaning the Hall of the Sultan, how when its door opens it is the disc of the moon splitting or a star rising, and the third gives a welcome to the Hall of the Sultan.

[231]

THE HAREM

II

SOMETHING of the air of majesty still pervades the Hall of the Sultan (Hünkâr Sofası), the most spacious room of the harem. It was the reception room where, from his throne against one wall, the sultan greeted the women of the harem on special occasions and to which he invited them for palace entertainment. The women trooped in attended by their slaves and dressed in their most magnificent costumes. They wore the harem trousers closed at the ankles, and over them a slash-skirted, long-sleeved dress whose low-cut neck was filled in with a chemise of delicate, transparent material. A jeweled belt encircled their hips, or perhaps a finely embroidered shawl. Over this was a robe of heavy satin or velvet, long and usually sleeveless, trimmed with fur or fur-lined, often with ermine, according to the season. Their hair was long and crowned with a high headpiece. They wore jewels wherever jewels could be worn—rings, bracelets, earrings, necklaces and innumerable pins, some attached to the headpiece, some to the front of the dress. The necklaces often hid tiny receptacles for verses from the Koran, and the pins might spell out in diamonds *maşallah* (what wonders God hath willed).

First making obeisance to the sultan, they seated themselves in the raised end of the room. The *valide sultan* and the princesses ranged themselves on the sofas before the windows at the rear; the *kadıns*, being forbidden so high a station in the sultan's presence, sank onto cushions on the floor. The slaves ranked themselves along the wall, motionless, their hands crossed in front of them.

The room is a long rectangle, and even deprived of the raised portion it has ample floor space for entertainment. It had long been attributed to Sinan and to the same date as Murat III's bedroom which flanks it, but the recent investigations have shown this supposition groundless. Its foundation is of an entirely different shape from that of Murat's room and the wall between them so thick as to suggest it was originally an outside wall. Furthermore in this wall have been found traces of two windows that must once have looked out onto a garden or court. To clinch the argument Holland has some late sixteenth-century pictures of this part of the harem in which there is no Sultan's Hall. The museum authorities now date the Hall of the Sultan to later in the sixteenth century than Murat's bedroom. Moreover certain evidence of decoration of the end of the sixteenth century has come to light under the present wall surface. The room has a central dome supported by large arches until recently painted in elaborate European patterns but now restored to Ottoman motifs. The interior of the dome, however, is still a mixture of early and late. Its center is a design of gilt Ottoman script on a green ground, whereas the rest of the dome shows a multitude of greyish-white painted designs of an indescribably complex nature on a red ground.

The room probably originally had Iznik tiles, since one of the panels of the Golden Way is thought to have come from here, to judge from the inscription in the Persian much used in the early court, which says: "May this sublime imperial hall bring happiness and blessing over the Moon of Fortunate Conjunction until the Day of Resurrection."

The only original tile work still showing in the hall is a frieze which encompasses the room just under the arches and which is inscribed with verses from the Koran. It is now composed of white letters on a blue ground as in its early days, but had at one time been painted and gilded. The room has been so much redecorated—one might say overdecorated—that it is difficult to visualize what it must once have looked like. Osman III did it over in the eighteenth century. It suffered from a later fire—how much is not clear—and was restored after that. The tiling now on the walls here and there in the lower part of the main section is of the formal European pattern of blue and white found in the Hall of the Valide, but nothing is apparent of what must be Ottoman floral sprays hidden behind this.

Over the far, railed-off end for the women rises a gallery for musicians who were either slave girls taught to play the instruments of the day or

The Hall of the Sultan showing the raised end for women and the gallery above it for musicians. The sultan sat under the baldequin.

pages trained in the Conservatory of the Palace School. If the latter, they were carefully blindfolded to protect the women from their forbidden eyes. The back wall under the gallery is lined with windows that overlook the Court with the Pond, at the far end of which is the Kiosk of Osman III. The side walls are mirrored and hide, on one side, a stairway to the gallery, on the other a door to the Room of Ahmet III. A railing of spokes with delicate spiral inlays of mother-of-pearl separates this section from the rest of the room.

The same spokes are found on the baldequin columns over the throne dais, which is close to the railed area. Even the grey marble posts of the raised area and the baldequin have the same capitals, making it clear they

[2 3 4]

date from the same period. The raised area's posts support a wide, heavily gilded cornice that runs the entire width of the room under the balcony and suggests nothing Ottoman.

The rest of the room boasts no less than three identical rococo fountains, one to a wall. All in all the room represents the apogee of ornateness that overcame harem decoration in the last century of the palace's active life.

Though the Sultan's Hall is now being freshened, it is being left rococo. The old Iznik tiles under its present walls are too dilapidated—and probably too few remain—to be brought to light. The room was filled with scaffolding when I last saw it, and so it was impossible to get a picture of it. The picture shown here is before the restoration.

The entertainment that went on here was for the most part music and dance, although Mahmut I used to like to watch plays in this room. The dancers were inevitably slave girls, young and agile, whose repertory included a dance called *tavṣan* or hare in which they ran and jumped about like that animal. It undoubtedly included the more sensuous dances, of which Lady Mary Wortley Montagu, who saw some of them in the harem of the wife of an Ottoman official, says: "I am very positive the coldest and most rigid prude on earth could not have looked upon them without thinking of something not to be spoken of." The girls had another accomplishment that delighted the sultans: leaping up and touching a crystal ball that hung before the throne.

The hall saw much music and dance in Selim III's time, for that sultan was particularly fond of these diversions. He was a musician himself and played the *ney*, the wooden flute of the Mevlevi or Dancing Dervishes. Very possibly the Karagöz, the shadow theater of the Turks, was given here, for women saw it notwithstanding its lubricious content. Other women's entertainment, such as listening to the story-teller (*masalçı*), went on in less formal quarters. More boisterous entertainments, such as acrobats performing feats of skill or actors imitating wild beasts, took place in the Hippodrome, where special kiosks were put up for the sultan and his woman. The Sultan's Hall was, after all, a place of elegance. Its other name was the Muayede Salonu (Greeting Salon). It was here that the women offered the sultan their congratulations on *bayram* days.

A corner of the Sultan's Hall is cut off to form part of a small, dark room which connects with the Hall of the Fountain. It was used for a short time as a bedroom by Pertevniyal, the mother of Abdülaziz who committed suicide. When she was moved from the Feriye Palace where the tragedy took

A corner of the Bedroom of Murat III.

place, she left without cloak or veil, but managed to bring along a box containing her wealth.

A door on the opposite side of the Hall of the Sultan takes one to the Bedroom of Murat III, of the sixteenth century and known to be the work of Sinan. It was built in 1578, was blessedly never redecorated, and is the gem of the harem. The fine original Iznik tiles still line its walls. One's eye lights first on a curvacious panel above the fireplace where sprays of tiny plum blossoms stretch upwards on a deep blue blackground. Tiles—floral tiles—are everywhere, lining the niches, in the upper part of the wide recess holding the fountain, on the high walls between the vaults that support the dome, in the panels with their contrasting borders that separate the components of the lower wall. The room has great harmony, partly from its high ceiling and square dimensions, and partly from the fact that in the lower range the tiles are all of the same coloring—blues and reds on a white ground with borders in which the red predominates. This deep, rich red disappears from the Ottoman tiles not more than a half-century later. The usual explanation is that the secret of making it belonged to one craftsman alone, and that when he died the secret died with him. The upper and lower sections of the walls are divided above the height of a man by a frieze of dark blue tiles on which white letters spell out verses from the Koran, among them the Verse of the Throne.

Murat's is a domed room, the interior of the dome holding the attributes of God in gold on a blue-green disc and otherwise decorated with painted motifs. Though every surface of the room is embellished, the details are subordinate to the whole, and the room is lofty and lovely. There are two ranges of windows, the upper ones divided into small panes by plasterwork, many of them colored glass. The fireplace, which dominates the room, is of bronze, tall like the room itself and big enough so that huge logs and even tree trunks used to burn there. Beside it on either side is a recess for the mammoth tongs needed to handle the logs.

On another wall is a *selsibil* or layered fountain larger than most, with three projecting basins over which the water flowed, each basin with its own faucet to add to the flow. Representations of vases of flowers decorate the topmost layer of marble. The fountain is framed in a solid piece of marble, like the doorways. The doors are inlaid from top to bottom with mother-of-pearl, and in them are finely chiseled locks. Behind what looks like the door of a cupboard one can see traces of a window that once looked outdoors.

It is curious to find that the sultan's intimate harem bath was separated from his bedroom by a court or garden. However, it may be that the bath

The bronze chimney piece of the Bedroom of Murat III. Notice the tiles of plum blossoms around the cone, a favorite 16th-century design, the tiled wall niches, and the inserts for fireplace instruments.

NECATI ORBAY

The tiered fountain set in a marble frame in the Bedroom of Murat III. The picture gives a clear idea of the calligraphic frieze and the upper and lower tile patterns, as well as of the classic mullioned Ottoman windows.

was built first and his earlier bedroom was nearer to it. In any event I would guess from the thickness of the walls of Murat's room that at least three of them were originally outside walls. We know that, except for its entrance hall, all the rooms contiguous to it are later.

The sultan for whom this bedroom was constructed was a great builder. He put up mosques, schools, and food kitchens for the poor, and added extensively to Topkapı's harem for the numerous ladies he brought from the Old Palace.

He too had a favorite, Safiye (Purity), a member of the noble Venetian family of Baffo who had been taken captive by Turkish corsairs while on her way to join her father who was governor of the Island of Corfu, then in

[239]

Venetian hands. Because of her beauty and station she was brought to the *saray*. Murat was so fascinated by her, he had no other concubine for twenty years. However, she bore him only one son, and this gave Murat's mother and sister a point on which to argue. Only one male heir made the dynasty unsafe, and on this the people agreed. Thus Murat was persuaded to accept other concubines, and two Hungarian girls were presented to him. At first Murat was impotent with them, and when his mother, Nur-u Banu, learned this she blamed it on sorcery inspired by Safiye. Certain Jewesses and harem women she claimed were Safiye's tools she had severely punished—the Jewesses beaten by eunuchs, the harem women exiled for a time to Rhodes.

Murat's impotence did not last, and Safiye's rivals were successful in making her share his amorous attentions. Eventually the slave girls awakened in him a taste for polygamy, and he took to bed numerous women by whom he had numerous progeny. Rumor credits him with a hundred and three, but actually only fifty-six can be accounted for.

Murat appears not to have been a strong-minded character. Neither was his father, Selim II, but Selim left affairs of state to the great grand vizier, Mehmet Sokullu. On his accession Murat confirmed Sokullu in the vizierate, but he was the sort of person who, without statesmanlike ability himself, still could not refrain from interfering. That, and his predilection for favorites, both men and women, ate into Sokullu's power. Many people, including the historian, von Hammer, date the beginning of the downfall of the Ottoman Empire from the decline of Sokullu's power, True, the Empire lasted several centuries longer, but it never again achieved its sixteenth-century greatness.

Murat III was a man of only medium stature, lean and pale, with well-marked dark brows over languid eyes and a long, reddish beard. His paleness and leanness were thought to be due to a fondness for opium, and when he stopped the habit and turned to wine, he lost these characteristics. He was interested in clock-making and painting. Mysticism attracted him, particularly mystic poetry. He used to spend his mornings in the company of the creative and the intellectual, then, after afternoon prayer, go to the harem to enjoy its delights. During his reign the cultural life of Istanbul flourished. The *Hünername* or *Book of Skills* (of the sultans) was written and illustrated with miniatures. Special albums of paintings were made for his enjoyment, including the one with designs that must have inspired the deer panels. Among his favorites were men of letters. Yet he was easily irritated and at times cruel. This was the man who rebuilt Topkapı after its first great fire and to whose use the palace's handsomest room was dedicated. The room is among those to be opened, and a better place to become acquainted with Ottoman interior decoration in its classic period can scarcely be found.

In the basement under it is an amazingly beautiful marble pool surrounded by a low pierced marble balustrade. A tiled room for the sultan overlooks it up a few steps at one end. Tradition has it that slave girls used to bathe here naked while the sultan watched from his perch and that İbrahim used to like to throw the girls in. I tend to put this down to gossip, in spite of having read Flachat's account of how Mahmut I liked to call his women to bathe in a large pool. He had them furnished with chemises such as they usually wore in the pool except that these were put together not with stitches but with paste. In the water the paste melted, and the chemises floated away. The women's reaction to this was a source of great amusement to the sultan. Flatchat says the sultan watched from a window, but there are only open archways that give a view of the pool. Since there are no steps down into it, these stories may well all be apocryphal. With its spouts from

A view of the pool under the Bedroom of Murat III.

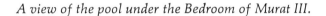

[2 4 1]

the marble columns within it and the spurting fountain toward the sultan's room, the pool may have been simply a place for the sultan to enjoy the sight and sound of rippling water, always a Muslim pleasure.

Next to the underground pool is another large pool, also of marble but open to the sky and shallower. For some unexplained reason it had been covered over with earth by Abdülhamit I and was brought to light only in the recent restoration. One looks down on it from the Court of the Favorites, from which a stairway leads under the Double Kiosk to the underground pool.

Also underground are the palace dungeons, surprisingly spacious but naturally dark with the only light slanting in from high apertures. One wonders who was put there and what their offenses were. Were they palace people who had transgressed palace rules or in some way offended the sultan, or were they outsiders? Historians are silent about them.

The Kiosk of Ahmet I in the harem.

NECATI ORBAY

The Doorway of the Circumcision Room

The Kiosk of Osman III as seen from Gülhane Parkı
and showing the inner wall of the Palace

Back upstairs, thrusting out from Murat's bedroom to the west, is another example of genuine Ottoman, the Kiosk of Ahmet I (1603–1617). It is a very small room, formerly called Ahmet I's Library because it was thought its cupboards once contained books. Actually there was no library in the harem. Books were brought to whatever room the sultan chose. The first thing that strikes one in this room is the pervasive blue-green light reflected from the blue-green of its wall tiles. In this ambience it is as if the architect had tried to encompass within a small space all the elements of Ottoman decoration—floral and plain tiles, mother-of-pearl and tortoise-shell inlay, marble frames surrounding inlaid cupboard doors, niches with tiled backs, a calligraphic frieze, poetic inscriptions, windows whose panes are separated by designs of plaster, a fountain enclosed in a cabinet, and all this covered by a dome on arches. Other rooms have these elements, but here they combine in a particularly dazzling display, perhaps because of the light that pours in through the windows. One of its inscriptions says: "That shah [Ahmet I] had this room built thinking he would be able to see the world," and when it was built he must have had an unobstructed view of land and sea. Now it looks out onto the Court with the Pond and the remnants of the garden beside it.

Another inscription dated 1608/9 compares Ahmet I to Alexander the Great, the gold centerpiece of the dome to the sun, and the running water in the fountain to the Kevser, a river of paradise. A third finds the windows of mystic beauty. There is a tale handed down in the palace that Selim III used this as a music room. It may well be true, for Selim's love of music is well substantiated, and certainly this sparkling little place would have made a more delightful hideaway in which to practice his flute than the nondescript room outside the *valide*'s prayer room.

Beside this kiosk is another of Topkapı's jewels, sometimes called the dining room of Ahmet III or, because of the painting of fruit on its walls, the Fruit Room (Yemiş, Odası). Dining room is a late appellation given it, and it is doubtful that it was ever used as such. There were no dining rooms per se in Ottoman times; trays were set up for eating in whatever room one chose. Very likely this was a room in which Ahmet III took his ease.

An eighteenth-century room, it illustrates the change in Turkish taste. Instead of tiles its walls are lined with painted panels of flowers and fruit. Instead of a high dome it has a low ceiling to which gilding and a square mirror are affixed. Its fireplace is marble with only its tiny niches tiled. This room also looks out onto the Court with the Pond, and at an angle to one of its windows is an *ışıklık*, a place for a candle or lamp, set into the wall.

NECATI ORBAY

The Fruit Room or Room of Ahmet III in the harem.

From window and light one might surmise that this was a favorite reading spot of Ahmet III's. A quatrain wishing Khan Ahmet happiness is written on a gold ground above the doorway, and a frieze of Arabic poems painted in gold on black extends around the room. Arabic, as well as Persian, was part of the equipment of an Ottoman gentleman, and without doubt Ahmet could read these lines. Since he built the room, they may have been some of his favorite poetry. He was a patron of poetry and, for that matter, of all the arts. A jutting ell is the entrance to the dais under the gallery of the Hall of the Sultan. An inscription dates the room 1705/6.

On the other side of the Bedroom of Murat III one comes upon three other small rooms, all tiled from floor to ceiling. The first one is the vestibule to Murat's room and, like it, the work of Sinan and one of the harem's distinctions. On each jamb of the door to Murat's room is set a green and white stone column that turns in its groove, smaller than but reminiscent of the turning column of the Green Mosque in Bursa. Over the handsome inlaid door is one of the depressed arches of contrasting stone the Ottomans liked so well, this one of pale pink and black porphyry against white marble. Above it is the date 1578. Like the classic Ottoman room that it is, it

[244]

contains cupboards with inlaid doors set in frames carved from marble slabs and sided by niches. The walls are faced with tiles of slender floral sprays that bespeak an early date. A dome tops it. The room lies in about the center of the sultan's private apartments, and from it doors lead in various directions.

Toward the south, linking them with the *valide*'s court, are two charming rooms, the small Hall with the Fountain (Çeşmeli Sofa) and the larger Hall with the Hearth (Ocaklı Sofa), each named for its salient feature. The

The Hall of the Fountain, showing the varied tile patterns. Through the door-way can be seen the entrance hall to the Bedroom of Murat III.

NECATI ORBAY

[245]

The Hall with the Hearth. It is a particularly good example of classic Ottoman decoration, showing tiled walls separated by a calligraphic frieze, mother-of-pearl-inlaid doors, painted pendentives, a painted decoration surrounding the dome, and the dominating fireplace, this one of bronze.

latter is part of the restoration ordered by Mehmet IV after the fire of 1665. Both are completely tiled, the Hall with the Fountain in nineteen different patterns, Ottomans having seldom seen any virtue in sticking to one. Both these seventeenth-century rooms must have been used by the sultan at times as a means of reaching the *valide*'s court, from which he had access to many parts of the harem. It is said that in the fireplace of the Hall with the Hearth the harem eunuchs heated the charcoal for the braziers to be set in the living rooms of the sultan.

One may easily wonder why the sultans built so many small rooms in the harem instead of fewer large ones more suited to majesty. The first explanation that comes to mind is that the Topkapı harem was the winter harem, and small rooms were easier to heat. There may also be a lack of tradition for large rooms for living space among the Turks. They built spacious mosques for worship, but, so far as has been indicated by the few old Turkic palaces that have been excavated farther east, their palaces consisted of large courts but small rooms. It was not until the Ottomans came to build Western-style palaces that rooms of great size came in.

Back at the anteroom of the Bedroom of Murat III and starting out to the east, one goes along a partly open corridor that connects with the Golden Way. This is the Council Place of the Jinns where, palace people believed, jinns met after dark to plan their mischief. It was a place to avoid at night, for who knew what jinn vengeance might be like if they were interrupted.

Off it are both the Court of the Favorites and what was long known as the Heir's Apartment (Veliaht Dairesi) or the Cage (Kafes). Hayrullah Örs has by now ascertained that it is instead a kiosk built for the sultan's pleasure. It was also known as the Şimşirlik (Place of Boxwood) because of its proximity to the Boxwood Gardens. A suite of two square, handsomely tiled rooms, it is presently named the Double Kiosk (Çifte Köşkü). Its exact date is unknown, but the museum authorities conjecture that it belongs to the period of Mehmet III (1595–1603). Originally of one story, in the nineteenth century its eastern room was divided horizontally to make a second. In the process its dome was covered with a flat ceiling and forgotten. Work on these rooms brought it to light in 1963. The restorers found a dome whose outside is covered with lead like all the domes of the palace, but over whose interior is stretched a sheet of linen affixed to the surface with heavy glue and, at intervals, heavy nails. On this surface is an overlay of gold on which tulips, carnations, stylized birds' wings, stylized waterlilies, and artichoke leaves shimmer in gold and green and crimson and other colors. The dome's center consists of wood inlaid in a geometric design, around it a stylized pattern interspersed with gold zigzag and all lightened by the use of vermilion on a ground of turquoise. Originally an ornamental pendant hung from the dome, an indication that it was a room used by the sultan, but all that remains of this today is the iron core.

The apartment is faced with fine tiles in a profusion of designs—cypresses, hyacinths, tulips and roses to which are added grape vines, all in greens and blues and whites, and a red that has gone brownish.

It is a handsome place, decorated at the windows with recesses lined with marble and deep enough so that there is room for little spigots from

The Double Kiosk in the harem, from the Paved Courtyard of the Favorites. Just inside the railing can be seen the lower door to the stairway that leads to the covered pool. Beyond the kiosk on the right can be seen a part of the exterior of the Bedroom of Murat III. The steps on the left lead to the corridor called the Consultation Place of the Jinns.

NECATI ORBAY

which water, piped from window to window, flowed into small basins. Running water has always been praised by Muslims, and it was plentiful in the palace, splashing both indoors and out. The room has its inscriptions, extolling the running water, wondering whether it comes from Zemzem, the sacred well of Mecca, or from the Tesnim, a river of paradise.

Both rooms have fine old fireplaces, narrow and tall and hooded. In the domeless room it has recently been discovered beneath the black paint at some period applied to it that the fireplace is made of brass which had originally been and is once again covered with gold leaf. The one in the domed room is made of plaster painted in the same motifs as the tiles.

The two tiers of windows of the kiosk give a view of what used to be called the Paved Court of the Cage. It occurs to me that the name may have come from the bars on the lower windows which are probably late additions. Now, with the changed opinion of the use of the kiosk, the court is referred to as the Paved Court of the Gözdes or Favorites (Gözdeler Taşlığı). The building itself juts out into the court, its outside walls agleam with pale blue tiles. From a midpoint of the building to the northern end of the court runs a low marble balustrade carved in an arabesque design. From it today one looks down on the newly excavated marble pool. Here, when it was covered, the jinns used to dance. Below it is the garden inexplicably called the Elephant Garden or in some cases the Boxwood Garden. In this lies the ground story of an old kiosk, now termed the Elephant House (Fiilhane), perhaps because it is in the Elephant Garden. The kiosk once rose along the wall that separates this garden from the next to the north. Along this wall and the one opposite it one can see points at which old beams must have been inserted and an old roof line that indicate old buildings were once here. In fact stone steps lead up from the open pool to what must have been a story above the Elephant House. A marble doorway opens high in the wall at its back, though it now has no place to which to lead.

On the upper floors between the Court of the Valide and the Court of the Gözdes the rooms of the princes, the Cage, were actually located. The custom of the Cage came in with the seventeenth century. Before that the sultan's sons were sent out in their teens as governors of provinces so that they might learn to rule. However, on the accession of a new sultan, all his brothers were executed to prevent intrigue and war over the throne. With the introduction of the Cage their lives were at least theoretically spared, although, as we have seen, in practice they were sometimes the victims of the bowstring.

Their suites are usually off a corridor that looks over the Favorites'

Court, and their only windows give onto this corridor. The windows to the court, and perhaps even the skylights in the rooms may have been eighteen-century innovations, for one reads much about the darkness of the Cage in the seventeenth century. The rooms have fireplaces and marble-framed niches. Some are tiled, some plastered and probably once painted. The painting that remains today is apt to be the ugly streaked colors that were in fashion in the *saray* at some late date. In 1910 Abdurrhman Şeref counted ten rooms for the princes, but another Turkish historian, İsmail Hakkı Uzunçarşılı, says there were twelve apartments, each with several rooms. Surely the number of apartments must have varied with the number of princes.

The Ottoman State did not follow the rule of primogeniture; the throne went to the eldest surviving male of the dynasty. Thus brother often succeeded brother, and the heir to the throne sometimes spent most of his life in the Cage, which in the seventeenth century was invariably dark. No wonder so many sultans proved unstable. Süleyman II, when he came to the throne at the age of forty-five, wrote to his grand vizier: "It is forty years that I was imprisoned in a dark place, despairing of life. I came into the world anew, and I found the world a confused mass."

When a prince's father was alive he had a certain amount of freedom. He accompanied his father to an imperial mosque for Friday prayer. He learned to ride a horse, to shoot with bow and arrow, to use a mace, and to hunt. Once his father died that freedom disappeared. He no longer went to the Princes' School but was taught by elderly women slaves. At the proper age he was allowed a sex life. According to one source only women past child-bearing age were assigned to him, according to another young girls who were fed certain beverages supposed to prevent conception and who perhaps used other practices. If these arrangements went amiss, the child was strangled at birth. Abdülhamit I seems to have been the only prince who, while in the Cage, had a child who was allowed to live. The women's costumes of the time could well conceal a pregnancy, and a daughter was secretly born to one of his slaves and smuggled out of the harem to a wet nurse. She was called Adopted Lady (Ahretlik, Hanım) until her father acceded, when she took her place as Dürr-ü Sehvar Sultan.

To pass the time the princes learned to make jewelry, do inlay and cabinet work, draw on Morocco leather, fashion bows and arrows and other articles. I have always doubted that the princes experienced as complete separation from the outside world as has been claimed. Women slaves were not likely to have had the knowledge to teach all these skills, and I suspect that craftsmen must have been allowed in to instruct the princes. Certainly Ahmet III, who entered the Cage at fourteen and spent twenty-seven years there, could not have become the excellent calligrapher he was without expert instruction. Nor did Mahmut I, who wrote Arabic poetry under a pseudonym, learn how to do so from a woman slave.

All sultans had to be horsemen, if only to ride to the mosque for Friday prayer. How did İbrahim, who entered the Cage at two and stayed there twenty-two years, learn to sit a horse, or Ahmet II who went in at five and came out forty-three years later? I suspect there must have been some loosening of constraint, perhaps at Edirne. The extent of it may have varied depending on who was sultan.

There was one exception to the incarceration of the heir before the nineteenth century, when it was abandoned—Selim III. He was carefully trained for the sultanate by his father, Mustafa III, and allowed a good deal of freedom by his predecessor, Abdülhamit I. He is known to have had contacts outside the palace and was even in correspondence with Louis XVI of France, asking his advice on the governing of a state. The result was an enlightened monarch, too much so for his time.

Despite the Cage, so well established in the public mind was danger to the princes that the populace sometimes asked for assurance that they were alive. We have seen that Murat IV had to produce his brothers for a council on foot, although in the end the suspicions of the populace were justified. During the rebellion that dethroned Selim III he was asked for confirmation that his cousins, Mustafa and Mahmut, were safe. Selim, who was a much more humane man than his ancestor, Murat IV, was deeply hurt at this lack of trust and wrote to his grand vizier, "May God increase the days of their lives."

Past the Meeting Place of the Jinns, where the Golden Way widens, one comes upon a stairway to the second floor. Its immediate goal is the area of the *gözdes*, where most of the rooms have painted decoration, even to their ceilings. Set in the walls between pairs of rooms are the *ışıklık* or little cupboards for lights, with a glass door opening into either room. One finds them often in the harem.

The second floor of the harem is not continuous, that is, it does not appear in all the buildings. However, by a series of twists and turns it wends its way past the Cevri Kalfa Staircase and around the Valide's Court to an apartment over a part of her suite. This, it is believed, belonged to the Haznedar Usta or Lady Treasurer. The second story at the south end of the harem, where Selim's suite and the second-story suite of the *valide* are located, are entirely separate from the rest of this floor and have stairways of their own.

From the part of the second floor we are now discussing stairways, usually steep and narrow, lead to up the third floor and even to attic rooms. Off a balcony from one of the third-floor rooms is the domed prison from which the Janissaries rescued Mustafa I by pulling him through a hole in the roof. At present it is rather pleasant, having a dome painted in leafy designs and equipped with both skylight and window. All this, however, came later. In Mustafa's day the room was dark and depressing. These upper-story rooms vary in decoration. Some are handsomely tiled, some are pleasingly painted, others are dilapidated or painted in splashy color. All have fireplaces and niches. Many were the rooms of slaves attached to the *kadıns*, favorites, or

The Mirrored Room of Sultan Abdülhamit I. This is also called the mabeyn, *the place between harem and* selâmlık.

princes. The upper stories are all waiting for restoration and, in the case of some, the rebuilding of stairways and balcony supports before they can be open to public view.

Down on the ground floor the Golden Way continues until at the anteroom at the end it gives access to the suite whose chief room is variously known as the Room of Selim I, the Mirrored Room of Abdülhamit I, and the *mabeyn*. It is almost entirely disengaged from the palace, having the Gözdes' Court on the left, a small court which adjoins the Corridor with Pillars on the right, and gardens beyond it.

The first building on this site may have been put up by Selim I in the early sixteenth century, or, more likely, by his grandson, Selim II, since his name is inscribed over one of the doors. Actually we know very little of its history except for what Abdülhamit I's confidential secretary has recorded, which is that an addition was made by that sultan in 1779. The new *mabeyn*, as it was called, was attached to a stone room called the tower which had at some period been transformed into a treasury. This has been identified as one of the Conqueror's watch towers. One can still see a corner of it where it protrudes into the Corridor with Pillars near the Mabeyn Door. Abdülhamit I built here a two-room suite, one a sort of anteroom, the other the Mirrored Room (Aynalı Oda). The latter was first called the Room with the Fountain because a *selsibil* (the kind of fountain, you will recall, in which water falls from layer to layer) was inserted in one wall. Abdülhamit lined the room's lower walls with mirrors except for a few windows, and the upper with stained glass. Watercolor scenes decorate its walls and an oil painting its ceiling. Though it has the time-honored religious frieze running around it, the fact that this is painted instead of tiled is evidence of its late date. The rooms bears the *tuğra* of Abdülhamit I. The anteroom to the suite harbors the door to a secret staircase, very dark and twisting, to the *gözdes'* quarters. Thus they could reach Abdülhamit without using the more public stairs in the Golden Way.

The suite is called the *mabeyn* because it lies between harem and *selâmlık* and was sometimes enjoyed by the women. It was Abdülhamit's favorite room. He liked to converse here with his statesmen and at other times proclaimed *halvet* or privacy and brought his harem women in to entertain him.

One day when he was sixty-four and ill, Abdülhamit saw off the yearly procession of the *sürre* to the Holy Cities, visited his sons who were not in the Cage but in the Revan Kiosk and the Circumcision Room, and presently came to the *mabeyn*. Here an official paper was brought him apprizing him of the loss to the Russians of a Turkish stronghold on the Black Sea. The current war with Russia had already worn him down. He asked for a pen but proved too weak to write his instructions. The doctor came, bled him, which must have used up the rest of his strength, and fed him medicine. Realizing all this was useless, he dismissed the men and called for his women. He would pass his last hours as pleasantly as he could. Toward morning he died here.

Abdülhamit I, though forty-eight when he came to the throne, was a great man for the ladies. Among his numerous women his favorite was Ruhşah. Not much is known about her except that she apparently did not like him very much. There are extant letters from him to her in which he calls himself her victim and pleads with her not to be angry with him. He was forever appealing to her to come to him at night, and apparently the lady did not always oblige. Come tonight, he entreats her, and writes that if she keeps on avoiding him he will die. At one point he wanted to pass over the other *kadıns'* turns for her. If he carried this out there must have been an uproar in the harem, for the *kadıns* were jealous of their nights with the sultan. Abdülhamit I was a gentle man, if not very effectual.

His successors continued to use this room as *mabeyn* and place of entertainment. However, in their day there seem to have been two *mabeyns*, this, which is probably the one they called the Upper Mabeyn, and another, the Şimşirlik Mabeyni, meaning the Mabeyn in the Boxwood Garden. Abdurrahman Şeref places the Şimşirlik below the north end of the harem, so its *mabeyn* must have been down there, especially as the sultans were fond of viewing sports from there. One March day in 1808 Mustafa IV watched from it while the pages threw snowballs. Their presence would indicate that this *mabeyn* was at some distance from the harem.

The Mirrored Room rests on tall concrete pillars that in turn rest on what was obviously once a ramp and interrupt another ramp above the first. The lower ramp runs from a group of dark rooms which, from the style of architecture, have been traced to the Conqueror. They lie underneath his Privy Chamber, now the Pavilion of the Blessed Mantle. This ramp went down to what was probably once a paved court—the paving stones may still be under the earth of the garden—and was very likely the start of the route by which the Conqueror reached the Tile Kiosk. The upper ramp also descends to the garden, but just how and where it was attached to the palace we do not yet know.

A heavy iron door connects the lower ramp to a set of rooms that lie underneath the Court of the Gözdes and look out onto the open pool. They must have been cool, what with being partially underground, and perhaps were once summer rooms for favorites.

In the wall that stretches out beside the ramps to separate the *mabeyn* garden from the harem garden, stone steps lead up from nowhere to the doorway we have mentioned above the Elephant House; tiled niches in the wall are further evidence of a building here. All this is proof, if it were needed, that Topkapı was more rebuilt than built.

There is one more area of the harem that we shall discuss, but in scant detail since it is un-Ottoman in inspiration. It lies to the west and south of the Sultan's Hall, and it stretches to the precipitous edge of the Inner Palace. Most of it was built by Osman III of the mid-eighteenth century and is replete with gilt and mirrors and landscapes. The first room we shall investigate, though sometimes credited to Osman III, far antedates him. It is the so-called Bedroom of Abdülhamit I though he may never have slept there. It lies within the main body of the harem, contiguous to the Hall of the Sultan and off the Corridor of the Bath. Architectural investigation has shown that it was built at the latest by Mehmet IV some time between the fire of 1665 and 1680. That it was done over by both Osman III and Abdül-hamit I is verified by the inscriptions over its door to the Bath Corridor. The corridor side of the door carries a couplet to the King of Kings of the time, Sultan Osman, Ruler of the World, and the inner side four lines dedicated to Hamit Khan, the Doer of Justice.

In Osman III's time it probably took on its present European character which became more pronounced and oppressive with each succeeding sultan. In his time it was perhaps used only as a passageway to his other construction. Abdülhamit divided both the room and its dome, thus forming a dark little area at one end, perhaps used as a treasury. Selim III added the windowed alcove to which his *tuğra* is attached and decorated the room anew, probably adding a frieze of selections from the description of the Prophet. Mahmut II made changes too, for his *tuğra* is found over the bed place. He covered Selim's more elegant decoration and calligraphic frieze with heavy-appearing frescoes and is responsible for much of the appearance of the room today. The earlier work was discovered by a discriminating scraping of the walls here and there.

The room is moderate in size and certainly the most obtrusively decorated of the harem. One feels that everything that could be thought of at the time was added here. Its upper wall is painted in busy, curvaceous shapes that would overpower the lower walls with their somewhat subdued Euro-

The so-called Bedroom of Abdülhamit I. The bed place, however, carries the tuğra of Mahmut II.

NECATI ORBAY

pean tiles if it were not for the ornate fountain and fireplace that interrupt them. The fireplace is especially fancy, rising in painted and gilded decreasing segments. The tiles here are thought to be the ones that passed through Belgrade in 1756, which would indicate that it was Osman III who had the room tiled.

Off the little treasury room Abdülhamit I made is a hall with a staircase in which, part way up, a niche is carved where slaves waited to serve the sultan. Up four steps farther is the Suite of Selim III. It lies partly over the Bedroom of Abdülhamit I and partly over the Court with the Pond where it is supported by columns. Its lead-covered dome and its decorated eaves rise slightly higher than its surroundings, so that the eaves slope gently on

[256]

The Prayer Room of Selim III on the second floor of the harem. The name of Muhammed is inscribed in the circle high on the left hand and next to it Omar, the second caliph. On the mirror over the cupboards is Selim's tuğra. *The room is heavily gilded in Ottoman baroque.*

one side to those of the Hall of the Sultan and on the other to the second-story suite of the Valide. Its main and really only room is Selim's Prayer Room, large and square and light, giving views in three directions to the palace gardens, the water, and the city. Panels high up on the wall encircle the names of the Prophet and His Companions, thereby indicating the room's purpose. Of eighteenth-century construction, it is a profusion of gilt. A mirror—a copy of the original which fell victim to an accident during the 1959 restoration—carries an inscription dating the room to Selim III. Off it is a small, dark but gilded cubicle called the Room of the Prophet's Beard because hairs from His beard were once kept here.

It was in this Prayer Room, according to present opinion, that Selim

[2 5 7]

met his death. Another version has it that he was killed in the ground-floor prayer room of the *valide*. This seems to me obvious nonsense for Selim would hardly have been spending his time in the apartment of a woman so jealous of his mother she had her name removed. Furthermore Cevdet Pasha, in his history of the period, says the killers headed for the apartment of Sultan Selim. There is another story about Selim's death that confuses me. A *kadın* of Mustafa IV, Peyk-i Dil, is supposed to have witnessed the killing. This room is so far from the *kadıns'* area, one wonders what she was doing here, unless out of grisly curiosity she followed the killers. Later, one reads, she was put to death for not having tried to help Selim.

Down on the ground floor at about this point Osman III decided to strike out afresh. He put up two pavilions and a court that are almost appendages to the palace, being attached to the older portion only by a corridor and supported by high and heavy piers set in the ground. One is the Room of Selim III. Though thought to have been built by Osman, it was named for Selim because he spent so much of his time here. Being semi-detached from the palace, it is a light room that thrusts out into the harem garden onto which long windows look on two sides. On a third side windows open onto the corridor to Osman III's Kiosk, which would seem to prove that this room is earlier than the kiosk. Almost one entire wall is taken up with a tile-backed fireplace carved in a swarm of curves and columns and surrounded by a filigree frame. Yet for all its overworked gilt the room has a pleasing quality that comes from the light that floods it. Selim, fond of music as he was, must have listened to many a performance of chamber music here.

The Kiosk of Osman III is even further afield, perched on the edge of the Inner Palace, its balcony overhanging Gülhane Parkı. It has perhaps the most dramatic location in the palace. From it the eye can sweep up and down the Golden Horn and the Bosphorus and over the city. The kiosk is a little palace of five rooms, a central large one and two small flanking rooms on each side, all thoroughly European, though the outside retains the wide eaves and the graceful fountains of the Ottomans. What we see today is Mahmut II's nineteenth-century renovation of the building, even to the heavy gilt furniture he imported from France. I am afraid that what I remember most clearly is a heavy gilt chair with arms made out of the backs and heads of lions and feet of lions' paws.

Osman III has been credited—or discredited—with the introduction of European baroque into the palace. Yet it is not fair to blame it all on him for, to judge from the changes made by his successors, it would have come anyway. However, he was such a negative character, one wonders what pleasure his building and decorating could have given him. The Hall of the Sultan must have seen few entertainments in his day, because he disapproved of musicians and drove from the palace those his predecessor had patronized. He had no use for women, had only two *kadıns* whom he apparently rarely visited since he had no children. His passion, besides building, was food, and it was his habit to go out from the palace in disguise and buy tidbits in the markets. He frequently dismissed and exiled his grand viziers. He executed his cousin, the heir to the throne. The remaining heir, who became Mustafa III, took pains to protect himself from poison. Only his mother had any influence on Osman; she prevented the death of at least one grand vizier. Osman had spent fifty-one years in the Cage, which may explain if it does not excuse his behavior. Mercifully his reign was short—1754–1757.

Yet he had an eye for the spectacular site and even some of the old Turkic love of the courtyard. His kiosk is separated from the Sultan's Hall by the wide and sunny Court with the Pond (Havuzlu Taşlık), sometimes called the Hanging Garden (Asma Bahçesi) because of the vines that twined around the columns and balustrade that once lined its open side. His rooms and Selim III's second-floor rooms are the last buildings to be added to the Topkapı harem.

The harem of Topkapı continued to house women after the sultans left it, if only retired *kalfas* and *ustas* (upper attendants). With the removal of the court to Yıldız under Abdülhamit II, Topkapı was to a large extent replaced by Dolmabahçe as a place of retirement. Ayşe Osmanoğlu says that in her father's time the elderly *ustas* who wanted to give up work "went to Topkapı Sarayı in order to receive the rights of their pension and lived there at least a year, because Topkapı was their hearth [guild]. . . . These *kalfas* came again to Dolmabahçe Sarayı, were pensioned and lived in ease."

It is my impression from what I have read that with Mahmut II the ex-*kadıns* were given houses of their own. As to the *valides*, some died before their sons, and the two who didn't were the mothers of dethroned sultans. Murat V's mother, who was living with him at Çırağan Palace on the Bosphorus, died just after visiting Yıldız, some think poisoned. The other, Abdülaziz' mother, spent the remainder of her life at the Palace of Feriye.

Women must have been entirely removed from Topkapı by 1910 or Abdurrahman Şeref would not have been allowed to inspect the harem. The silence enforced in the palace was by then complete.

THE OUTER PALACE

THE OUTER PALACE is usually neglected by visitors to Topkapı Sarayı Museum. In the first place it is not part of the museum and there is no present guide to it. Furthermore this area, which besides the First Court included the gardens, kiosks, and wall that surrounded the entire enceinte, has been swept clean of its old character. To bring it back to life needs even more imagination than did the First Court which after all still has a good many remnants to steer by. Nor is one much helped this time by the *Hünername* miniatures which, for one thing, are early, before Palace Point became really built up, and for another take the usual liberties with space. Still, the Outer Palace was an important part of the *saray*, and if one wants to know the old palace, one will want to learn something about it.

We have some sources to go by. Because it was the one part of the palace that could be observed from the European quarter across the Golden Horn and which some Europeans were able to enter, the gardens and especially the kiosks have been described by numerous Westerners. Since what they saw differed from century to century, and since their accounts are at times at odds and incorrect, they often confuse as much as help. Nevertheless some of them contain valuable descriptions of certain kiosks. As to pictures, many tried their hand at views of the palace from a distance, and though the wall, the Cannon Gate (Top Kapı) and the Shore Kiosk (Yalı Köşkü) are usually plain to see, what else the artist chose to show varied.

The only extant map that gives a clear if not entirely truthful picture is one by the German architect Melling, based on and supposedly corrected from a map by Kauffer, an architect and engineer in the suite of the French ambassador, Choiseul-Gouffier, who was sent to Istanbul at the end of the *ancien régime*. The trouble is, Melling did not correct it enough. Still, it is useful for indicating how the gardens surrounded the Inner Palace, for the placement of the shore kiosks, for some detail on the Marmara slope, and for its location of the arrangements of the area at Palace Point (Sarayburnu). Otherwise the plan is best ignored. The only others I have come upon on a sufficiently large scale to make them intelligible are one made by Abdurrahman Şeref in 1910 and another, really only a sketch, by Tahsin Öz, the former director of the museum. There is no use reproducing Abdurrahman Şeref's map, since it is annotated in Ottoman Turkish. However, in trying to resuscitate the Outer Palace I have largely relied on it, for his companion on his tour was a palace attendant who had known the kiosks and the walls before penury and the railroad played havoc with the palace grounds.

Both land and sea walls, much of which are still standing, can be walked or driven around. Since this is rather fun, we will leave it to the last and, the First Court having already been discussed, begin by considering the area that slopes down to the Marmara. The first place to catch a glimpse of this is from the weedy plot just past the site of the Boot Gate in the First Court, but there is no use expecting much. Better chances come farther down, from the outer porch of the Treasury and the Mecidiye terrace. The ground down from the Boot Gate has been usurped, as far as the railroad tracks, by the Educational Press, the warehouses of Customs, and an army hospital on the site of an older one built by Mahmut II. It was under Mahmut that the army began to make inroads into the palace grounds. On this slope once were vegetable gardens and vineyards, and farther down the Place of the Armory (Cebehane Meydanı). Here the sultans and princes used to practice their mace-throwing and shooting. If one could get down there, which the visitor cannot, one would see two stone shafts with inscriptions praising their skill. The lower one, three sides gracefully sculpted in a long spray of flowers, tells how Sultan Selim III hit an egg first from 408 and then from 434 paces, and the other, of a later design and sided by a fountain, that Mahmut II was equally successful. A third, far simpler marking stone stands nearby. As far as I could see it has no date, but it may be the one Abdurrahman Şeref says commemorates the mace-throwing of Bayezit II's son, Prince Ahmet, in 1503/4.

[261]

Selim's and Mahmut's columns are sculpted at the top with cabbages and okra, apparently because the guild homes or hearths of the cabbage and okra growers were nearby in the long-gone turrets of the gate to the Place of Gülhane (Gülhane Meydanı). Abdülaziz, who lived in Dolmabahçe and had little interest in keeping up the old customs of Topkapı, turned the turrets into pigeon houses. Apparently, since there was a gate between them, a wall separated the Place of the Armory from the Place of Gülhane beside it.

The Place of Gülhane (the Rose House), probably named for a building that used to distill perfumes for the palace, was a fairly large area that extended from the Inner Palace to the sea wall, roughly down from the kitchens of the Second Court. It is now all either ruins or Customs territory. Yet in the nineteenth century it was famous. Mahmut II drilled his new army here after he suppressed the Janissaries. In a pavilion known as the Gülhane Kiosk, which Mahmut seems to have restored from an older one, there met for the first time in 1838 the newly formed Supreme Council of Judicial Ordinances (Meclis-i Vâlâ-ı Ahkâm-ı Adliye) whose purpose was to prepare judicial regulations that would reflect Mahmut's policy of Westernization.

Mahmut died the next year and was succeeded by his son, the sixteen-year-old Abdülmecit. Nevertheless his ideas bore fruit, and shortly after his death there was read, at a tribunal set up in front of the kiosk, one of the most important documents of Ottoman history, the Imperial Rescript of Gülhane or the *hat-ı şerif* (noble rescript). The edict was enunciated by the famous Westernizing foreign secretary and later grand vizier, Mustafa Reşit Pasha, the Great Reşit, whose work it was. It proclaimed, among other things, the security of a subject's life, honor and property and his right to a public trial whatever his religion, thus putting Muslim and non-Muslim on the same legal footing. It initiated a long period of reform, the Tanzimat-ı Hayriye or Auspicious Reorganization, which lasted until Abdülhamit II came to the throne in 1876. Though enforcing the edict's provisions was by no means as easy as proclaiming them, still it was a landmark in Ottoman reform and a goal for which to strive. The ambassadors of foreign powers were gathered in the Gülhane Kiosk for the occasion.

The kiosk, which stood near the crest of the hill, has disappeared, having been pulled down by Abdülaziz so that part of its walls could be used as a lion house (*arslanhane*). He had a favorite old lion, called Beşir, which he used to let loose to play with. Abdülaziz had a passion for animals surpassing even that of his ancestors, who had all kept lions, tigers and other wild beasts in a menagerie outside the palace up the hill from the Great

Stable. Of Abdülaziz' lion house only some few stones of the back wall are left.

It was under Abdülaziz (1861–1876) that the Outer Palace became a no man's land. First of all the kiosks had been allowed to run down after the sultans left the *saray*. Then the director of the Military School, which was now on the grounds, persuaded Abdülaziz that keeping them up was too expensive. So down they came, with the exception of three which are still standing. The final blow to what was left arrived with the railroad, which you can see running close inside the wall from either the Treasury porch or the Mecidiye terrace. This is the line that connects Istanbul with Europe over which the famous Orient Express ran. The route through Istanbul was debated at length in the Council of Ministers, where one pasha argued vigorously that it should not pass through and deface the palace grounds. The sultan and the grand vizier would not listen, believing that a rail link to Europe transcended other claims.

At the time there was still living an eighty-year-old man, Memiş Efendi, who had been chief barber to Mahmut II. When he heard that the rails would destroy a certain grove of boxwood trees, he lamented, "Alas, in that grove of boxwood every Wednesday night the king of the jinns holds council. Where will he go now?" Boxwood grove and whatever else was in its path, including the wall around Saray Point, were swept away with no care for either intrinsic beauty or historical significance.

At the northern end of the Place of Gülhane was probably the earliest pavilion, next to the Tile Kiosk, to have been built in the Outer Palace. It was the Ishakiye and stood between the Place of Gülhane and the Privy Garden. Its sponsor was Ishak Pasha, an early grand vizier whom we will have occasion to mention again. It was built for the Conqueror's son, Bayezit II, when Ishak was an old man and shortly to die. The pavilion lasted at least through Selim III and Mahmut II, for it was from here that they made the shots marked by the columns in the Place of the Armory. The starting points were also marked near where the old kiosk stood. At that distance they must have been shooting with rifles.

Near the site of the Ishakiye the Privy Garden (Has Bahçe) began. Much of this is now a public park, Gülhane Parkı. It is curious that it should have been given this name, since everything connected with Gülhane was on the Marmara side of the palace, whereas the park extends around the area overlooking Palace Point and along the land side of the inner wall. It can be entered—on foot—from the Shore Road or from directly inside the Gate of the Fountain of Fresh Water. It is worth investigating for several reasons. There is the view from the elevated area in back of the Fourth Court of the palace. Here, before the land dips, it was called the Fifth Place. At a point at the top of the incline near the Gülhane Place end of the park you will find the gate that leads to the Mecidiye. Though connecting the Fourth and Fifth Courts, it is called the Third Gate. Just outside it in a clearing rises a pre-Ottoman monument, the Goths' Column, a shaft of granite all of a piece, slightly less than fifty feet high. It commemorates the victory of the Roman Emperor Claudius over the Goths at Nish in 259, but was probably erected much later. From the style of lettering on its base it is conjectured that it belongs to the time of Constantine the Great. It carries a Corinthian capital that was once toppled by an earthquake, and there is a tradition that at one time a small observatory topped it.

There is an amusing order issued by the sultan in 1581 stipulating that the official tasters (çaşnigirler) must learn horsemanship for a palace celebration (düğün), which was undoubtedly the circumcision of Murat III's son that took place in 1583. Here in the Fifth Place in the open area around the column is where they practiced.

Farther toward the land side is another gate, the Elephant Gate (Fiil Kapısı) that leads to the lower, neglected garden one can see from the Baghdad Kiosk. So far as anyone knows, it had nothing to do with elephants. There is no record of there having been any at the palace. It was from here that the sultans emerged at night when they wanted to tour the city incognito. On the way to it stand some Byzantine columns.

Down from the Goths' Column outside the park, along where the Marmara wall once ran, was the New Garden and its terraces, the only section laid out in formal Western fashion. It was the work of Jacob Ensle, brother of the gardener of Vienna's Schönbrun, whom Selim III imported from 1792 to 1802. Ensle liked to smuggle in Western friends, at least two of whom, Pouqueville, an ex-French consul who had been imprisoned in the Seven Towers during the war with Napoleon over Egypt, and Clarke, an English traveler, have left accounts. Melling, who was also a visitor, has shown the garden on his map, where most of it is marked Ieni Batkché. Here I follow Melling, since he actually saw the garden which had disappeared by Abdurrahman Şeref's time and had probably fallen into neglect by the time of the youth of his guide.

It spread along the shore and rose through a hyacinth garden bordered with Dutch tiles and a slight elevation to a little terrace. One end of this led to the Summer Harem, the other to a pavilion, the Hasan Pasha Kiosk, which an inscription connects with Mahmut I, and indeed he had a grand vizier by the name of Hasan. According to Pouqueville it was open at one end and had a gilded and mirrored ceiling, but had been neglected and left to the swallows. Clarke, who saw it at about the same time by peeping through a window, gives an entirely different impression of a pavilion ready for use with glass cases containing books in manuscript, gilt cages with artificial birds, a bench with water vessel, basin and towel ready for the sultan, and a portfolio embroidered in silver on yellow leather, perhaps a Koran case. A Gobelin tapestry—a new fashion—was on the floor, and the walls were hung with arms.

The grounds were apparently terraced up from the New Garden, and Pouqueville describes, in what must have been the privy garden, "a square, which encloses a sort of garden filled with rose-bushes and other odoriferous shrubs, interspersed among old beams and heaps of rubbish." Ensle apparently did not consider this part of his domain, although in a location above the New Garden and not far from the Elephant Gate to the Inner Palace he built a massive, fenced-in arbor where jessamine bloomed and jet fountains played. Pouqueville thought it built "as if to defy the injuries of time." Traces of it may have lasted into the twentieth century, for Abdurrahman Şeref locates what he calls an old covered place of enjoyment just above the railroad in the position Pouqueville indicates. All these sites are now lost. They are even difficult to imagine, so changed is the area.

A more concrete experience is to walk from the Fifth Place down to the lower level of Gülhane Parkı, of which there is a Palace Point offshoot across the Shore Road. We shall take this in later. The park is a pleasant place of shaded paths, trees and shrubs arranged in Western style by the Municipality in this century, but telling us little about the profuse confusion of an old Turkish garden. Abdurrahman Şeref has filled it with a botanical garden, a terraced lawn, a vegetable garden, and a wooded area. Clarke says on the way to it he passed an aviary of nightingales and found the old garden gloomy and neglected. More likely he just didn't understand old Turkish gardens, where trees, shrubs, vines and flowers mingled and through which walks wound and fountains splashed. I have seen such un-laid-out gardens on a much smaller scale behind Turkish houses in the provinces.

The sultans were proud of their gardens and at great pains to see that they were well supplied. Many orders have been discovered for plants and bulbs for them—500,000 hyacinth bulbs to be sent from Aleppo and its vicinity in 1595; 40,000 each of white and blue bulbs from the high pastures and mountain places of Maraş in eastern Anatolia in 1592/3; red and white rose shoots from Edirne, and all manner of trees from Izmit in Asia Minor—

plane trees, ash, lime trees, elm, oak, bay trees, Judas trees, wild pear and others, 4,000 young and symmetrical plants in all. Another order for saplings from Izmit instructs that they be sent in instalments to the head gardener. These edicts range through the sixteenth and seventeenth centuries.

Barnette Miller says there was a vegetable garden in what is now the park, planted to berry and melon patches, probably the *bostan* (vegetable garden) Abdurrahman Şeref locates just below the inner wall. The *ağaçlık* or wooded place (place of trees), where many of the saplings must have grown to treehood, he makes a large plot along the outer wall. Dallam, who entered this way, reported "statly siprus . . . betwyxte them and behind them, smaler tres that bearethe excelente frute." A host of gardeners tended the palace gardens, 947 of them in 1660. On fair days the women used to be driven in carriages along roads here, at which times black eunuchs went ahead of them shooing away gardeners and any other males in sight.

Passing through today, you may be walking under some of the old trees on the outer path. Nevertheless it is worth while also to explore the inner path where you will see rising beside you the inner wall of the palace, even to the overhang of Osman III's kiosk, and realize how remote from the city and how protected the Inner Palace was. Unfortunately the ground close to the wall has in part become a dumping ground for old iron. Nevertheless the place is of interest because of an old blocked-up ramp that comes down here from a gateway of which there is now no sign within the Inner Palace. It is tempting to think it was the exit used by the Conqueror when he left his ramp below the Court of the Gözdes.

Gülhane Parkı debouches just inside the Gate of the Fountain of Fresh Water (Soğuk Çeşme Kapısı) where a road goes up the hill to the First Court. Part way up, to the left, you will come to a plateau once called the Place of the Ağas (Ağalar Yeri), the Lawn of the Ağas (Ağalar Cayırı) or the Ağas' Garden (Ağalar Bahçesi). It now includes three museums: the Archaeological Museum, a late nineteenth-century building housing classical antiquities which include the supposed sarcophagus of Alexander the Great (I have seen busloads of tweedy Englishwomen with walking sticks heading for it); the Museum of Early Eastern Art which once was an art school; and the lone survivor of the earliest Ottoman days, the Tile Kiosk (Çinili Köşk), raised by the Conqueror in 1472/2 and once called the Glazed Kiosk (Sırca Köşkü). An old chronicle describes it as a "gladness-increasing place," and indeed, light and colorful as it is inside and out, it must have been so. It was the work of an architect who must have been an Anatolian, for it shows the influence of both Bursa, the first Ottoman capital, and the Seljuk cities. You will see nothing like it in Istanbul.

It was often used by the sultans to watch games and displays of horsemanship in the flat area of the Ağas' Garden in front of it.

The building is in the shape of a Greek cross with the angles filled in and an apse at the back. Today it is many windowed, although originally some of these apertures were merely curtained. A columned stone porch, a later addition, has been affixed to the front, probably in the eighteenth century to judge from its non-Ottoman capitals. It replaced a simpler wooden porch that must have lacked the balustrade and the number of columns that cut off the view. This seems particularly likely since the façade of the building is decorated with mosaic Seljuk-type tiles in ivans and doorway which the architect would scarcely have wanted to hide. Seljuk mosaic tiles were more difficult to produce than the later and finer Ottoman plaque tiling, but had the advantage of being able to conform to any shape. The tiles were shaved to fit the required form and then set in plaster in a frame. Not until the plaster was set would they be raised to the wall. The entrance ivan, deep set in a pointed arch, has its walls and ceiling tiled with these mosaic tiles which are divided part way up by a tile inscription of religious significance. This is bordered by a design of leaves, tendrils and flowers, *hataî*, an old Turkic motif from Central Asia. The side ivans are similar, and the predominant colors in all of them are dark blue and turquoise with some white, except for the calligraphic frieze which introduces yellow and a brownish red.

Since the structure rises from a declivity, the front is of one story and basement, the rear of two. The glory of the kiosk was its interior where some of the rooms are still ablaze with colored tiles and give an example of the brilliance here when, as originally, it was entirely tiled. These tiles are not the floral panels of the palace proper, which came later, but rather go back to the earliest period of Ottoman tile work. The interior tiles are navy blue and turquoise, hexagonal or triangular in shape, virtual replicas of those found in Bursa, many of them having gold decoration which was laid on after the tiles were baked. In contrast in the sixteenth and seventeenth centuries the colors were all painted on before baking. I particularly recall one stunning room of hexagonal tiles in turquoise and dark blue with some of the gold decoration still clinging to them. This room has a fountain decorated with a peacock painted on marble and an inscription which ascribes it to Murat III. However, historians who have investigated its chronogram—a favorite Ottoman method of dating—have found that it does not add up to the time of any Murat. To me it seems more probable that there is a mistake in the chronogram, complex as chronograms are, rather than in the name.

In the late nineteenth century before the Archaeological Museum was put up, the building was used to house the first collection of classical antiquities. In those years the antiquarians in charge, having no interest in Ottoman art, managed to do more damage to the kiosk than time and fire had wrought. They covered the mosaic tile of the porch first with whitewash and then with plaster, which at least preserved it. They actually destroyed some of the inside tiles when they made structural changes, and they even broke the symmetry of the façade by adding an outside stairway. The kiosk has since been restored and the stairway removed, but the very old inside tiles can never be replaced. The building is now a tile museum in which Turkish tile work of all periods, from Seljuk on up, is on display.

Behind it in the early days there was a pond, which shows up on the left side of *Hünername* Miniature No. 5. The Tile Kiosk is probably the larger of the two buildings there. Positive identification of the other is not possible, but it may be the pavilion the architect Ayverdi mentions as being south of the Tile Kiosk and which he calls the Kiosk of the Sürre Procession. Directly opposite the Tile Kiosk, a writer of Mehmet II's time has reported, the Conqueror built a pavilion of somewhat later inspiration. Nothing of it remains, except that in digging for the Archaeological Museum they came across the ruins of a foundation and some tile fragments.

The number of kiosks that once stood in this area depends on whom you read. We have mentioned a possible Sürre Procession Kiosk (Sürre Alayı Köşkü). There is a tradition that the *sürre*, the yearly gift of money and valuables to the two Holy Cities, Mecca the Revered and Medina the Enlightened, started out from one of the kiosks here, sometimes said to be the Kiosk of Mehmet III which Ayverdi locates near the Tile Kiosk. If it went from any place on this level it must have been in the earlier years when the *sürre* ceremony was more simple. A register of the Department of the Master of Ceremonies describes a *sürre* of 1768/9 as beginning with an elaborate ceremony in front of the Divanhane of the Second Court, where the camel bearing the treasure was loaded, prayed over and handed to the custodian of the *sürre* who would be in charge of its journey. The procession left the palace through the Imperial Gate, passed the Procession Kiosk and the Iron Gate to the Vizier's Dock on the Golden Horn where it embarked for Üsküdar on the Asiatic shore for the long overland journey. The money and other gifts, usually of jewels, were carried on the camel's back in what was called the sacred litter (*mahmil-i şerif*). The museum has one of hand-worked leather, a rather tent-like affair, but it is not now on display. Apparently no kiosks were participating in the start of the *sürre* by the eighteenth century.

One runs across mention of other kiosks in the palace gardens, but not of anything much concerning them. From the plateau of the museums the road runs up to meet the First Court at the Gate of the Guardians of the Walnut Tree.

We are now free to follow the wall and learn a little of the magnificent kiosks that looked out from it. If you are a good walker, by all means walk. The distance around the palace is about three and a half miles. If not, take a taxi and tell the driver *yavaş yavaş* (yavash yavash) which will indicate you want him to go slowly. If you want him to stop so you can look more closely, say *dur*.

The wall divides into land wall and sea wall, the former the work of the Conqueror, the sultan's wall (*sur-u sultaniye*), and the latter built by several Byzantine emperors and strengthened from time to time by Ottoman sultans. A guard walk once ran along it. Defense towers still rise here and there on both land and sea walls, twenty-eight of them in all, four-sided, eight-sided, nine-sided. The sea and at one point the land wall were topped by ceremonial and pleasure kiosks to which the sultans sometimes invited officials and at other times their women. A number of gates of greater or lesser importance broke the walls, inserted at different times, each one guarded, each having a special purpose and admitting only those who had a right to use it. Some of these are still to be seen. Of certain vanished ones, probably small gates, I have been able to learn almost nothing and shall omit them.

For a circumnavigation of the walls I suggest that you start at the Imperial Gate and turn directly toward the sea down the Hill of Ishak Pasha, where the wall stands high and crenellated and several towers still rise. A short way along and you will come to a gate that opens into the Educational Press (Maarif Matbaası). It is no use trying to enter it; there is nothing to see except a group of utility buildings that house the press and its offices. In late imperial days it was the Takvimhane (Calendar House) where were printed the official newspaper, the *Calendar of Events* (*Takvim-i Vekayi*) and the works of the Imperial Press (Matbaa-ı Âmire). Both were started elsewhere earlier and moved to the palace in 1860.

A way past here the land wall is hidden by houses except for a tower or two, but the Street of Ishak Pasha continues. Ishak Pasha had been a grand vizier of both the Conqueror and his son, had built a mosque nearby, and despite the fact that the mosque has gone his name has remained attached to the neighborhood. Though you would never guess it today, it had once been a fashionable place to live because of its proximity to the palace. Great *konak*s or mansions had been built here. Since they were made of wood, they have either burned or fallen to pieces, except for one old house that still stands a few blocks from the palace. This is not a guide to old Istanbul, but if you would like to see a moderate-sized house of the old days, follow the street as it goes under the railroad near the station of Cankurtaran and turn right. You will be in the neighborhood of Akbıyık (White Mustache) —neighborhoods were small in old Istanbul—and soon come to the little Akbıyık Mosque. On your right across a side street from it stands a wide wooden house, its unpainted boards weathered until they are silver in some lights. On one side of its carved central doorway the lattices *(kafes)* of the harem section still crisscross the windows. There are also, diagonally across from the mosque, two old Ottoman fountains in which very likely children will be playing. Back at Ishak Pasha, just this side of the point where the railroad leaves what was once the palace grounds, is the Haystore Gate (Otluk Kapısı), near where the land and sea walls joined. The gateway remains, domed and pillared, but now painted white, the entrance to the army hospital. Melling called this Kara Kapısı (Land Gate), and Barnette Miller is apparently referring to it when she mentions a Gate of Ten (Onluk Kapısı). This is obviously a misreading of the Ottoman word, *otluk*, the difference between them in the Ottoman alphabet being a matter of only one dot. In late times it seems to have been known as the Gülhane Gate because it was the entrance to the Gülhane Hospital, now across the Bosphorus.

To your right near the shore was the Great Stable (Büyük Ahır) of which there is now no vestige though it was vast enough to accommodate some 2,000 horses for the Palace School. Every day a corps of gardeners carried hay here from the sheds at the Haystore Gate. Near the gate, inside the grounds, another group of gardeners nurtured swans whose wing feathers were in great demand for use on arrows.

Follow the street until you go under the railroad and keep to the right until you come to a break in the wall, a very short distance. You will be at Ahır Kapı, the Stable Gate, which will take you out beside a fish restaurant to the Shore Road (Sahil Yolu) that runs along the Marmara. From here the sea wall stretches in both directions. To follow the palace you will want to turn left. The wall along here is that of Constantine and the gates are all sea gates, for the Shore Road is a recent improvement. Not very far along, perhaps where the wall takes a jog inward, was the Fish House Gate (Balıkhane Kapısı). It had a second story in which the fishermen stored their nets which otherwise were stretched from a wooden platform offshore to the sea to make their catch. Men still fish the Marmara here. If you walk some distance down to the right from the Stable Gate you will come upon women mending colorful fishing nets, and if you walk or drive along here at night you will find the sea atwinkle with the little lights of the fishing boats.

In the sultans' days the Fish House Gate had another and more sinister purpose. It was from here that grand viziers were sent into exile, if they were lucky enough to escape with their lives. A curious custom gave them a sporting chance. When an official was condemned the head gardener, who was also the chief executioner, was dispatched to the Fish House Gate, to which the condemned man was forced to go. If he arrived before the head gardener, he went into exile. If he found the head gardener awaiting him, he lost his life then and there and was thrown into the sea.

There is only one known instance when the head gardener was waiting, yet the condemned man got away. It happened in 1817/8 with the grand vizier Mehmet Emin Rauf. He had an enemy at court, one Halet Efendi, who was determined to get rid of him and managed to persuade the sultan, Mahmut II, to send him into exile, hoping to turn the exile into execution. The head gardener of the time, whose name was Deli (Mad) Abdullah, reached the gate first, but no victim appeared. Presently Halet Efendi arrived. Fearful that Deli Abdullah would give up the vigil, he exhorted him, "Don't go yet, Abdullah Ağa. Walk around instead. Because of a *kallâvi* [the tall, tapering turban], I have not yet been able to obtain the edict of execution."

Up at the palace the edict had been submitted to Mahmut, but instead of approving it, he had said, "The *kallâvi* suits the head of Mehmet Emin Rauf. I cannot condemn that handsome head."

Meanwhile Mehmet Emin Rauf, unaware of the sultan's clemency, reached the gate and found the head gardener there, a shock he never got over though he lived forty-three years more.

Past Balıkhane the shore comes to a small point on which a lighthouse, the Stable Gate Lighthouse (Ahır Kapı Feneri), still rises from the wall. A lighthouse has been here since 1755 when Osman III had one erected after a ship from Egypt dashed itself to pieces against the wall. Next probably was the Little Iron Gate (Küçük Demir Kapı), called little to distinguish it from the more important Iron Gate on the land side. Not much is known about it except that it dates from Byzantium.

A little farther on and you come upon the stone arch supports of one of the most famous of the shore kiosks, known as the Pearl Kiosk (İncili Köşk) from a cluster of pearls that hung from the dome, or the Kiosk of the Great Sinan Pasha (Koca Sinan Paşa Köşkü). It was the work of the chief architect, Davut, successor to Sinan, erected on the foundation of the Byzantine Church of the Savior. There is a legend that it was erected in forty-five days to be ready for the circumcision of Murat III's son which is celebrated in the *Surname*, some of whose miniatures we have discussed in the section on painting. The trouble with this legend is that the dates do not support it. The circumcision occurred in 1583, and the kiosk bears an inscription saying that Murat ordered its building in 1588/9. That would seem to be the date of its conception rather than its completion, for Murat issued edicts connected with the erection of this building as late as 1591/2. In 1588 he ordered that tiles be sent from Iznik for a pavilion being built at the palace, and another order to Davut in 1591/2 commanding him to find carpenters and stoneworkers for the imperial pavilion being built on the shore. The same year he called for certain master carpenters, whom he named, to be brought from Gallipoli. These seem all to have been Greek. The date of completion could not have been before 1592/3.

The Pearl Kiosk is believed to have been one of the most beautiful of the shore kiosks, a rectangular building whose walls were faced with Iznik tiles in floral designs, the interior of whose dome was gilded and set with precious stones, and whose furnishings were of the finest gold- and pearl-worked fabrics. Gold and diamond balls hung from its dome along with a sparkling chandelier. On one side it faced the sea with a view of the Anatolian shore and on the other a playing field now lost to the railroad cut where the pages of the Palace School put on games. From the kiosk's porch the sultans watched wrestlers, and the game called *tomak* in which pages divided into two teams and tried to hit their opponents on the back with a small ball like a golf ball on a leather thong, or played the swift, mounted game of *cirit* (jirit) in which opposing teams charged one another with iron-tipped wooden lances. It was a dangerous exercise in which a man could be and sometimes was killed if he was not able to turn his horse quickly and race out of reach.

The Pearl Kiosk was a favorite of Murat III's. He used it to carouse and converse with companions and to listen to music. In fact no sooner had

The Pearl Kiosk (İncili Köşk) on the palace wall along the Marmara shore.
An eighteenth-century view from Choiseul-Gouffier.

Dallam's organ been set up in the Corridor with Pillars than Murat had it moved down here. Two pages led Dallam to the kiosk along a "waye [which was] verrie pleasante throughte the garthens, whear did grow store of siprus trees and many orther good frute trees in verrie comly and desent order." He found Turks riding on a green, and then described the kiosk:

> Close to the sea sid Dothe stande a prittie fine litle buldinge which theye cale a Cuske, made for a bancketinge house; but espetially, as I persaved, it is a place wheare the Grand Sinyor dothe use to meet his Congquebines twyse in the weeke. It is finly covered with Leade, and bulded squear on the topp; in the midle a litle square tour like a pera-madese (pyramid?) on a greate heighte, and on the top of that a litle turret well gildede, and on the side nexte to the sea a faire large gallarie wheare men may stande and se bothe up and doune the rever of Hellisponte [the Dardanelles; he really means the Marmara], and lik wyse over it into Asia.
>
> On the other 3 sids towards the grene ar verrie larg pentazis [pent-houses], supported with fine marble pillers, the flore spred with fair

[273]

carpites, the roufe under the pentas verrie Curiusly wroughte withe gould and collors; but cominge into it is a litle wonder, I cannot duly discrib it. . . .

Dallam began to set up his organ and then had to flee when the sultan and his women, "and 4 neageres or blackamoors cam runinge towardes me with their semetaries [scimitars] drawne. . . . Now, as I was runinge for my life, I did se a litle of a brave show, which was the Grand Sinyor him selfe on horsebacke, many of his conquebines, som ridinge and som on foute, and brave fellowes in their kinde, that weare gelded men, and keepers of the conquebines."

At the beginning of the illness that brought on Murat's death he went down to this kiosk and asked his musicians to sing a song that included the words, "My illness waits, O Hour of Death, take my soul tonight."

It so happened that that day the fleet returned from Iskenderun and, learning that the sultan was at the Pearl Kiosk, proceeded to salute him there with cannon. The kiosk rattled and filled with smoke. Superstitious as most Ottomans were, Murat said, "It is a sign that this is the last time I shall come to this kiosk."

The kiosk was renovated by Mahmut I who added a solid silver throne. It fell into ruins in Mahmut II's reign and was finally pulled down in the money-saving spree of 1861.

Within the arches of its foundation was an *ayazma* or sacred spring of the Greeks to which they used to come each year on the Feast of Transfiguration to drink the water which they supposed to have medicinal properties. On this day a gate was opened for them until 1821 when the Greek independence movement motivated the sultan to refuse them access.

Important events took place in the Pearl Kiosk. Murat IV held one of his councils on foot here, and this time he won. A grand council of state gathered here in 1732 and decided to accept peace in one of the many wars with Russia. At another time Osman III (1754–1757) reviewed a naval procession that included a vessel captured from the Knights of Malta. Selim III was fond of using the place as a vantage point from which to watch naval spectacles when the fleet, simulating war action, set off its cannon in great roars.

Not very far past here is a small open gate through which one can enter and climb to the high ground siding the railroad tracks. It is a good spot from which to view the outside of the kitchens, Treasury and Mecidiye and brings home a realization of the ruin that has beset the Marmara grounds. Frequent trains will run below you, for these lines are interurban as well as transcontinental. By the local people the gate is called the Gate of the Third Fort (Uçüncü Kale Kapısı), which may possibly mean the third tower along the Marmara.

The wall continues some distance, zigzagging in and out until it turns into a low fence. Along here were the Gate of the Refuse-Carriers (Mezbel-eşan Kapısı) where the palace refuse was thrown into the sea, and the Mill Gate (Değirmen Kapısı) near a palace mill and bakery. It used also to be called the Gate of the Sick (Hastalar Kapısı) because the palace hospital and its small mosque (Tabhane Mescidi) were just inside the wall here. From the terrace of the Mecidiye one can easily see closed-up arches that must once have been these gates. It is just past a point below the Mecidiye that the wall ends. It does not start up again until the Iron Gate, some distance up the land side. However, the sea side sidewalk of the Shore Road continues, though not so pleasantly since it begins to be lined with trucks waiting to embark on the ferry that will take them to the Anatolian shore.

Around the turn of the nineteenth century Selim III built along here for his mother the Şevkiye (Place of Joy). The wall apparently projected here and gave the pavilion a superb view of Asia and the Princes Islands. It had several names: the New Kiosk (Yeni Köşk), the Tas Köşkü (Stone Kiosk) and the Serdap. This last means an underground reservoir or cool underground apartment. Turkish sources say it was given the name because of its fountains, but since it actually had an underground story, I surmise that resulted in its being called Serdap. The basement could have been an old Byzantine cistern—the palace grounds are full of them—which had been made part of the kiosk. It was paved with marble and had a little nook for the sultan's yellow morocco slippers. The lowest grade of slaves slept here, who in this case were the lucky ones. It must have been the coolest summer quarter of the entire Topkapı, for though the shore is bathed in sea breezes, they do not penetrate the buildings at night.

The kiosk, itself of marble, was approached from the New Garden by three broad marble steps which led to a large waxed and painted curtain instead of a door and which lent the kiosk, on this side, the appearance of a tent. Pushing it aside, the visitors entered the main room, which was elliptical. Its walls were lined with cloth on which a colonnade had been painted and with mirrors and painted flowers in vases from which water flowed. Singing canaries inhabited cages that contained little handles they had been taught to turn in order to get water. And of course the room had a fountain. From its dome hung a crystal chandelier which Lord Elgin had presented to Selim on behalf of the King of England. When the women came down to the kiosk the chandelier was taken down to keep it safe from their high spirits.

Some think the New Kiosk was the work of Melling, but there is no evidence that he ever had a commission at the *saray*. In fact the inaccuracy of his map, except for the portion at the point shown him by Ensle, suggests that he was not really acquainted with the palace. However, we know that Selim was interested in Melling who had worked for his sister, and he had even given him a commission elsewhere. It is possible that he sent his chief architect to study Melling's work, so pervasive is European influence in Selim's changes in the palace. Whoever designed it, the Serdap was all charm and a favorite place of relaxation of Selim III. He used frequently to watch dancing here and to bring his harem women with him.

Keep on along the sidewalk and you will come to the sadly run-down little park at Palace Point (Sarayburnu). Here, at the northernmost tip of the palace, was once a cluster of kiosks. Nothing is left of them now. Today a colossal statue of Atatürk marks the change in Turkey's ways. Just off the point was Cannon Gate (Top Kapı), at first simple enough but from the seventeenth century on sided by solid-looking marble towers, each carrying a small kiosk. The gate appears in *Hünername* Miniature No. 4, slightly misplaced, in its simple form but already guarded by cannon which one can see along the shore. (In Ottoman days there seems to have been a narrow strip of land between wall and sea, at least until well down the Marmara. It shows up in *Hünername* Miniatures Nos. 4 and 5.) Palace Point was a logical site for a sea gate, and one had stood there guarding the Acropolis under Byzantium.

The Cannon Gate was much used by the Ottoman sultans and by the harem women when they embarked for a sea outing. Two caïques stood off-shore ever in readiness to carry the sultan across to Asia or up the Bosphorus or the Horn. The gates' artillery never had to fire on an enemy, for Istanbul has never been attacked under the Turks. The guns sounded off only to announce celebrations, the end of the Ramazan daily fast or important events such as the birth of an imperial child. The gate was demolished in 1817 when Mahmut II decided to use its marble elsewhere, probably in renovation of the nearby shore palace, the first to be called Topkapı, after the Cannon Gate which it all but adjoined. One of the Balyans, the father of the architect of Dolmabahçe Palace, worked on this palace, presumably during Mahmut II's reign.

Like the larger palace up the hill that adopted its name, the first Topkapı was more rebuilt than built. Its initial stage was the work of Ahmet III who erected a small kiosk of wood in the style of Ottoman city houses with overhanging second story. His successor, Mahmut I, put on an extension and called it the Place of the Beloved (Mahbubiye). He then decided it was too small and enlarged his and Ahmet's structures into what became known to Westerners as the Summer Harem, built around a court behind Cannon Gate. An order of Mahmut's calls for great stones of marble to be cut, undoubtedly on the Island of Marmara in the Sea of Marmara, the source of most marble, and brought down from the mountain and moved to Istanbul for "the imperial buildings situated in Topkapı situated in my imperial New Palace [today's Topkapı]." Von Hammer, describing Mahmut's construction, says it had columns of marble the color of dawn. The men Ensle smuggled in when it was not in use were invariably impressed with its beauty.

Some three hundred women used to move here during the warm months. It had *selâmlık* and harem, quarters for eunuchs and its own kitchens. The harem encompassed a large apartment for the *baş kadın* with a view of the court, suitable apartments for the other *kadıns*, quarters for a multitude of slaves, and the *pièce de resistance*, a sort of throne room overlooking the sea for the *valide sultan* on the first floor. Edward Daniel Clarke, in his *Travels in various countries of Europe, Asia and Africa*, described this room as "surrounded with enormous mirrors," and at one end of it a throne, "a sort of cage, in which the Sultana sits, surrounded by latticed blinds." The palace, for it grew to be more than a kiosk, was decorated in European fashion and even had some European pieces of furniture which Clarke scoffed at as being inferior. F. C. H. L. Pouqueville (*Voyage en Morée à Constantinople, en Albanie and dans plusieurs autres parties de l'Empire Ottoman*) was particularly impressed with its baths which, since he had never seen the other baths of the palace, he refused to credit to the Turks.

Consisting mostly of wood despite the "large stones," the first Topkapı was consumed in 1862/3 by a fire that started in a brazier, that object which was the source of so many Istanbul fires. The small palace and the military school which then stood nearby on the palace grounds were completely destroyed despite the efforts of the entire fire department of Istanbul. Apparently many valuable objects perished, for a palace page was put to searching for precious stones after the ashes had cooled.

A Swedish friend of Clarke's, on a similar tour with Ensle, was interrupted by the arrival of women. Hiding, he managed to secure a look at them, finding them with long hair dusted with diamonds and wearing pantaloons (*şalvar*) embroided in gold and silver, and long spangled robes open in front to show their necks and breasts. Their faces, which were uncovered, he found very beautiful.

Topkapı stretched along the Marmara side of Palace Point. Just to the Golden Horn side a very old kiosk, the Marble Kiosk (Mermer Köşkü) had been built in 1518 by a treasurer of Selim I. He had had the marble imported from Egypt. This must be the pavilion that stands next to the Cannon Gate in the miniature on page 110. No one has left a bona fide description of it, but no other shore kiosk along the Horn was that close to Palace Point.

Today's little park takes in only the tip of the point. The sea wall, however, continued along the Marmara.

A bit past the Marble Kiosk came the Wood Gate (Odun Kapısı) and near it the storehouse for firewood. To this gate ships brought wood from the sultan's lands along the seacoasts. Very near it was the imperial boat-house (kayikhane) that housed the long, graceful imperial caïques, several of which may be seen in the Naval Museum at Beşiktaş. The rowers' quarters were in the same area, as was the lodging of the head gardener, since he was in charge of the sultan's caïques and of the policing of the shores. None of these survive, only the Basketmakers' Kiosk (Sepetçiler Köşkü), until recently forlorn among the welter of rails and sheds along the shore. It survived the demolition of the wall on which it was built probably only because the army was using it at the time.

If you want to see it, walk along the quay past the park until you come to a building on high arches and in the process of reconstruction. It stands on the site of an early kiosk of Bayezit II which Murat III had ripped down. He then ordered Sinan Pasha, the sponsor of the Pearl Kiosk, to build a new one, which was sometimes called the Sublime Pavilion (Kasr-ı Âdil) and sometimes the Sinan Pasha Kiosk which, since the Pearl Kiosk also bore that name, is very confusing. Barnette Miller says its purpose was to signal the fleet, but though it may have done so, old descriptions of it make it seem primarily a pleasure kiosk. Grelot, a Frenchman (Relation nouvelle d'une voyage de Constantinople, Paris, 1680), shows it rising on high arches, and calls it the Sinan Kiosk. Over the arches were three richly decorated rooms, their various roofs pulled together by a dome. Grelot thought it was built for the women, which is very probable. The name Sinan Pasha Kiosk seems to have stuck, although Sultan İbrahim changed it to the Basket-makers' Kiosk when he repaired the building in 1643. Since he had learned basketmaking as a prince and therefore was inclined to favor the basket-makers' guild, the guild contributed to its repair. His reward to them was to give the kiosk their name. The change in name seems at first not to have been widely known, and thus many have thought the Basketmakers' Kiosk and the Sinan Pasha Kiosk on the Horn were two different buildings. Even Barnette Miller, who researched carefully, and Penzer who followed her in the Thirties, fell into this trap. Some people call it the Sinan Ağa Kiosk, thus further complicating the situation. This name suggests to me the possibility that the architect Sinan, who would have been called Sinan Ağa, was responsible for its rebuilding under Murat III. We have seen that he did extensive work in the palace for Murat. Like all the shore kiosks it was a good place from which to watch the boats at sea, and we find Mustafa IV doing just that from here in 1808.

Only the arches and two rooms of the old kiosk have come down to today, and the rooms are very dilapidated. Therefore most of it above the arches will be reconstruction, but in its own style. It is slated to become either a restaurant or a museum. Though rails run right beside it, its rooms on those high arches will have a long view over them.

The land wall came down to join the sea wall where the railroad yards

The Palace of Topkapı and Gülhane Parkı as seen from the entry to the Golden Horn. The building on arches on the shore is the Basketmakers' Kiosk.

now spread out, and just outside that jointure on the Golden Horn a gate led to what was one of the most important and famous of the palace pavilions, the Shore Kiosk (Yalı Köşkü). It was sixteenth century, formerly thought to have been built by Süleyman, but lately credited to his father, Selim I. Its one story had a porch whose many marble pillars supported a cornice shadowed by eaves. The spaces between the pillars could be closed by red curtains, reminding one of the early Corridor with Pillars. Though its roof was topped by a windowed dome, it was often said to resemble a tent. Its three large rooms were rich with sofa cushions worked with gold and silver thread on Bursa velvet. As time went on, mother-of-pearl inlaid tables and stools were added. Here was traditionally held the ceremonial farewell to the head of the navy, the *kaptan paşa*, at the hour set by the chief astrologer for the fleet to set out to sea to fight the enemy. The sultan on a silver throne, the *şeyhülislâm*, the grand viziers and other dignitaries assembled to do him honor. Prayer was offered for his success, and he left the sultan's presence clothed in a robe of honor trimmed with sable, a diamond dagger thrust into his sash. A small boat took him out to the fleet, which then sailed past the kiosk, the *kaptan paşa's* flagship at its head. Cannon saluted the padishah from the warships, and the guns at Cannon Gate answered.

The kiosk also took part in *donanma*s, which means a decking out for a celebration. In 1759 Princess Heybetullah was born, the first child born to a sultan in three reigns, and though she was only a girl, the birth was made a gala affair. Yalı Kiosk, the Kiosk of Pearls, the shore Topkapı and the imperial gardens were all strung with garlands and ribbons, the whole city was illuminated, and the First and Second Courts were ablaze with 400 torches.

In addition to ceremonial occasions the sultan sometimes came here to rest. In the journal of Selim III's confidential secretary there is an entry telling how, on the fifth of June, 1791, Selim withdrew to the Shore Kiosk to eat and pray after watching a performance of wrestlers and an exhibit of three lions, one leopard, and a number of dogs and cocks, all accompanied by the palace band.

During the Crimean War the area of the Yalı Kiosk became, of all things, a steel factory, which must have robbed it of its old character. In 1870 the kiosk fell victim to the railroad, and the factory was moved up the Horn. This is probably the kiosk placed outside the wall in the *Hünername* Miniature on page 111.

The sea wall continued along the Horn and was pierced not far from the palace by the Vizier's Dock, its site somewhere along Sirkeci quay, where foreigners disembarked on their way to the palace. They lived in Pera across the Horn, which had no bridge until the nineteenth century. They entered the palace grounds through the Iron Gate (Demir Kapı) of the land wall, and that is where we shall go next. The easiest way to get there if you are touring the wall is to cross the Shore Road from the park at Palace Point, keeping your eye quick and your feet nimble for dodging traffic, and follow the road over the tracks right next to the one that leads to Gülhane Parkı. It will take you to the Iron Gate. Otherwise you will have to go all around Sirkeci Railroad Station.

The massive gatehouse still dominates the wall here, a sturdy stone structure with a high, deep-arched passageway and a crenellated top. Its name comes from the iron leaves of the gateway. It led to the Privy Garden, and because it was appointed to the gardeners' use it was also called the Gardeners' Gate (Bostancılar Kapısı). The *Hünername* Miniature on page 110 shows the gardeners' quarters at the upper left near the wall. They are labeled Bostancılar Odası, the Gardeners' Room.

Certain others besides foreigners and gardeners came through this gate, officials who were in the sultan's favor, the chief black eunuch, and the proxy or *vekil* of the imperial bridegroom who represented him at the *nikâh*, the short legal marriage ceremony. Sometimes the sultans used it. Mahmut I went out this way one day to a mosque for Friday prayer. He was sick when he left the palace, and as he returned he died in the passageway of the Iron Gate.

Presumably you have already walked through the park, so now go out through the Iron Gate and turn left up the hilly street. From here a good way up the wall has been taken over by industry. Right next to the gate stands a yellow industrial building unredeemed by the late fountain (1877/8) beyond it. For a time you will be able to see only a tower or two for the little automotive repair shops that have been built against the wall, and at first there is no sidewalk. If a car goes by, just squeeze up against a building. But persevere upwards, and meanwhile recall that this too was once a fashionable neighborhood. You will emerge at a structure built into the wall, the Post, Telefon and Telegraf Fabrikası. It encompasses the gate said to have been used by Süleyman's grand vizier, İbrahim. İbrahim's own palace was at the top of the hill at the far end of Sultanahmet Square (the Hippodrome) opposite the Mosque of Sultan Ahmet. After the vizier's death it was used as a preparatory school for the Palace School. What was finally left of it is now being made into a museum for fine old rugs.

By now a sidewalk has appeared, more or less, and as you walk along it you will pass another fountain and a small, closed gate, this one used by the great grand vizier, Sokullu Mehmet Pasha. Actually there is some doubt as to who used which gate. Neither was conveniently located to the mansions of these viziers and must have been used only to reach the sultan privately, without the fanfare and the public attention attached to entry via the First Court.

At an angle of the wall about halfway up the hill comes the Procession Kiosk (Alay Köşkü), a polygonal marble building raised by Mahmut II in 1810 on the foundation of a tower of the wall. A lead roof, gathered into a spire, tops it. Though late, it has a distinctly Ottoman aura. Across the street from it stands Bab-ı Âli, the Sublime Porte (formerly called the Pasha's Gate) which was once the office of the grand vizier and is now the State Archives. The kiosk is on or near the site of a former Procession Kiosk built in the sixteenth century by Murat III and is a fine vantage point from which the sultans watched processions. On going to war the army marched past here in all its panoply, followed by the guilds of artisans who attended it in the field. The guildsmen brought along miniature workshops with which to display their skill. Millers ground wheat in little mills they carried in their arms. Bakers were accompanied by portable ovens. Shepherds led plumed sheep by ropes of gold. There were tailors, cobblers, knife-makers, sword-makers, carpenters, bricklayers, and even herbalists and surgeons.

At times less resplendent events took place at the Procession Kiosk. In 1656 a council on foot was held. A war over Crete, lasting for years, had so depleted the treasury that the government had devalued the money. The armed forces found themselves being paid in coin the tradesmen would not accept. It was the reign of Mehmet IV, a boy of fifteen at the time, and the army blamed his advisers for the situation. On their demand for a council on foot Mehmet appeared at the Procession Kiosk, which was chosen to keep the crowd away from the Imperial Gate. The street outside was thronged with people as far down the hill as the Iron Gate, both armed soldiers and bystanders. The *ağa* of the cavalry, who were at the forefront of the confrontation, pulled out a sheet of paper and read a list of the names of thirty persons whom the cavalry demanded be executed. Then he thrust forward a handful of the debased coins as evidence of their complaint.

Mehmet tried to compromise. He suggested that the wealth be confiscated from those whose names were on the list and they be sent into

The Procession Kiosk as seen from the street outside the palace wall. At the left may be seen the entrance to Bab-ı-Âli, formerly the headquarters of the grand vizier and now the state archives.

exile. The cavalry was not to be easily placated. A great cry went up from the throats of the multitude demanding the lives of the officials. Fear gripped Mehmet. With the crowd in so ugly a mood, it could be only a short step from calling for the lives of officials to calling for the throne of the sultan.

[283]

Then and there he had an order made out condemning the thirty men to death and handed it to the chief executioner. First on the list were three harem eunuchs who were straightway killed and their bodies stripped and thrown onto the palace wall.

The kiosk had other uses, depending on the character of the sultan. Mehmet IV (1648–1687) used to sit here and keep track of who went to see the grand vizier. He also watched the passersby on the street to make sure Christians were wearing only the costumes assigned to them. (In the old Ottoman Empire everyone had a particular style and color of clothing.) Selim III used it for ceremonial occasions, to appoint a governor, to watch the bridal procession of a princess whose sumptuous presents were carried in wicker cages for all to see. The goings-on in the street on a Ramazan evening, when gaiety was the rule, would amuse him too, and he often sat here and watched. The kiosk is still intact though not open. Its exterior can be viewed from either the street or the area just inside the Gate of the Fountain of Fresh Water.

This gate (Soğuk Çeşme Kapısı), just a stone's throw from the kiosk, is a vehicle gate that today is an important entrance to the palace grounds. Since Gülhane Parkı starts here, it is more often called the Park Gate. The main gate is a wide affair opened in the seventeenth century by Sultan İbrahim. Smaller entrances on either side are the work of the Municipality under the Young Turks in this century. Its fountains too date from early and late. The earliest, built by Ahmet I in 1605/6, antedates the gate. It bears the *tuğra* of Selim III who must have repaired it. Another fountain was donated by Abdülhamit II when he had work done on the gate in the late nineteenth century. What with all this restoration it has lost its air of antiquity and has a rather rundown appearance. Inside it is made more pleasant by the curves of the wrought iron and the carvings of the fountains which, when they flowed, were supplied with water from the Byzantine cistern, Yere Batan, across the street and up the hill.

There remains only to climb the rest of the hill where the wall rises beside you stern and forbidding, along the little street, Soğuk Çeşme Sokağı (Street of the Fountain of Fresh Water) that separates the palace from Santa Sophia where you can see old houses built into the wall. Back very soon at the Imperial Gate, you will have encircled the Palace of Topkapı, the home of the "majestic, divinely-inspired, felicitous, merciful padishah" in the city of Istanbul the Well-Protected (by God), the threshold of felicity.

[2 8 4]

OTTOMAN SULTANS

with the dates of their reigns

1. Osman I	C.	1288–1324
2. Orhan		1324–1360
3. Murat I		1360–1389
4. Bayezit I (Lightning)		1389–1402
Interregnum during which Bayezit's sons fought for the sultanate		1402–1413
5. Mehmet I		1413–1421
6. Murat II		1421–1444
7. Mehmet II		1444–1446
Murat II*		1446–1451
Mehmet II (The Conqueror)		1451–1481
8. Bayezit II		1481–1512
9. Selim I (The Grim)		1512–1520
10. Süleyman I (The Magnificent)		1520–1566
11. Selim II		1566–1574
12. Murat III		1574–1595
13. Mehmet III		1595–1603
14. Ahmet I		1603–1617
15. Mustafa I		1617–1618
16. Osman II (Young Osman)		1618–1622
Mustafa I**		1622–1623
17. Murat IV		1623–1640

* Murat II at first retired from the throne in favor of his son, Mehmet II, but because Mehmet came to be considered too young to rule in the face of the danger to the Empire, Murat II resumed the throne. Mehmet II acceded again on his death.

** Mustafa I was deposed in 1618 because he was mad. Osman II, who succeeded him, was deposed by the Janissaries four years later and Mustafa I reinstated on the throne. He was so obviously unfit to rule, he was again deposed within a year.

18.	İbrahim	1640–1648
19.	Mehmet IV	1648–1687
20.	Süleyman II	1687–1691
21.	Ahmet II	1691–1695
22.	Mustafa II	1695–1703
23.	Ahmet III	1703–1730
24.	Mahmut I	1730–1754
25.	Osman III	1754–1757
26.	Mustafa III	1757–1774
27.	Abdülhamit I	1774–1789
28.	Selim III	1789–1807
29.	Mustafa IV	1807–1808
30.	Mahmut II	1808–1839
31.	Abdülmecit I	1839–1861
32.	Abdülaziz	1861–1876
33.	Murat V	1876
34.	Abdülhamit II	1876–1909
35.	Mehmet V (Reşat)	1909–1918
36.	Mehmet VI (Vahiteddin)	1918–1922

BIBLIOGRAPHY

*These items are guides to the Topkapı Palace Museum and may be purchased at the entrance to the museum. At the moment of writing new guides are in preparation by the museum staff.

SOURCES IN WESTERN LANGUAGES

Alderson, A. D. *The Structure of the Ottoman Dynasty.* Oxford, 1956. Useful for keeping straight the sultans and the members of their families.

Arif Pasha, painter. *Official Costumes of the Ottoman Empire at the beginning of the nineteenth century.* Istanbul, n.d. Reproductions of 16 paintings.

Arnold, Sir Thomas W. *The Caliphate.* Re-issue of the original 1924 edition, London and New York, 1966. The classic study of the Islamic Caliphate, including that pertaining to the Ottomans.

Arseven, Celâl Esat. *L'Art turc.* Istanbul, 1939. A study of Turkish art throughout the centuries by a member of the Academy of Fine Arts in Istanbul.

———. *Les Arts decoratifs turcs.* Istanbul, n.d., but post 1939. Contains many illustrations of the decorative arts at which the Ottomans were adept.

Aslanapa, Oktay. *Turkish Arts.* Translated by Herman Kreider; revised by Sheila M. O'Callaghan. Istanbul, 1962. Color plates of Seljuk and Ottoman carpets, tiles and miniatures, some from Topkapı Palace.

Babinger, F[ranz]. *Mahomet Il le Conquérant et son temps (1432–1481).* Translated from the German by H. E. Del Medico. Paris, 1954.

Bon, Ottaviano, Venetian *bailo* in Istanbul 1606–1609. *See* Withers.

Boppe, A. *Les Peintures du Bosphore au dix-huitième siecle.* Paris, 1911.

Bowen, Harold. *See* Gibb, H. A. R.

Brindisi. *Official Costumes of the Ottoman Empire at the beginning of the nineteenth century.* Istanbul, n.d. Reproductions of 22 paintings.

Brockelmann, Carl. *History of the Islamic People.* Translated from the German by Joel Carmichael and Moshe Perlman. New York, 1960. Includes sections on the Turks of Central Asia and on the Ottoman Empire.

[287]

Brunschwig, R. " 'Abd," *EI²*, i, pp. 24–40. An article on slaves in Islam.

Busbecq, Ogier Ghiselin de. *The Life and Letters of*. Translated from the Latin by Charles Thornton Forster and F. H. Blackburn. 2 vols. London, 1881. Busbecq was ambassador to Süleyman I from the Holy Roman Empire.

Choiseul-Gouffier, Comte de. *Voyage pittoresque de la Grèce*. 3 vols. Paris, 1782–1822. Author was the French ambassador to the Porte in 1776 and 1778. Illustrated with engravings of Topkapı Palace, but some of the kiosks are wrongly captioned.

Clarke, Edward Daniel. *Travels in Various Countries of Europe, Asia and Africa*. London, 1891 (1st edition 1816–24). Some description of Palace Point by an antiquarian, minerologist and traveler.

Covel, Dr. "Dr. Covel's Diary," *Early Voyages and Travels in the Levant*, pp. 101–280. Reprint of Hakluyt Society edition, New York, n.d. An account of his experiences in the Ottoman Empire in the seventeenth century by the chaplain to the British ambassador of the time.

Creasy, Edward S. *History of the Ottoman Turks*. Beirut, 1961. A reprint of an earlier edition that takes us up to 1878. Creasy's history is frankly based on von Hammer, and his treatment of the years after 1774, which von Hammer does not cover, is considerably less interesting. Written far too early to take advantage of modern research into the beginnings of the Ottoman State, it is nevertheless a readable and balanced account.

*Çiğ, Kemal. *Topkapı Museum*. Istanbul, n.d. High spots of the Topkapı Palace Museum by its assistant director, in Turkish, English, German and French. The English translation does not do justice to the Turkish text. Color photographs.

*———. *Topkapı Museum (Guide to the kitchens, which exhibit porcelains, silverware, glass and copperware.)* Istanbul, n.d. In Turkish, English, German and French. Color photographs.

———. "A Unique Ceiling-Style Newly-Discovered in the Harem of the Topkapı Palace," *Atti del Secondo Congresso Internazionale di Arte Turca, Venezia, 26–29 Settembre, 1963*, pp. 57–60. Naples, 1965. An article describing the ceiling of the domed room of the Double Kiosk.

Dallam, Thomas. "The Diary of Master Thomas Dallam, 1599–1600," *Early Voyages and Travels in the Levant*, pp. 1–98. Reprint of the Hakluyt edition, New York, n.d. The diary of the man who installed in Topkapı Palace the organ Elizabeth of England sent to Mehmet III.

Deny, J. "Wālide Sultān," *EI¹*, iv, pp. 1113–1118. An article on the *valide sultan*.

Emler, Selma. "Le Palais Royal de Topkapı et ses Restaurations," *Atti del Secondo Congresso Internazionale di Arte Turca, Venezia, 26–29 Settembre, 1963*, pp. 65–72. Naples, 1965. An article on Topkapı Palace by a former harem architect.

Encyclopedia of Islam, first edition. Leyden, 1913–1934. Referred to as *EI¹*.

Encyclopedia of Islam, second edition. Leyden, 1960–. Referred to as *EI²*.

Erdman, Kurt. "Die Fliesen am Sünnet odası des Top Kapı Saray in Istanbul, aus der Welt der islamischen Kunst," *Festschrift für Ernst Künel zum 75. Geburstag am 26. 10. 1957*, pp. 144–153. Berlin, 1959.

*Erkins, Zia. *The Topkapı Palace Museum*. Prepared and arranged by Niyazi A. Banoğlu. Istanbul, n.d. Color and black and white photographs; floor plan; gives detailed guide to sections of Sultans' Robes and Treasury. Unfortunately some photographs are incorrectly captioned.

Esin, Emel. *Turkish Miniature Painting*. Rutland, Vt., and Tokyo, Japan, 1960. Color plates.

Ethem, Halil. *Le Palais de Topkapou (vieux serail)*. 1931.

Evliya Efendi (Çelebi). *Narrative of Travels in Europe, Asia and Africa in the seventeenth century*. Translated from the Turkish by Joseph von Hammer Ritter. London, 1834. A partial translation of the *Seyahatname*.

Flachat, Jean Baptiste. *Observations sur le commerce et sur les arts de l'Europe, de l'Asie, de l'Afrique, et même des Indes orientales (1740–1758)*. 2 vols. Lyons, 1776. Author was a Christian merchant who lived in Istanbul and Izmir for several years and supplied the palace.

Gibb, H. A. R. *Mohammedanism, an historical survey*. New York, 1955. Many useful books on Islam might be mentioned, but this is one of the most concise as well as being by an outstanding Arabist.

———— and Bowen, Harold. *Islamic Society and the West*. So far only Vol. I, in two parts, has been published. London, New York, Toronto, 1957. A study of the Ottoman Empire in the eighteenth century.

Giese, G. "Čighalezāde Sinān Pasha," *EI¹*, p. 855. An article on the Ottoman general and grand vizier, Ciğaloğlu Sinan Pasha.

Goodwin, Godfrey. "The Marble Quarries of Marmara Island," *Golden Horn*, 1965, pp. 47–54. Istanbul, 1965.

Grelot, Guillaume Joseph. *Relation nouvelle d'un voyage de Constantinople*. Paris, 1680. A seventeenth-century traveler who illustrated his book with engravings showing Topkapı Palace from the water. Some of the kiosks are wrongly named.

Grube, Ernst J. *Muslim Miniature Paintings from the XIII to the XIX Century from Collections in the United States and Canada*. Venice, 1962. Catalogue of an exhibition at Asia House in New York. Black and white plates.

Gurlitt, Cornelius. *Die Baukunst Konstantinopels*. 2 vols. Berlin, 1912. Author a German architect who was allowed to make plans of the Second, Third and Fourth Courts but not of the harem. He has done nothing with the gardens.

Habesci, Elias. *The Present State of the Ottoman Empire*. Translated from the French. London, 1784. Author was a Greek of Istanbul who was in the service of both the Ottoman Empire and Russia.

Hammer(-Purgstall), J. de. *Histoire de l'Empire Ottoman depuis son origine jusqu'à nos jours*. 18 vols. Translated from the German by J. J. Hellert. Paris, 1835–1843. Except for the earliest days of the Ottoman Empire, where recent research has superceded it, this is still the fullest and most authoritative account of Ottoman history in a Western language, based as it is on the Ottoman chroniclers. Unfortunately it stops with the reign of Abdülhamit I.

Ibn Battūta. *The Travels of, A.D. 1325–1354.* Translated with revisions and notes from the Arabic text edited by C. Defrémery and B. R. Sanguinetti. Prepared by H. A. R. Gibb. 2 vols. Vol I, Cambridge, 1962. This gives certain information on the early days of the Ottoman Empire.

*Koçu, Reşat Ekrem. *A Guide to the Topkapı Palace Museum.* Istanbul, 1968. Photographs in color and black and white. Floor plan.

Köprülü, M. Fuat. *Alcune Osservazione Intorno all'Influenza della Instituzioni Bizantine sulla Instituzioni Ottomane.* Rome, 1953. Translated from the Turkish "*Bizans müesseselerinin Osmanlı müesseselerine tesiri hakkında bazı mülâhazalar* (Some observations concerning the influence of Byzantine institutions on Ottoman institutions)," *Türk hukuk ve iktisat tarihi mecmuası,* (Magazine of Turkish legal and economic history), i, 1931, pp. 165–313.

———. *Les Origines de l'Empire Ottoman.* Paris, 1935. A basic work on the subject described by its title.

Kramers, J. H. "Şokolli, Mehmet Pasha, *EI*^{i}, iv. pp. 474–475. An article on the great grand vizier, Sokollu Mehmet Pasha.

———. "Sultān," *EI*^{i}, iv, pp. 543–545.

Lampé, Melek Celâl. *Le Vieux Serail des Sultans.* 2nd edition. Istanbul, 1963. Illustrated with sketches.

Lewis, Bernard. *Istanbul and the Civilization of the Ottoman Empire.* Norman, Okla., 1963. The author is a member of the faculty of the School of African and Oriental Studies of the University of London. Has some information on Topkapı Palace.

Lybyer, Albert Howe. *The Government of the Ottoman Empire in the Time of Suleiman the Magnificent.* New York, 1966. A reprint of a standard work.

Mamboury, Ernest. *The Tourists' Istanbul.* Translated from the French by Malcolm Burr. Istanbul, 1953. For long the authoritative guide to Istanbul. In using it, however, one must keep in mind that the street car routes he mentions have disappeared. The section on Topkapı Palace is out-of-date.

McCullough, Francis. *The Fall of Abd-ul-Hamid.* London, 1910. Has some information on the dispersal of Abdülhamit II's harem.

Melling, Antoine Ignace. *Voyage pittoresque de Constantinople et des rives du Bosphore d'auprès les dessins de M. Melling.* 2 vols. Paris, 1819. The volume of plates has some charming scenes of old Istanbul, including some having to do with Topkapı Palace. The map is not accurate except for Palace Point.

Miller, Barnette. *Beyond the Sublime Porte.* New Haven, 1931. The first modern study of Topkapı Palace to be published in English. The author taught at

Wellesley and at the Girls' College in Istanbul. She has done a scholarly job of research, but much has come to light since her day. Her map of the palace is inaccurate. An excellent bibliography.

————. *The Palace School of Mohammed the Conqueror.* Cambridge, 1941. This excellent study of the Palace School illuminates the Third Court. Unfortunately the author has not given us her bibliography. Has some interesting old floor plans.

Montagu, Lady Mary Wortley. *Letters from.* New York, 1906. Lady Mary's letters from Istanbul are justly famous and very illuminating. She was the wife of the British ambassador to the Porte in the early eighteenth century.

Mordtmann, E. H. "Ibrahim Pa__sha__," *EI*[1], ii, pp. 442–443. An article on Nevşehirli İbrahim Pasha.

Mordtmann, J. H. -(H. W. Duda). "Ewliyā Čelebi," *EI*[2], ii, pp. 717–720. An article on the famous traveler and author of the *Seyahatname*, Evliya Çelebi.

Mordtmann, J. H. "Ibrahim Pa__sha__," *EI*[1], ii, pp. 441–442. An article on Süleyman I's grand vizier, İbrahim Pa__sha__.

————. "Die jüdischen Kira im Serai der Sultane," *Mitteilungen des Seminars für orientalische Sprachen an der K. Freidrich-Wilhelms-Universität zu Berlin: Westasiatische Abteilung,* January, 1955, pp. 1–38.

Motraye, A(ubrey) de la. *Travels through Europe, Asia, and into Part of Africa; with Proper Cutts and Maps.* 2 vols. London, 1723.

Nicolay, Nicolas de. *Les Navigations, Peregrinations et Voyages, Faicts en la Turquie.* Paris, 1709 (reprint of a Lyons edition of 1567).

d'Ohsson, Mouradgea. *Tableau général de l'Empire Othman,* 3 vols. Paris, 1787–1820. Dedicated to and apparently prepared for the King of Sweden, it is one of the most celebrated studies of the Ottoman Empire.

Oygar, İsmail Hakkı. "Les Origines de la Céramique Seldjoukide et Ottomane," *Türk sanatı tarihi araştırma ve incelemeleri,* pp. 583–606. Istanbul, 1963.

*Öğütmen, Filiz. *Miniature Art from the XIIth to the XVIIIth Century.* Translated from the Turkish by Michael J. L. Austin. Istanbul, 1966. An excellent English translation of the guide to the Miniature Section of Topkapı Palace Museum, by a member of the museum staff.

Öz, Tahsin. *50 Masterpieces.* The Topkapı Sarayı Museum, [1952?]. By the former director of the museum. Illustrated. Sketch of Outer Palace.

[————]. *Guide to the Museum of Topkapu Saray.* [Translated from the Turkish by Seniha Sami Moralı.] The museum's early days, by its first director. Istanbul, 1936.

————. *Turkish Ceramics.* Turkish Press, Broadcasting and Tourist Department, n.d. Plates in color and black and white. A rare and illuminating book.

Penzer, N. M. *The Harem, an account of the institution as it existed in the palace of the Turkish sultans with a history of the Grand Seraglio from its foundation to the present time.* Philadelphia, n.d. The author was apparently guided through Topkapı Palace by Tahsin Öz sometime in the Thirties before much of the restoration had been accomplished. Hence his description of the palace is spotty, through no fault of his. More serious are his attempts at linguistic and historical analysis without any apparent background for judgement. The book's many pictures are interesting. The map is out-of-date.

Pickthall, Mohammed Marmaduke. *The Meaning of the Glorious Koran.* New York, 1953. A translation of the Koran from the Arabic by an Englishman who became a Muslim.

Pouqueville, F. C. H. L., MD. *Travels through the Morea, Albania and Several Other Parts of the Ottoman Empire to Constantinople.* Translated from the French. London, 1806. The French edition was published in Paris in 1805. He was among the Europeans who were able to visit the gardens and kiosks on Saray Point.

Redhouse, Sir James W. *A Turkish and English Lexicon.* Constantinople, 1921 (a reprint of the original 1890 edition). This Ottoman-Turkish-English dictionary has never been superceded and is a mine of information, since Redhouse, who was a famous Orientalist, was familiar with Ottoman institutions.

Rycaut, Sir Paul. *The History of the Present State of the Ottoman Empire.* 3 vols. London, 1670. This also has a French edition published in Paris in 1709. The author was the secretary to the British ambassador to the Porte from Charles II and later consul of Izmir (Smyrna).

Sevin, Nureddin. "Ottoman Court School which also trained hundreds of artists between the fifteenth and the nineteenth centuries," *Atti del Secondo Congresso Internazionale di Arte Turca, Venezia, 26–29 Settembre, 1963,* pp. 235–243. Naples, 1965.

Siyavuşgil, Sabri Esat. *Karagöz, its history, its characters, its mystic and satiric spirit.* Ankara, 1955. Color plates.

Sourdel-Thomine, J. "Hamam," *EI²,* iv, pp. 139–144. An article on the history of the bath in the eastern Mediterranean.

Tavernier, Jean Baptiste. *Nouvelle relation de l'Intérieur du Serrail du Grand Seigneur.* Paris, 1675. Tavernier was for a time part of the French ambassador's suite and therefore had entry to the Second Court and the Throne Room. His descriptions of other parts of the palace, though detailed, are second-hand. There is an English translation of this book published in London in 1678.

Thévenot. *The Travels of Monsieur de Thévenot into the Levant in 3 Parts.* Translated from the French. London, 1688. Part Two deals with Turkey.

Ulucay, Çağatay. "The Harem in the XVIIIth Century," *Aktes des Vierundzigsten Internationalen Orientalisten Kongresses, München, 28. August bis 4. September,* 1957, pp. 394–398. Wiesbaden, 1959.

UNESCO. Turkey, *Ancient Miniatures.* Preface by Richard Ettinghausen, present curator of Islamic Art at the Metropolitan Museum of Art, and introduction by M. S. İpşiroğlu and S. Eyeboğlu, both of the University of Istanbul. Paris, 1961. Color plates.

Ünver, Dr. Süheyl. *Levnî*. Istanbul, 1951. Color plates.

Withers, Robert. "A Description of the Grand Seigneur's Seraglio or Turkish Emperor's Court," *Hakluytus Posthumus or Purchas His Pilgrims*. New York, 1905 (reprint of the 1625 edition). This is an unacknowledged translation of Ottaviano Bon, Venetian envoy to the Porte. Withers was attached to the British embassy in Istanbul c. 1620.

Wittek, Paul. *The Rise of the Ottoman Empire*. London, 1958. (Reprint of 1938 edition). A basic work on the beginnings of the Ottoman Empire.

SOURCES IN TURKISH

Abdurrahman Şeref. "Topkapı Sarayı hümayunu (The Imperial Palace of Topkapı)," *Tarih-i Osmanî encümeni mecmuası (Ottoman Historical Society Magazine),*" Nos. 5–12, December 14, 1910–December 14, 1911. By the last imperial historiographer *(vakanüvis)*. The first first-hand study made of Topkapı Sarayı.

Aktepe, M. Münir. "Mahmut I," *IA*, vii, pp. 158–165.

——. *Patrona isyanı (1730) (Revolt of Patrona)*. Istanbul, 1958.

[Altınay], Ahmet Refik. *Eski İstanbul (Old Istanbul)*. Istanbul, 1931.

——. *Hicrî 10cu, 11ci ve 12ci asırlarda İstanbul hayatı (Istanbul Life in the 10th, 11th and 12th centuries of the hegira)*. Istanbul, 1935, 1931, 1930. Documents dating from 1553 to 1785.

——. *Lâle Devri (The Tulip Period)*. Istanbul, 1932.

And, Metin. *Kırk gün, kırk gece (Forty days and forty nights)*. Istanbul, 1959. A brief history of Turkish entertainments.

Arseven, Celâl Esat. *Sanat ansiklopedisi (Art encyclopedia)*. 4 vols. Istanbul, 1947–1951.

Aslanapa, Oktay. *Anadolu'da Türk çini ve keramik sanatı (Turkish tile and ceramic art in Anatolia)*. Istanbul, 1965. Plates. Also available in German.

——. "Sinan," *IA*, section 108, pp. 655–661. Article on the great architect, Sinan.

Ayverdi, Ekrem Hakkı. *Fatih Devri mimarisi (Architecture of the period of the Conqueror)*. Istanbul, 1953. By a former architect of the Topkapı Palace restoration. Has a large, illustrated section on Topkapı Palace.

——. *XVIII Asırda lâle (The Tulip in the eighteenth century)*. Color plates. Istanbul, 1950.

Baykal, İsmail. "Selim III devrinde 'imdad-ı sefer' icin para basılmak üzere saraydan verilen altın ve gümüş avanî hakkında. (Concerning gold and silver vessels given from the palace to be coined into money 'for help for the campaign' in the period of Selim III," *Tarih vesikaları (Turkish documents)*, iii, 13, August, 1944, pp. 36–51. By the former librarian of Topkapı Palace Museum.

————. "Silâhtar-ı Şehriyarî ve Darüssaade Ağası tâyinleri hakkında hat-ı hümayunlar (Imperial decrees concerning the appointment of the ruler's sword-bearer and the Ağa of the House of Felicity)," *Tarih vesikaları,* ii, 10, February, 1943, pp. 338–341.

————. "*Topkapı Sarayı Müzesi kitaplıkları* (Collections of Books of the Topkapı Palace Museum)," *Güzel sanatlar (Fine arts),* vi, 1949, pp. 75–84.

————. "Hat sanatı (Calligraphic art)," *Güzel sanatlar,* ii, 1940, p. 33–48. Illustrated. 1 color plate.

————. "Hazine-ı hümayun ile Bağdat Köşkü ve Revan Odası kütüphaneleri hakkında iki hat-ı hümayun (Two imperial decrees concerning the libraries in the Imperial Treasury, the Baghdad Kiosk, and the Revan Room), *Tarih vesikaları,* ii, 9, October, 1942, pp. 188–192.

Baysun, M. Cavit. "Kösem Sultan," *IA,* vi, pp. 915–923.

Bikkul, Ahat U. "Topkapı Sarayında Hasahır (The Privy Stable in Topkapı Palace)," *Güzel sanatlar,* vi, 1941, pp. 118–131. Illustrated. Author is a former member of the staff of the Topkapı Palace Museum.

Celâl, Melek. *Türk işlemeleri (Turkish embroideries).* Plates, some color. Istanbul, 1939.

Cenkman, Emin. *Osmanlı sarayı ve kıyafetleri (The Ottoman palace and its costumes).* Illustrated with sketches. Istanbul, 1948.

Cevdet Pasha. *Tarih-ı Cevdet (Cevdet's History).* 12 vols. 2nd printing. Istanbul, 1309 (1891/2). Vol. 8 deals with the saving of Mahmut II in Topkapı Palace.

Cezar, Mustafa. "Osmanlı devrinde İstanbul yapılarında tahribat yapan yangınlar ve tabiî âfetler (Fires and natural calamities that damaged Istanbul buildings in the Ottoman period)," *Türk sanatı tarihi araştırma ve incelemeleri (Research and investigation in Turkish art history),* pp. 327–414. Istanbul, 1963.

Çetinas, Sedat. "Türkler'de su-çeşme, sebil (The water fountain and public fountain among the Turks), *Güzel sanatlar,* v, 1944, pp. 125–147. By a former member of the staff of the Topkapı Palace Museum.

Çiğ, Kemal. "Hattat padişahlar (Padishah calligraphers)," *Tarih dünyası (World history),* i, 5, June 15, 1950, pp. 196–197. Written by the present assistant director of the Topkapı Palace Museum.

Eldem, Sedat Hakkı. "17nci ve 18inci asırlarda Türk odası (The Turkish room in the 17th and 18th centuries)," *Güzel sanatlar,* v, 1944, pp. 1–28. Illustrated.

Emler, Selma. "Topkapı Sarayı restorasyon ve çalışmaları (Restoration and work on Topkapı Palace)," *Türk sanatı tarihi araştırma ve incelemeleri,* pp. 212–227. Istanbul, 1963. Article going into detail on the restoration and construction of certain rooms in Topkapı Palace, by a former harem architect.

Eren, A. Cevat. "Selim III," *IA*, section 105, pp. 441–457.

Erkins, Ziya. "Osmanlı haremi, ne zaman kuruldu? (The Ottoman harem, when was it founded?)" *Tarih dünyası*, i, 9, August 15, 1950, pp. 362–365.

———. "Selim III ve Alemdar Mustafa Paşa (Selim III and Alemdar Mustafa Pasha)," *Tarih dünyası tarih kütüphanesi (Turkish world history library)*, No. 3, entire issue. Istanbul, 1950.

Erksan, A. Cemal. "Saltanat arabaları (Carriages of the Sultanate)," *Tarih dünyası*, June 15, 1950, pp. 184–187.

Eyice, Semavi. "Yeni Saray (The New Palace)," *IA*, 53 A.B.C. sections, pp. 1214/49–1214/54.

Giz, Adnan. "2. Mahmud'un otuz günü (Thirty days of Mahmut II)," *Belgelerle Türk tarihi dergisi (Turkish historical magazine with documents)*, 5, February, 1968. The first thirty days of Mahmut II's reign from the records of his confidential secretary.

———. "İki padişahın otuz günü (Thirty days of two padishahs)," *Belgelerle Türk tarihi dergisi*, 4, January, 1968. The last thirty days in the reigns of Selim III and Mustafa IV, taken from the records of their confidential secretaries.

———. "17. yüzyılda Osmanlı padişahlarının günlük yemek masrafları (Daily food expenses of the Ottoman padishahs in the seventeenth century)," *Belgelerle Türk tarihi dergisi*, 6, March, 1968, pp. 76–78. Lists of food sent to the harem.

Gökbilgin, Tayyip. "İbrahim," *IA*, vol. 5/1, section 49, pp. 880–885. Article on Sultan İbrahim.

İnciciyan, P. G. *XVIII asırda İstanbul (Istanbul in the eighteenth century)*. Translated and annotated by Drand D. Andreasyan. Istanbul, 1956.

İslâm ansiklopedisi (Islam encyclopedia). Istanbul, 1950–. Based on the English-French *Encyclopedia of Islam* but has many more and fuller articles on Ottoman matters. Referred to as *IA*.

Karal, Enver Ziya. "Ahmet III," *IA*, i, pp. 165–168.

———. "Mahmut II," *IA*, vii, pp. 165–170.

———. *See* also Uzunçarşılı, İsmail Hakkı.

Karatay, Fehmi. "Giriş (Introduction)," *Topkapı Sarayı Müzesi Kütüphanesi türkçe yazmalar kataloğu (Turkish manuscript catalogue of the Topkapı Palace Museum Library)*, i, pp. x–xi. Istanbul, 1961.

"Kıyafetname (Book of Costume)," *Tarih vesikaları*, ii, 9, October, 1942, begins facing p. 192; ii, 11, February, 1943, begins facing p. 338. Color pictures of palace officials in costume from a book made in the time of Selim III. Ahmet III kütüphanesi, #3690.

Koçu, Reşat Ekrem. *İstanbul ansiklopedisi (Istanbul encyclopedia)*. Istanbul, 1946–. Illustrated.

———. *Türk giyim kuşam ve süslenme sözlüğü (Turkish dress and adornment dictionary)*. Istanbul, 1969. Illustrated with sketches.

————. *Topkapu Sarayı (Topkapı Palace)*. Istanbul, 1960. A popular history of the palace, not entirely accurate historically.

————. *Yeniçeriler (Janissaries)*. Istanbul, 1964. Illustrated with sketches. A popular history of the Janissaries.

Köprülü, M. Fuat. "Hadım (Eunuch)," *IA*, v/1, pp. 45–47.

Meriç, Rıfkı Melül. "Bayramdarda padişahlara hediye edilen sanat eserleri ve karşılıkları (Works of art presented to the padishahs on *bayrams* and their gifts in return), Türk sanatı tarih vesikaları (Documents of Turkish art history)," *Türk sanatı tarihi araştırma ve incelemeleri*, pp. 764–786. Istanbul, 1963.

Musahipzade Celâl. *Eski İstanbul yaşayışı (Old Istanbul Life)*. Istanbul, 1946. Illustrated with sketches.

Nedim. *Hayatı, sanatı, şiirleri (His life, his art, his poems)*. Istanbul, 1959. Poetry of Tulip Period.

Nüzhet, Selim. *Türk temaşası (Turkish entertainment)*. Istanbul, 1930. A history of the *meddah* or story-teller, Karagöz or shadow theater, and the *ortaoyunu* or theater-in-the-round.

Orgun, Zarif. "Kubbealtı ve yapılan merasim (Under the Dome and the ceremony performed)," *Güzel sanatlar*, vi, 1949, pp. 91–108. Illustrated. Color plates. By a former Topkapı Palace archivist.

————. "Osmanlı İmparatorluğunda Kaptan Paşalara ve donanma yapılan merasim (Ceremony performed for the Captain Pasha and the decking out in the Ottoman Empire)," *Tarih vesikaları*, i, 2, August, 1941, pp. 135–144.

————. "Osmanlı İmparatorluğunda name ve hediye getiren elçilere yapılan merasim (Ceremony performed in the Ottoman Empire for ambassadors who brought letters and presents)," *Tarih vesikaları*, i, 6, April, 1942, pp. 407–413.

————. "Osmanlı İmparatorluğunda tuğ ve sancak (The *tuğ* and banner in the Ottoman Empire)," *Tarih vesikaları*, i, 4, December, 1941, pp. 245–255; i, 5, February, 1942, pp. 345–355 plus plate.

Osmanoğlu, Ayşe. *Babam Abdülhamit (My Father, Abdülhamit)*. Istanbul, 1960. Intimate glimpses of Abdülhamit II and of her own life by his daughter, Ayşe Sultan.

Öz, Tahsin. "Çinilerimiz (Our tiles)," *Güzel sanatlar*, ii, 1940, pp. 5–26. An article on tiles by the former director of the Topkapı Palace Museum. Color and black and white illustrations.

————. "Hünername ve miniatürleri (The Hünername and its miniatures)," *Güzel sanatlar*, i, 1939, pp. 3–15. Illustrated. Some color plates.

————. "Selim III, Mustafa IV ve Mahmut II zamanlarına ait birkaç vesika (Some documents belonging to the times of Selim III, Mustafa IV and Mahmut II)," *Tarih vesikaları*, i, 1, June, 1941, pp. 20–29.

————. "Selim III 'ün sırkâtibi tarafından tutulan ruzname, (Day book by the confidential secretary of Selim III)," *Tarih vesikaları*, iii, 13, August, 1944, pp. 26–35; iii, 14, October, 1944, pp. 102–116; iii, 15, May, 1949, pp. 185–199.

——. "Tavanlarımız (Our ceilings)," *Güzel sanatlar*, v, 1944, pp. 29–38. Illustrated. Color plates.

——. "Topkapı Sarayı Müzesi onarımları (Topkapı Palace Museum repairs)," *Güzel sanatlar*, vi, 1949, pp. 6–74. Illustrated. Color plates.

——. "Türk el işlemeleri ve resim dairesi (Turkish hand embroidery and picture area)," *Güzel sanatlar*, iv, 1942, pp. 29–52. Illustrated. Color plates.

——. *Türk kumaş ve kadifleri, ii, XVII–XIX yüzyıl ve kumaş süslemesi (Turkish fabrics and velvets, II, XVII–XIX centuries and ornamented fabric)*. Istanbul, 1951. Color plates.

Pakalın, Mehmet Zeki. *Osmanlı tarih deyimleri ve terimleri sözlüğü (Dictionary of Ottoman historical phrases and terms)*. 3 vols. Istanbul, 1946, 1951, 1954.

Sertoğlu, Mithat. *Resimli Osmanlı tarihi ansiklopedisi* (Illustrated Ottoman historical encyclopedia). 1 vol. Istanbul, 1958.

Sinan, Mimar. *Tezkiretülebniye (Memorandum of buildings)*. Prepared by Rıfkı Melül Meriç. Ankara, 1965. This is a transliteration from Ottoman into modern Turkish of a short autobiography of the architect, Sinan.

Siyavuşgil, Sabri Esat. *Karagöz*. Istanbul, 1941. The Turkish shadow theater.

Şehsuvaroğlu, Halûk Y. *Asırlar boyunca İstanbul (Istanbul during the centuries)*. Published as a supplement to the Istanbul newspaper, *Cumhuriyet*, n.d. A collection of articles and sketches by a former director of the Topkapı Palace Museum. Many have to do with the palace.

——. "Topkapı Sarayı Müzesi Kütüphanesine bir bakış (A look at the Topkapı Palace Museum Library)," *Topkapı Sarayı Müzesi Kütüphanesi türkçe yazmalar kataloğu*, i, pp. v–ix. Istanbul, 1961.

Tayanç, Muin Memduh. "Duvar çinilerimizdeki yaprak motifi (İstanbul devri) (The leaf motif in our wall tiles (Istanbul period))," *Türk sanatı tarihi araştırma ve incelemeleri*, pp. 606–656. Istanbul, 1963.

Tunalı, Tahsin. "Bestekâr padişah III. Selim (The music composer padishah, Selim III)," *Hayat tarih mecmuası*, February, 1965, pp. 48–49.

Tuncay, Rauf. "Türk nakış sanatı ve nakkaş Molla Kasım (The art of Turkish painting and the painter Molla Kasım)," *Belgelerle Türk tarihi dergisi*, 13, October, 1968, pp. 71–77.

Uluçay, M. Çağatay. *Haremden mektuplar (Letters from the harem)*. Istanbul, 1956. Letters of imperial women, with commentary.

Uzunçarşılı İsmail Hakkı. "Mustafa III'ün kızı, Şah Sultana borç senedi (Document of debt of Shah Sultan, daughter of Mustafa III)," *Belleten (Bulletin)*, xxv, 1, pp. 97–100, 1961.

——. "Nizam-ı Cedit ricalından Valide Sultan kethüdası meşhur Yusuf Ağa ve Kethüdazade Arif Efendi (The famous Yusuf Ağa, steward of the *valide sultan*, of the important men of the New Order, and the Son of the Steward,

Arif Efendi)," *Belleten*, xx, 79, July, 1956, pp. 485–523. An article on the steward of the mother of Selim III and on one of his famous descendants.

———. *Osmanlı Devletinin saray teşkilâtı (The palace organization of the Ottoman State)*. Ankara, 1945. A book basic to the understanding of the groups that served the palace and how they worked. Plates.

———. *Osmanlı Devleti teşkilâtından kapıkulu ocakları (The groups of the slaves of the gate of the organization of the Ottoman State)*. 2 vols. Ankara, 1943. Vol. I gives the history of the Janissaries.

——— and Karal, Enver Ziya. *Osmanlı tarihi (Ottoman history)*. 7 vols. Ankara, 1951–1964. The Ottoman history published by the Turkish Historical Society.

Ülgen, Ali Sâim. "Hamam," *IA*, v, pp. 174–178. An article on the bath.

Ünal, İsmail. "Çin porselenleri üzerindeki Türk târsiâtı (Turkish jeweled ornament on Chinese porcelains)," *Türk sanatı tarihi araştırma ve incelemeleri*, pp. 677–714. Istanbul, 1963.

———. "Türkler'de sedefçilik (Mother-of-pearl work among the Turks)," *Güzel sanatlar*, vi, 1949, pp. 132–147. Illustrated. By a former member of the Topkapı Palace Museum staff.

Ünver, Prof. Dr. Süheyl. "Hattat Mustafa Râkim Efendi (The calligrapher, Mustafa Râkim Efendi)," *Tarih dünyası*, i, 7, July 15, 1950, pp. 271–275. An article on the calligrapher who designed the *tuğra* of Mahmut II.

———. "Süsleme sanatı bakımından Topkapı Sarayı Müzesi (Topkapı Palace Museum from the point of view of decorative art)," *Güzel sanatlar*, vi, 1949, pp. 109–117. Illustrated. Color plates.

———. *Müzehip ve çiçek ressamı Üsküdarlı Ali (Gilder and flower artist, Üsküdarlı Ali.)* Istanbul, 1954. Text in English and Turkish.

———. "Resime göre Tanzimat-ı hayriye ilân merasimi (The ceremony announcing the Auspicious Reorganization according to a picture)," *Belleten*, xxviii, 112, October, 1964, pp. 701–704.

Vakanüvis (Chronicler). See Wickerhauser, Moriz.

Wickerhauser, Moriz. *Eine Deutsch-Türkische Chrestomathie*. Vienna, 1853. An interesting selection, in Ottoman Turkish, from the chroniclers or imperial historiographers such as Naima, Raşit, Sami, Şakir and Suphi, İzzi Süleyman, Vasif, with a German translation.

Yenal, Şükrü. "Topkapı Sarayı Müzesi Enderun kitaplığı (Ahmet III kitaplığı) (Collection of books of the Enderun of Topkapı Palace Museum (Ahmet III collection))," *Güzel sanatlar*, vi, 1949, pp. 85–90. By a former Topkapı Palace Museum librarian. These books have now been moved to the New Library.

Yetkin, Suut Kemal. *İslâm mimarisi (Islamic architecture)*. Ankara, 1959. Illustrations. Glossary.

INDEX